The 1903 World Series

The 1903 World Series

The Boston Americans, the Pittsburg Pirates, and the "First Championship of the United States"

ANDY DABILIS *and* NICK TSIOTOS

McFarland & Company, Inc., Publishers
Jefferson, North Carolina, and London

LIBRARY OF CONGRESS CATALOGUING-IN-PUBLICATION DATA

Dabilis, Andy.
　　The 1903 World Series : the Boston Americans, the Pittsburg Pirates, and the "first championship of the United States" / Andy Dabilis and Nick Tsiotos.
　　　　p.　cm.
　　Includes bibliographical references and index.

　　ISBN-13: 978-0-7864-1840-4
　　(softcover : 50# alkaline paper) ∞

　　1. World Series (Baseball) (1903)　2. Boston Red Sox (Baseball team) — History — 20th century.　3. Pittsburgh Pirates (Baseball team) — History — 20th century.
I. Tsiotos, Nick.　II. Title.
GV878.4.D33　2004
796.357'646 — dc22　　　　　　　　　　　　2004009590

British Library cataloguing data are available

©2004 Andy Dabilis and Nick Tsiotos. All rights reserved

No part of this book may be reproduced or transmitted in any form or by any means, electronic or mechanical, including photocopying or recording, or by any information storage and retrieval system, without permission in writing from the publisher.

On the cover: Huntington Avenue Grounds, Boston, before the start of the first game, October 1, 1903 (*Boston Public Library*)

Manufactured in the United States of America

McFarland & Company, Inc., Publishers
　Box 611, Jefferson, North Carolina 28640
　　www.mcfarlandpub.com

This one is for my late uncle, Dick Jackson, who took me to my first baseball game at Fenway Park in 1959. The Boston Red Sox and Cleveland Indians were tied 9–9 after three innings, making me think that all games were going to be as exciting and wonderful. I got to see the greenest green of my life, the grass and the Green Monster of the left field wall, and feel the wonderment about the game that would last forever. And I got to see and appreciate Ted Williams, my uncle's baseball idol.

But I didn't get there in time when my uncle passed away. I hope that somehow, if there is baseball in heaven, he knows how much what he did meant to me.

— *Andy Dabilis*

To my late, beloved uncle Panos Condakes, another immigrant who fell in love with baseball. He first introduced me to the game when I was five years old as we watched the great Ted Williams on our black and white Motorola TV. There we were, lying back on the couch and dipping delicious Greek koulourakia cookies into a glass of Hood's milk, inning after inning.

— *Nick Tsiotos*

Acknowledgments

Special thanks to our agent, Susan Julian Gates, and attorney, Chris Tsiotos, for their tireless guidance and friendly efforts on our behalf.

Thanks also to Ted Spencer, curator of the National Baseball Hall of Fame in Cooperstown, N.Y., along with Scot E. Mondore, senior researcher for the Hall of Fame and Museum, Timothy J. Wiles, director of research for the National Baseball Library and Archive, and Patricia Kelly, director of the photography collection for the Hall of Fame Library. Our appreciation is extended to Jack Grinold, sports information director of Northeastern University in Boston, and Aaron Schmidt of the Boston Public Library. We are indebted to the staff of the *Boston Globe* library for their professional assistance. We must also thank our colleague Caroline Louise Cole, who found "Tessie" and located the home of Edward Doheny, and Harold Criger and Jeannette Done, for their revealing recollections of their grandfather, Lou Criger, the Boston Americans' catcher.

Thanks are owed to newfound friends in Pittsburgh, including Lizabeth S. Gray of the *Pittsburgh Post-Gazette* library and Fritz Huysman, assistant managing editor of sports; to New Englander Ben Bouma, who wound up in Pittsburgh as assistant director of media relations for the Pirates; and to the staff of the Pennsylvania room and the microfilm room of the Carnegie Library in Pittsburgh. Steve Krah of the Elkhart, Indiana, *Truth* provided much of the material on Criger, for whom a chapter of the Society of American Baseball Research is named.

And to old friend Dick Johnson, curator of the Sports Museum of New England, who with his writing colleague and fellow sports historian Glenn Stout has written extensively and masterfully about Boston sports history, the first World Series, and the Royal Rooters.

Table of Contents

Acknowledgments	vii
Introduction: An Invitation to Play	1
ONE. Today They Assault the Citadel	5
TWO. End of the Elysian Field	17
THREE. Barney Builds His Dynasty	30
FOUR. Murnane's Baseball	38
FIVE. Play Them, But You Must Beat Them	47
SIX. An Awful Boom in the Ninth Inning	67
SEVEN. They Didn't Do a Thing But Turn the City Upside Down	103
EIGHT. "Tessie"	141
NINE. Echoes of the Game	174
Conclusion: The Bronze Man	185
Appendix: 1903 World Series Statistics	189
Bibliography	201
Index	211

Introduction:
An Invitation to Play

Barney Dreyfuss had a lot to be happy about in the summer of 1903. From the window of his office, he could see the emerging steel city of Pittsburg evolving into an industrial giant in the new century, propelled by newfangled machines that made work easier and more efficient, and by waves of immigrants, mostly from Europe, who were the human fuel for the growing might of the United States. Pittsburg was smoky and busy and filled with eager men whose desire to work was matched by the desire to play: and it was baseball to which many of them were taking, drawn by the colorful heroes of the game — men with names like their own and with backgrounds like theirs, players who would swear and spit and fight on the field, and drink with their fans in the city's many saloons afterward.

It was like that in most of the major cities of the United States, a country where most of the population lived in 19 major urban areas. The streets of the cities were bustling with people heading off to work, many to mills where they labored hard just to have enough to eat. They could identify with the players, even if the ballplayers were making sums as high as $4,000 a year, half a dozen times and more the average annual wage of a working man.

Dreyfuss wanted the game to appeal, too, to the growing middle class of America and to families. He wished it to escape its legacy of being too rowdy, trouble that had come during the heyday of the National League when it was a monopoly run by autocrats who didn't care much for public opinion. Dreyfuss was a well-dressed, tidy man with a penchant for business, who in his younger days had fallen in love with the game of baseball.

And now, the professional baseball team he owned, the Pittsburg Pirates, was heading toward its third consecutive National League championship behind the greatest player of the day, shortstop Johannes Peter Hans "Honus" Wagner. "The Flying Dutchman," was a massive, barrel-chested man who sped like a runaway bull, scooped ground balls out of the dirt like a machine, and terrorized pitchers with his defiant stance at the plate. He had an incomparable ability to hit, especially line drives that screeched past bewildered infielders who could only look up and see the big-cheeked, big-boned Wagner rumbling toward them with a deadpan look on his face.

The upstart American League had become surprisingly successful in luring fans. It had been launched only two years before by a group of entrepreneurs who created a baseball war with the older, established National League owners. The new league wa popular even in cities where the older league had been playing for years, and Dreyfuss, like his colleagues in the National League, could no longer ignore its successes. But Dreyfuss still felt his team couldn't be beaten by anyone in a series.

Wagner had a lot of support. Dreyfuss' team was coached by left fielder Fred "Cap" Clarke, a tough man who kept the players in line, and it featured a great hitter and runner in speedy center fielder Ginger Beaumont. It still had a strong pitching staff, although the team had lost two of its pitching stars, Jack Chesbro and Jesse Tannehill, to the American League in 1902. Dreyfuss had been happily surprised by the pitching performance of a crafty left-hander named Ed Doheny, who had a fireball fastball mixed with an assortment of off-speed pitches and a desire to win rivaled only by Wagner, it seemed. Doheny had become a favorite, although Dreyfuss was increasingly worried that the left-hander was getting too intense. There were signs of stress, Clarke had warned, moments where Doheny couldn't keep his temper and fought with players, including some on his own team. Doheny's demeanor became more and more distant, and he had the eerie, fixed-eye stare of aman who was lost in a different world. There was talk that it was just Doheny's desire to win that made him that way.

Dreyfuss had barely been able to keep his other players, including the great Wagner, from being lured away to the new league by lucrative contracts that challenged the foundation of the game and the monopoly the National League owners had enjoyed for decades. There was even talk that some of the American League's better teams — like the Philadelphia Athletics and the Boston Americans, who in 1903 were fighting for the pennant — could give the Pirates all they could handle. It was heretical talk in the National League, where a combination of defiance and arrogance prevailed among the owners.

Dreyfuss saw an opportunity his colleagues did not. He had worked his way up in the business world and then in the baseball world because of his strong management skills and an ability to see what was coming before his rivals could. He was a good businessman and a good man. In the early 20th century, workers were like fodder for the capitalist mills, commodities on whose backs profits could be made. They were often interchangeable, even in baseball, unless they were among the game's elite, but Dreyfuss gave them respect and in return they gave him loyalty. He regarded his players well and wanted to win at the game he had grown to love when he was younger, although he had been a mediocre player himself.

Dreyfuss was a small man with big ideas. He was especially good at figuring out ways to get what he wanted without being caught. Dreyfuss had an idea he thought could pre-empt the upstart American Leaguers — especially the insufferable president Ban Johnson, a gargantuan man, a former sportswriter who had parlayed a bellicose management style into taking on the National League and whose publicity grabbing was taking headlines away from it. Dreyfuss was confident his team could beat any in the American League, even though the new junior circuit had spirited away some National League stars, like pitcher Cy Young, who was leading the Boston Americans toward a pennant over the defending champion Philadelphia Athletics. Even worse, the teams in Boston and Philadelphia were outdrawing their National League rival Boston Beaneaters and Philadelphia Phillies. Dreyfuss wanted to get the fans back and show Johnson and the American Leaguers who the real champions of baseball were.

All he had to do was convince the best American League team to play his team at the end of the regular season, to bring the pennant winners together for the first time. It was a concept he thought would get the fans' attention, especially from the sportswriters who loved hanging around the teams. In Boston, *Globe* baseball editor Tim Murnane, who had played professional baseball and was among the most respected writers, would be sure to whet the fans' appetite.

Dreyfuss had to get permission from A.H. Soden, owner of the Beaneaters, to let the Pirates play an American League team in their city. Dreyfuss wanted to write to Americans owner Henry Killilea about his idea, but first he needed to contact Soden because there was talk in Boston about a series at the end of the year between the Americans and Beaneaters, an intracity rivalry that was sure to make a lot of money. Soden would have to give up his share of the take if the Pirates played the Americans instead. Dreyfuss sat down at his desk and wrote Soden. He didn't have to wait long. Several days later, in mid–July, he got his reply.

> My dear Mr. Dreyfuss;
>   Your letter at hand and contents satisfactory. Answering your request, I will say that if the Pittsburg club of the National League and the Boston club of the American League win the championship of their respective leagues, the Boston National League most cheerfully extends to the Pittsburg club an invitation to play in the city of Boston any games they may desire with the said Boston American League club.

Trusting that the results of said games may establish more firmly the supremacy of the National League, I am,

                                      Truly yours,
                                      A.H. Soden, President

Dreyfuss had to make the arrangements with Killilea, which he would work on that summer. The Pirates owner was confident in his great team. Wagner, Clarke and Beaumont could supply the hitting, and the great Pirate pitching staff of Deacon Phillippe, Sam "The Goshen Schoolmaster" Leever, Brickyard Kennedy — and Doheny, en route to a great season — would be too much for the Americans, Dreyfuss felt sure.

Then came word from Clarke. Doheny was going mad.

ONE

Today They Assault the Citadel

The first World Series would be a best-of-nine affair with the first three games to be played in Boston at the Huntington Avenue Grounds. The first game was set for October 1, 1903. On that Thursday morning, the *Boston Globe* front page bannered its lead story over a cartoon depicting a gang of pirates, their ship in a harbor behind them, on land trying to scale a hill on top of which were thick intellectual books for a bunker. Titles included *Ethics of Baseball* by noted Bostonian Ralph Waldo Emerson, and *Baseball as Taught at Harvard*, poking fun at Boston's working-class-city opponents. Behind the Boston players, who were decked in their uniforms, Golden Dome of the State House was shining in the sun. The pirate ship carried the flag "Smoke Town" while the pirates on land bore the black skull-and-bones of the raiders. This was war.

The lead pirate, with a polka-dot bandanna, a cutlass in one hand and single-shot revolver in the other, was Honus Wagner, spouting, "I vill make me dose ten home runss alretty yet," and the caption cloud had him signed as Hans Vogner. Another pirate, bearded and brandishing his cutlass, said, "Dis is fer cuttin' into Old Cy."

The barb, of course, was directed at Boston's — and baseball's — best pitcher, Cy Young, who was nestled behind a stack of books on top of the hill, holding a baseball bat and saying to Wagner, "You mean 'Nein,' don't you, Hans?" telling Wagner he was going to get nothing out of the grand old man of the game. They talked up the Americans' great player-manager, Jimmy Collins, who had jumped from the National League Boston Beaneaters two years before.

The Pirates had arrived by train the day before at Boston's Hotel Vendome on elegant, tree-lined Commonwealth Avenue. It was an imposing gray stone building of ornate design. They were surprised to see so many fans, and gamblers, in the lobby of the well-appointed hotel. The atmosphere quickly became testy. The scrappy Pirate outfielder Beaumont, the fastest man in the game, was having none of the razzing that was starting up and he snapped at some of the fans who were getting too close.

"Well, what the heck are you staring at?" he said between chaws of tobacco. Then he spit close to the crowd and the tension heightened, especially when one Boston fan recognized the quiet, gentlemanly Wagner and got on him.

"Hey, Dutchman, we're going to give you and the Pirates a licking you'll never forget," he said. That was too much even for Wagner.

"Who with? With that old man, Cy Young? Why, we chased him out of the National League years ago," Wagner said, harshly and uncharacteristically. Other players spat profanity and the fans gave it back. Gamblers flashed wads of bills as the scene verged on chaos, and no one made any pretense of hiding the betting interests on the game.

On the eve of the first game a well-dressed young man walked into the lobby and looked for some Pirates backers to bet against. He was holding a big roll of bills in his hand, looking smug and ready for some betting action. "Where's the Pittsburg Rooters?" he tooted. But the Pittsburg fans had gone out sightseeing and to the theater. He walked up to some of the players sitting in the lobby.

"Tell your boys I'll be at the game tomorrow with $10,000 ready to put up on Boston at 10 to 8," he smiled. "I'll be in the third row of the grandstand with a pink pin in the lapel of my coat and I'll accommodate anyone who has money to bet against Boston." Then he walked out without giving his name.

But other Bostonian bettors had already put big money down on the game, raising some fears that the games might not be on the level. There had been plenty of talk about some regular season games being tossed if they were meaningless so the players could bet and supplement their salaries, but already the stakes were high for the series and the players and fans of both cities had taken it personally. It was a chance for the upstart American Leaguers to show they could play on the same field with the seasoned National League and especially the vaunted three-time pennant winners, the Pirates, and their star, Wagner.

Sportswriters from most of Pittsburg's newspapers, eager to record the monumental event and enjoy the trip, accompanied the Pirates. The *Pittsburg Leader* captured the mood of intensity. "The eyes of the whole baseball world are on this city today, for this afternoon will open about the most important and widely interesting series in the history of the national game," the paper reported. *Pittsburg Post* sportswriter John H. Gruber, also the team's official scorer and unofficial cheerleader, was surprised nonetheless to see the degree of excitement in the city. The Pirates, of course, had come to Boston often to play the National League Beaneaters, but this was a different foe for a higher stake.

Gruber wrote his lead for the next day's paper: "The Pittsburg champions arrived in Boston this morning and found the old town all agog over the coming struggle for the world's championship. Everybody here is talking about the games." He noted the intense gambling too, although he said Pittsburg's player-manager, left fielder Fred Clarke, had warned his players to stay away. "There is no betting by the Pittsburg players, on the advice of Clarke who thought it would influence their play."

A lot of money was being bet, and the story said there would be a keen eye placed on the players. "Errors may be looked for, as the players have much at stake, and they are more likely to miscue than when there was little or nothing at stake," the *Post* cautioned.

Knowing those stakes, Clarke privately was worried about the staff that had thrown six consecutive shutouts and 56 scoreless innings during a summer run that saw them pulling away from the field en route to an impressive pennant-winning performance, but now had come up lame. He was especially downcast about Doheny, the left-handed pitcher who had a mental breakdown and was now with his wife and child in nearby Andover, 25 miles north of Boston. Clarke had hoped that Doheny would somehow recover and be able to play, and he was worried that the Pirate staff, thin from injury, wouldn't be able to hold back the Boston hitters. Before the series, he had sent Doheny a telegram to see if he could play, and told reporters wondering about the pitcher: "If he shows his old time skill, he certainly will be used as he is the only left-hander on the squad." But that was for show only. Clarke also had several everyday players nursing injuries. Wagner had a bad leg, and the team was without Otto Krueger, a catcher the Pirates had picked up who had been beaned late in the season and was still unable to play. Clarke was beginning to wonder if the challenge to play Boston was such a good idea since he was so short-handed.

Boston had two left-handed hitters in the lineup in leadoff man Patsy Dougherty, who was fast and big at 6'2" and 190 pounds, and cagey veteran Chick Stahl, while first baseman Candy LaChance was a switch hitter. Clarke hoped his team's lineup — which included left-handed hitters Beaumont and himself at the top of the order, and young Jimmy Sebring followed by second baseman and switch hitter Claude "Little All Right" Ritchey — would cause problems for Boston's lineup of big right-handed power pitchers. Clarke had already decided to go with Deacon Phillippe, his shy right-handed ace, to open on the mound. Phillippe had the manner of a preacher.

Although adored for his genuine niceness, he was a hard competitor who would give no quarter. He said:

> If I am chosen to work for Pittsburg I will pitch the best ball of my career. I was never in better shape for hard, grueling work in my life. I have been on edge right along and the rest I have had has put me in the best possible physical condition. If I pitch, I am confident of winning. There is not the least doubt in my mind as to the result of today's game. Our boys will get after Collins' men from the start and the pace the Nationals will set will be too hot for the Americans to follow. If we do not win, it will be a great disappointment.

Especially for Dreyfuss, who had put the prestige of the National League on the line.

Of course, the Pirates had Wagner as the leader on the field, although his manner was even more reserved than Phillippe's. But while Wagner was the team's spiritual leader, third baseman Tommy Leach was a sparkplug, even at 5'6" and 150 pounds. He was a terrier, a scrapper whose bellicose style of play was belied by his choirboy good looks, slicked-back black hair and hint of a little boy smile. He still had a swollen finger from an injury, but said he would play nonetheless, even wearing a bandage. There was a good deal of swaggering and boasting going on — mostly among fans — and Leach felt the Pirates could not lose, although he had to be drawn into saying so:

> You see, it's not up to me to have much to say. You had better see Mr. Dreyfuss or Fred Clarke. They'll tell you all about it. Personally, I think we have it all over them. I don't see how we can lose. We know the Boston Americans are in the upper class as a ball team and nobody but a lunatic would deny that. Still, we have been playing together a long time and our pitchers are all in good shape. The Boston Americans will realize they are up against the toughest proposition yet when they stack up against Pittsburg today. It will be [a] fight from the drop of the hat, and no doubt the better team will win the series.

Clarke said he was so sure of victory now that "I can't see the result any other way. The team to a man feels the same way. Reports about Leach's injury are exaggerated and he will be in the game in good shape. Boston people have not seen us play on fast grounds such as those on Huntington Avenue, which are like our own, and we will show them some speedy baseball." That was for public consumption.

Of course, Clarke told another Pittsburg sportswriter that he also felt the Pirates might be able to sweep the first five games and run the Boston team out of the series before they could even catch their breaths or make sure their spikes were on tight. "I feel confident that we shall win, although I expect it will take eight games to settle it. I figure that we shall win two out of three in Boston," he said.

Even the quiet and businesslike Dreyfuss was feeling good about the Pirates' chances. "I've come a long way from the west to see my boys take two out of three here. I do not underrate the Boston Americans but I do think the Pittsburg team has something on them. Of course, I've made a wrong guess before, but I think candidly and truly that the Pittsburg team is the best in the country, and I know that right here in Boston, you have one too," said Dreyfuss.

Clarke, known as "Cap," was a 5'10", 165-pound Iowan, who was in his tenth year with the team, including four in Louisville. He had finished second in hitting in the National League at .351, just behind Wagner's .355. He told a reporter: "All I care to say is that I never went into a game yet that I did not expect to win. You can say that we will be in the game with heads, hands and feet tomorrow."

On the day before the first game, the Boston players were at the Huntington Avenue grounds practicing loosely, looking confident. The Americans had a lot of veterans from the National League and were not daunted by the prospect of playing men they had faced before. The Americans' manager, Collins, walked over to Cy Young. "You'll be in the box tomorrow," he said. Young would be the starting pitcher.

"All right," Young smiled, pulling up his 6'2", 210-pound frame. "I will try to be there," he laughed. Clarke's prediction that the Pirates would sweep the Bostonians held no sway with Collins. "I am not underrating the men from Pittsburg, but will not take Fred Clarke's word for it when he says they will win in five straight," Collins said, no levity in his manner, stance or voice. But then he smiled and said, "We will pick up a few games, all right."

Collins said he was confident because seven of his starters, excepting only LaChance and Dougherty, had been together since the team was formed two years earlier, at the beginning of the American League, and knew each other's movements well. "They know each other to the dot," he said. "I know that Pittsburg will face a much stronger team today than they have been up against all year."

After the practice, the club manager and money-handler, Joseph Smart, made sure the field was roped off, anticipating a big crowd and big payday. He had hired a small army of Boston police for security. National League President Harry Pulliam, a former Pirates executive, came into town the night before and would sit in a front row seat with Dreyfuss, who was informed by Smart that he would have to pay for the seats for his entourage. This riled the usually calm businessman.

"Did you ever hear of such a thing," the indignant Dreyfuss said. "They made me pay to see my own players!" He could afford it, of course, but he didn't like the idea. Besides, despite his disdain for anything that would hurt the integrity of the game, Dreyfuss and his Pittsburg friends had bet $30,000 on the Pirates to win the series and his gentlemanly demeanor didn't mask his competitiveness.

Smart was a businessman, though, and he also enforced a pay policy for sportswriters who were not from Boston or Pittsburg, and even for the owners of the National League rival Boston Beaneaters, a tactic that did not endear him to those who had expected to sit for free. Tickets were $1 for the grandstand seats, up from 50 cents, and 25 cents to stand in the outfield, although many with grandstand tickets would find themselves behind ropes in the outfield, thanks to an on-the-field standing room only policy to bring in more fans.

Boston was bracing for a chaotic weekend. Besides the first games of the World Series, the city would host the Ancient and Honourables, a marching guard from England that was expected to draw as many people to the narrow streets of the city as the series would draw to the ballpark. Usually reserved Bostonians were getting excited now and the city took on the air of a huge celebration. Working-class men and women were going to be jockeying for spots in the ballpark with men in their best suits and women in their best dresses.

The Grip of Enthusiasm

Boston was ready for the clash of cultures and teams. The first game of the first real World Series had become a social affair as much as a sporting event. At Mike "Nuf Ced" McGreevey's Third Base Saloon near the park, players, politicians, celebrities and fans crowded together in anticipation of a battle royal, games where the ball field would become a battlefield for bragging rights between the two cities, Smoke Town and the Athens of America, even though most of the ballplayers came from the same Irish and German-American working-class backgrounds. McGreevey would lead his maniacal Royal Rooters and their band. The Pirates had been to Boston plenty to play the Beaneaters at the next-door South End Grounds, but hadn't been able to see the Americans play, although they knew the National League veterans who had jumped leagues.

In Pittsburg, residents picked up the *Pittsburg Gazette* on the day of the game to see the headline, "The Pirates Are In Fine Fettle For The Fray," and were told, "People [were] baseball crazy." It was going to be a good day for it, mild weather for New England, with the temperature at about 60 degrees.

The series had engulfed both cities with fervor and passion, pitting ideas and cultures against each other as much as ballplayers. Even with talk that betting money was swapping hands openly and influencing the series, the players' pride was coming to the fore. Everywhere in Boston, people were in good spirits and the most common greeting when people met was, "Going to the game?"

Reporters who got assignments to mingle with the crowd and keep their ears open for comments were up against the hardest kind of proposition, especially when they got to the ballpark and found it submerged in humanity. The Huntington Avenue Grounds wouldn't hold more than 9,000 people comfortably and even the large contingent of police Smart had hired wasn't enough to handle the crowds that suddenly swarmed down the broad path of Huntington Avenue the late morning of October 1.

The path to the park's entrance went along the first base side, while the 12-foot-high outfield fence, bordered on Huntington Avenue, was not high enough to keep fans from getting on each other's shoulders and trying to shimmy up to see. Others resorted to climbing telephone poles and perching precariously to get a sight. It seemed like the crowd estimates of 15,000 would be too low.

Early arrivals to the park sometimes found usurpers in the seats and police reluctant to intervene because they were busy trying to control the growing crowd. Absent, though, was American League President Ban Johnson, for whom the series meant so much. His absence made for taunting by a Pittsburgh newspaper which said he "remained away to avoid a pain in the region of his heart."

A gate behind the Boston players' bench was closed and the crowd sent around back of first base behind a roped-off area. There were so many fans that Smart recruited some of the players for help, including Young, who showed up to work at a ticket booth before putting on his uniform. It was apparent that spectators would spill into the outfield and watch the game from behind a roped-off barrier. Coming down Huntington Avenue were men in suits, some in tails and high hats, and women in full dress gowns.

The air was filled with the sounds of thousands of excited people: the Royal Rooters marching over from McGreevey's saloon, filled with the intoxication of liquor and the fervor of the game; the hoi polloi hobnobbing with the wealthy and the politically connected; the shouts of hawkers and peddlers and gamblers, the wide-eyed heart-pounding joy of the game upon them; the Pittsburg fans unable to understand how their three-time pennant winners were suddenly the underdogs to the gamblers. For several hours before the game, all the roads and avenues leading to the ballpark were jammed with hordes of happy people, chortling in anticipation and delight. There was a constant murmur of greetings, laughter, chatter, and stoked-up cries of exultation. This game would produce the largest crowd thus far to see a baseball game in Boston.

Besides Pulliam, Boston Mayor Patrick Collins, former mayors, and many prominent business leaders were there, along with those working-class

12   The 1903 World Series

people who could afford to take off the time and raise the admission price. Ministers sat next to laborers, politicians next to men who carried ice and delivered coal, gamblers next to priests. But Boston owner Henry Killilea was still in Milwaukee and not due to arrive until the morning of the second game. Everybody else seemed to be there. Businessmen rubbed shoulders with their clerks and city hall politicians and their heelers were on an equal footing — this was how the *Boston Post* described the scene. "Like a Harvard-Yale football game, almost everyone of any importance was to be seen," the paper said. Baseball had been popular in Boston and throughout the country, but this series had elevated it from the sporting ranks to grand entertainment on a scale transcending economic classes and constituencies.

Pittsburgh had even brought along an unofficial rooter in a mascot named "Nuf Ced"— the same nickname as Boston's saloon owner — but who represented Pickering's Furniture Store and who carried a megaphone to cheer on the team. "It was a big surprise to see a Pittsburg furniture house leading the Champion rooters and led the Pirates to believe that Fred Clarke and his men must be solid with the business men of Pittsburgh," the *Pittsburgh Times* noted. The furniture store Nuf Ced, though, would be no match for what McGreevey and his Royal Rooters had planned for the Pirates.

By 2 P.M., an hour before game time, the first base bleachers and those behind third were packed; there were no outfield seats or seats along the first and third base sides. Each successive trolley car that came up Huntington Avenue poured out people like cattle and a dozen extra police were called into duty. The stands behind home plate and a short distance along the first and third base lines were jammed. Trying to move a foot there "meant stirring up of testy natures," as a reporter quickly found. When one tried to squeeze into the stands, he was met with loud cries of opposition, "What d'yer want? What d'yer want?"

"It was no use to complain it was a business necessity," the reporter said. To move a foot meant a great deal of exertion and to push on for a row was likely to precipitate a fight. Shortly after 2 P.M., the huge throng on the field and in the stands suddenly erupted into a loud cheer when the first Boston players — Hobe Ferris, Chick Stahl, Dougherty, and catcher Lou Criger came out for batting practice. Then the cheers grew voluminous when several more — shortstop Fred Parent, LaChance, manager Collins, American League home-run king Buck Freeman, and pitcher Big Bill Dinneen came out. But the crowd exploded when Cy Young walked onto the field.

A few minutes later, the first of the Pirates came in through a side gate,

Opposite: **Fans jumped fences, sneaked in and otherwise did what they could to get into the sold out first game, including flooding the field. They were pushed back by game time but still filled much of the outfield (courtesy Boston Public Library).**

headed by Clarke. They walked straight past the Boston bench and took off their blazers. Clarke turned to a contingent of newspapermen in the stands, winked, and said, "A great crowd, isn't it," before nonchalantly strolling out onto the field with the team. Wagner walked out behind second base to stretch. A crowd of McGreevey's Royal Rooters, each with an American flag, ran onto the field to greet the Pirates and cajole them with an overly warm reception. Wagner and first baseman Kitty Bransfield, a local boy from Worcester (about 50 miles west of Boston) who had played for the Beaneaters five years before, got some genuine applause as the Pirates took infield practice.

By 2:30 P.M., there were more than 12,000 fans in the stands and on the field. Many women and their escorts tried to get into the grandstands but were pushed back behind the outfield ropes. Hundreds of other fans who had seated themselves on the grass along the third base line were directed back to the roped-off outfield by swarms of police.

The players' benches were at ground level; the bats were lined up in front of them on the ground. The police, in their high, round hats, stood guard by the players because of the propensity of the fans to shout loudly, argue with each other, scream at the umpires, and even to try to come out on the field. The Royal Rooters had brought their own band, including a large drum, hoping to disconcert the Pirates. Lined up behind the first-base side, the uniformed brass band played tunes trying to hop up the crowd, while the Pirate fans occupied front seats directly over the Pittsburg playing bench.

The official attendance in the field with a capacity of about 9,000 was 16,242. Killilea, who had put up a lot of money, was especially anxious and anticipating a profit. A Boston sportswriter said the fans owed Killilea for putting the team together. "By personal sacrifices, by business sacrifices, by the application, earnest and steady, of a mind that has no superior, he has placed Boston at the head of the American League and he has the gratitude of all Boston lovers of clean baseball." Now it was time to play ball.

The two team managers, Clarke and Collins, walked out to home plate and met with the umpires, Hank O'Day of the National League and Tom Connolly of the American League, the only two who would call the game. As they came together, the crowd grew silent. From a constant clatter and din there fell a calmness and sudden stillness and surprised the four men at the plate. No one moved in the stands, no sound came from the thousands in the outfield and teetering on the fences. The four men talked briefly about the ground rules, which called for hits going into the outfield crowd to be triples. They surveyed the scene and walked away as the silence broke with a loud eruption of cheering from every quarter, intensifying when the mighty Young strode out to the mound.

Young took his first few easy warm-up throws and the Americans began a banter of chatter in the infield to support him. There was high anxiety

The Royal Rooters of Boston made sure they had a band ready for the games in Boston, and hired one when in Pittsburg. They wanted musical accompaniment to their constant singing (courtesy Boston Public Library).

everywhere and it would soon show in the field. In the stands and out on the field, the crowd shuffled in anticipation. The big Young, with his 28 wins, blazing fastball and fearsome reputation, was an odds-on favorite to handle the Pirates, who were going to oppose him with 25-game winner Phillippe.

While Young was big, he was more pear-shaped than muscular, but his shape belied how quickly the ball came to the plate. Phillippe was tall, pencil-thin and reticent and avoided publicity. He had a sturdy oval face, a strong jaw and dark hair parted in the style of the times, just left of the center, and he had a strong curving bender he thought might confound the Americans.

Connolly, behind the plate, and O'Day, on the bases, had set ground rules because of the large crowd. Even ground-rule triples into the crowd would be quite a feat. It would have to be a prodigious hit for most of the players because left center field was 440 feet and dead center was 635 feet, although the right field fence was only about 280 feet. But in those days, fans lined the outfield in front of those distant fences. Young was concerned since the Pirates' first two hitters, Beaumont and Clarke, were left-handed hitters, as was Sebring, while Ritchey was a switch hitter.

Young would have to be wary of Beaumont, who had led the National League in runs with 137, hits with 209, and total bases and runs produced with 198. Clarke's .531 slugging average led the league, ahead of Wagner in second place; they were the top of a lineup that had produced a league-leading 793 runs. While Phillippe would open on the mound, Clarke thought it might be Sam Leever who could be his ace, especially with the left-handed Doheny out. That's if Leever could pitch, for his arm and shoulder were still sore from an injury in a trap-shooting contest, and he also had a cold. Leever's 25–7 mark was just ahead of Phillippe's 25–9 in leading the league in winning percentage, and Leever had a league-leading seven shutouts and the lowest earned run average, at 2.06. Phillippe also had the best control of any pitcher in the game, walking less than one man a game.

While the Pirates were confident they could handle Boston, Clarke knew the Americans had plenty of power in Buck Freeman, who had a league-leading 13 home runs. Dougherty led the American League with 107 runs and 195 hits, and Freeman was the RBI leader with 104 and a batting average of .331. Young was the workhorse on the mound, with 341.2 innings pitched, 34 complete games, and seven shutouts. He was rated with Cleveland infielder Nap LaJoie, Wagner, and New York Giants pitcher Christy Mathewson as the best players in the game.

At 3 P.M. the Boston players were in position under a cloudy October sky, on fresh cut grass that had been watered a little while before, and they looked into a sea of people in the stands and surrounding the field. For this moment, there was no other event that mattered anywhere, and the anxiety and elegance of the well-dressed audience had hearts racing, even among the cynical sportswriters. Men in bowlers and women in feathered hats were ready to roar. The Pirates were resplendent in bright blue caps with the big yellow "P" representing their city and the National League, handsome in gray wool uniforms with the bright blue collars. Young was firing fastballs in his warm-up and looked to be in what the writers called "gilt-edged style."

Boston was in its home uniform, white wool with turned down collars, lacing part way down the front and big blue capital letters on the chest spelling out "Boston." Belted, loose trousers with built-in quilted padding for sliding protection came to just below the knees and bright blue stockings went over the shoe tops. The caps were pillbox shaped with a single thick blue stripe around the crown.

Then Beaumont stepped to the plate as the cry of "Play ball!" was heard. The crowd went wild.

TWO

End of the Elysian Field

Former sportswriter Bancroft "Ban" Johnson saw an opportunity for the game he loved — baseball — as America awoke to the 20th century and the new millennium. "Hail to a Century" was the banner headline in the *Boston Globe* on January 1, 1901. Celebrations around the country at midnight had ushered in the new era for the United States, especially urban centers, which were the nucleus for a growing Industrial Revolution that had burgeoned at the end of the 19th century but was now really catching steam. Optimism abounded as 1901 dawned.

In Pittsburg, steel mills may have poured black smoke into the air, but they were putting to work the immigrants and sons of immigrants who had come from Europe, many from Germanic and Scandinavian countries, and who settled into the hard hills of the city with a determined resolution, a work ethic and a desire for play and sport. They were hard-working family men, to be sure, but they populated the saloons after hard days in the mills, liked gambling, drinking and singing, and had taken to a game new to many of them when they arrived: baseball. It was all the more appealing with a winning home team. The Pirates had finished a close second to Brooklyn in 1900, and Dreyfuss felt his team was on the verge of a dynasty that he would build with shrewd player moves. The National League had ruled the sport since it began a quarter-century before, despite limited competition from several major leagues that made a run at its popularity.

In Boston, waves of Irish immigrants had settled, in sometimes sharing the city uneasily with the established and moneyed upper class. The steel mills were in Pittsburg, but the Bostonians thought they were building an intellectual center. In both cities, the downtowns were teeming with an exploding population and starting a crescendo of work, driven by the new engines of technology.

Despite baseball's popularity, some warning signs of public discontent were starting to show. The National League had finished a profitable year in 1900 and the owners had tried to ignore the trouble brewing. Complaints of rowdyism by players, of umpire baiting, and even of assaults on umpires had sullied the game for many. The National League owners, smug in their monopoly, were unafraid of Ban Johnson and his new American League, which had been formed out of the minor Western League. Johnson was a formidable figure with his huge frame and slicked hair parted in the middle. He was a hard-charging dictator who could be vain and arrogant and publicity-hungry, but he didn't suffer fools gladly, and he thought there were plenty of them amongst the National League owners. He wanted to challenge them and make the American League a major league too.

The level of play in the American League might not be able to yet match the National League with all its stars, but Johnson was able to get the backing of the sportswriters and the fans, because he would not allow rowdyism and stood by his umpires in having them control games. He had become the arbiter of what he thought fans wanted and he was going to give it to them. Soon, *The Sporting News* said Johnson's able and professional leadership and business skills had pushed the new American League into success because it lacked "the cowardly truckling, alien ownership, syndicatism, hyppodroming, selfish jealousies, arrogance of club owners, mercenary spirit and disregard of public demands" the National League had demonstrated.

Frank Richter, editor of *The Sporting Life,* had written in 1900 that the National League owners were apparently blinded by their own ambitions and couldn't see what they were doing to their game and businesses. He said the league was marred by "gross individual and collective mismanagement, their fierce factional fights, their cynical disregard of decency and honor, their open spoilation of each other, their deliberate alienation of press and public, their flagrant disloyalty to friends and supporters and their tyrannical treatment of the players."

By the end of the 1900 season, the National League was in disarray with wavering attendance and continuing factionalism. Johnson was ready for competition that would bring the American League into a major league status. It was bold and risky, but he thought the timing was right with the National League owners at each other's throats. In September of 1900, he decided to expand into the East in areas where he thought the National League was most vulnerable. It was also where he would provoke them.

In January of 1901, he declared the new American League would become a major league. It would abandon Minneapolis, Kansas City and Indianapolis and place teams in Baltimore, Washington, Philadelphia — and finally Boston. Charles Somers would put up the money and become owner of the new Boston team which would be the flagship of a the new major league which would go head-to-head with the National League in many cities where the older circuit had been operating for years.

The Symbol of the Century

Even with the infighting, baseball was still what Mark Twain had called "the very symbol, the outward and visible expression of the drive and push and rush and struggle of the raging, tearing, booming 19th century," and newspapers and magazines of the day said the game had taken hold of the American public. But now it was losing its grip and Johnson knew it. The *Boston Globe* promised it would dedicate plenty of space to baseball no matter what else was going on in the world — and there was plenty, with the Spanish-American War and a new century underway. It said stories about baseball would abound even though "Emperors may be shot down by the dozen, gigantic political frauds may be exposed; steamships may collide and go down with all hands on board; Europe may be plunged in bloody and universal strife." Baseball was still the bread-and-circus for the common folk, and Johnson sensed a new audience was looming.

The population of the United States had grown rapidly, from about 31 million in 1860 to more than 76 million by 1900, with many of those concentrated in the major cities. This helped take baseball from the rural playing fields into the populated metropolises, where ample coverage by multiple newspapers made it easy for baseball to be followed even by people who couldn't get to the parks. And while many working people found it difficult to attend weekday afternoon games or couldn't afford to go, a growing urban middle class, mostly men, who had time and money, created a new audience. Most of the games were scheduled for late afternoon so these fans could attend. The fast pace of games, with most lasting under two hours, ensured a finish during daylight.

And even with growing troubles in baseball because of mismanagement, it was still the most followed game, mostly because of the sportswriters, who were the conduit between the fans and the players and the owners and the game. The *Boston Globe's* Tim Murnane was paramount among them, but they were a colorful cadre, including John Gruber of *The Pittsburg Post*, Frank McQuiston of *The Pittsburg Dispatch*, Walter Barnes of *The Boston Herald*, J. Ed Grillo of *The Cincinnati Commercial-Tribune*, and Richter. With the telegraph, baseball writers could travel with their hometown teams and transmit stories as soon as the games were over, allowing fans to follow the action all over the country, and it was the writing of the reporters that made many of the baseball players national figures.

A curious symbiosis had developed between many players and sportswriters too because the writers liked mingling with the men and being able to partake of the sport in a vicarious way although some, like Murnane, had been players themselves. The writers wrote of the exploits as if they were jousting matches for honor, in colorful and illustrative terms that were a mix of elegance-and-sensationalism that could, in the same sentence, show baseball as a metaphor for life and go over-the-top with purple prose that was embarrassing. But then they would unfurl phrases and imagery that was uplifting. If Boston and Bostonians liked to think of themselves as the intellectual capital of the country — producing hospitals and schools like Boston Latin and Harvard — Pittsburg was the muscle, producing the steel and sweat that would be the foundation and building blocks of the new America. The Irish had found a home in Boston, where wealthy Yankees ruled, and the Germanics found theirs in Pittsburg, bringing cultures that would create identities for their cities and their baseball teams.

A portrait of "Nuf Ced" McGreevey, who ruled the Rooters and had his famous saloon near the ballparks of the Americans and the National League Beaneaters (courtesy Boston Public Library).

Work was hard and long for too little pay for most people, and they looked to embrace entertainment and sport they could afford and to which they could relate and like. Boston's population had reached 560,892 by 1900; many of them newly arrived from Ireland, arriving to find whole neighborhoods of their countrymen, while Pittsburg was at 321,616.

The Boston Beaneaters, a National League team, that had been a mini-dynasty a decade before, played at the South End Grounds, about a mile further down Huntington Avenue from Symphony Hall, and over a couple of blocks, near some railroad yards. It was also close by Michael T. "Nuf Ced" McGreevey's bar, at the corner of Ruggles Street. McGreevey had gotten his nickname, "Nuf Ced," from listening to many a baseball argument and settling it with his declaratory judgment: "Nuf Ced."

McGreevey was also an inveterate gambler who loved the rough-and-rowdy atmosphere of his elaborate saloon, all wood and brass and filled with baseball souvenirs and memorabilia. He was a handball player and one of a group called the L Street Brownies, named for a street in South Boston which ended at Boston Harbor, into which the Brownies would annually make cold plunges in the dead of winter to show their mettle. With a big mustache and sharp, piercing eyes, McGreevey would hold court in his own establishment like the character he was. Beaneater players were regulars at his saloon, as were many of the city's leading Irish-American politicians, including Mayor Honey Fitzgerald.

McGreevey had opened his place in the late 1890s and called it the Third Base Saloon because it was said it was "the last stop before you steal home," a double metaphor for the games at the South End Grounds and for the folks who would have a last drink there before calling it a day. Inside, the place was usually filled with laughter and drinking and cigar smoke. Patrons chewed tobacco and argued over baseball and politics and gossip. McGreevey had decorated it with scores of photographs of ball players and ballparks. Even the light fixtures in the ceiling were made from players' bats, at the bottom of which were baseball-like light bulbs. There was a grandfather clock with a pendulum made of a bat and ball. McGreevey was so proud of his nickname he had it spelled out on the saloon's mosaic tile floor. Above the entrance was a full-sized mannequin called "The Baseball Man" dressed in a Boston uniform.

A Short and Popular Death

The minor American League had a successful season in 1900, and Johnson was ready to make his move early in 1901. He had been battling with the National League owners over their drafting of his league's players. He had plenty of support from Charles Comiskey, whose Chicago team, built with rejects from the National League and some young new ballplayers it had overlooked, had won the first American League pennant. Johnson made overtures to lease a park in Philadelphia, and in Boston, where the National League did not want competition for the Beaneaters. Johnson needed more players, and better players, so he had an idea. He would go after the best players the National League had, not just the castoffs. This was a direct threat not only to what the National League owners saw as the integrity of the game, but to their business and monopoly. This was war. And Boston would be a prime battlefield for a revolution.

There was worry in the National League although, as Dreyfuss — for one — thought Johnson might make a go of his new enterprise and was concerned Pittsburg might be a site for a prospective American League team. Dreyfuss was cagily assessing the new threat and, unlike his bombastic fellow owners, he tried to position himself and his team for what he felt was the inevitability of the new league succeeding and challenging the senior circuit.

He had just put all his resources into getting ownership of the Pirates, and wisely knew that peace was more profitable than a war. "Maybe we better see what Johnson and those American League fellows want," he said to his fellow owners. But most of them were still opting to resist, not believing that Johnson and his backers, even though well-to-do, could get the players they needed without putting up so much money they could not make a profit when there was just the attendance for revenues.

But on January 5, Murnane reported that Boston would have two teams playing in the 1901 season, and that owner Charles Somers had surreptitiously had been coming to the city to scout ballpark sites, including the Charles River Park, alongside the river that separated Boston from Cambridge, and which led right to Boston Harbor. "His mission here is to show ... how strong is the American League and what a winner they could make of Boston," Murnane said. "Mr. Somers is perfectly willing to back the team from here, and being a man of means could no doubt make good," although Murnane said Somers hadn't succeeded yet in convincing the fans of Boston. If the National League succeeded in getting the American Association going, including in Boston, that would "mean a death blow to Johnson's league," he said. And Murnane reported that some National Leaguers were ready to jump ship if a new major league could offer them more money.

Soden, the Beaneater president, was asked what he thought about having a rival in Boston and tried to deflect it. He smiled and said, "We will try to do business just the same and hope the game will be benefited. The Boston club has no jurisdiction over the territory as long as the new club is outside the National Agreement." Murnane's conclusion? "The fans are rooting for a lot of good baseball here next season," he wrote.

And Johnson, as *The Globe* reported a few days later, was proving very aggressive, both as a businessman and in marketing his idea. "Ban Johnson, president of the American League, is proving one of the best press agents seen in the baseball business for years," the paper reported. With Boston being eyed for another major league team, the newspapers in the city were aggressively reporting the story, trying to outdo each other for readership with ever more behind-the-scenes stories and speculation about what was happening. Still, Johnson to that point had been content to send Somers to the city and had not visited Boston himself.

Then the *Globe* reported a new ballpark site was being eyed on Huntington Avenue, close to the city's working class Roxbury neighborhood, right near the Beaneater's home field, the South End Grounds. Murnane wrote though Johnson hadn't come to the city yet, "Even to carry out his bluff, so that the chances of worrying the Boston magnates is a waste of powder." But Johnson had called for a meeting the following week and there were reports that the new American League would probably consist of Boston, Philadelphia, Baltimore and Washington in the east, and Chicago, Cleveland, Detroit and Milwaukee in the west. "Johnson says that Philadelphia and Boston are the best ball towns in the country and that is why his league will invade the territory, placing in Boston a lot of youngsters with two or three old heads," the paper said.

But Johnson still needed parks in the cities where he would be going head-to-head with the National League. Somers, who now had been convinced by Johnson to finance the new Boston team, had to move fast. The season would start in only a few months, and still the new Boston team had no place in which to play. On January 18, Somers closed a five-year lease with the Boston elevated railway company for grounds on Huntington Avenue near the outskirts of downtown. Johnson had put his threat literally in the National Leaguer's backyard.

The Beaneaters, at least publicly, claimed no concern, as the team's director, Arthur Conant, said "The public will have all the baseball it wants next season if the American League makes good its threat to come here. It costs a lot of money, and I will not believe it is coming until the season opens."

Five days later, on January 23, Johnson came to Boston himself, and brought Somers with him. Somers signed the final lease papers for the Huntington Avenue Grounds, which the two men visited after breakfast. An architect was already at work on rough plans for the grounds, which would face south, in an opposite direction from the layout of the nearly adjacent South End Grounds, almost as if the American Leaguers were turning their back on their rivals.

Johnson said, "The American League is not looking for a fight: we think we have something in the way of baseball that the public wants, and will play the string out with good, fast, clean ball conducted by sportsmen." He said he had high regard for the Beaneaters, but believed the city could support two ball teams, and he totally discounted talk of a new National League–backed American Association putting a team in the city. "If they do," he smiled, "It will be a short and popular death."

War with the National League

On January 27 the American Leaguers held a summit in Chicago to outline the workings of the new major league. "It is expected that this meeting will make important baseball history," the *Globe* reported. Indeed, for such a public meeting, Johnson and his cohorts were trying to keep the National Leaguers from knowing what was going on, but it was being reported that the new major league had enough good players ready to begin their inaugural season and challenge the older league.

On January 29, reorganization of the American League and its declaration as a major league was finished. Johnson said, "The American League will go ahead regardless of any other organization, though as far as that is concerned, we do not anticipate any serious conflict from the schedule." Somers was named vice-president. Boston had its new team, called the Americans, and one of Somers' first plans was to try to sign the great Boston Beaneater third baseman, Jimmy Collins, a great player and leader who was a favorite of McGreevey's Royal Rooters too. Collins was an often taciturn and sometimes surly sort, but a firebrand on the field who would brook no slackers, even though he was not overly dictatorial to his players. He was a better than .300 hitter with the Beaneaters, and the kind of leader Somers wanted. And to steal him away from the National League team in the same city would be a real coup. But the calendar was against Johnson in some respects. For all his talk, his new major league still needed more and better players, and parks for his teams. In Boston, there were reports it would cost about $50,000 to build the Huntington Avenue facility.

The *Globe* said the public would be expecting more than just a new park though. They would want ballplayers. The Beaneaters had been a dominant team in the 1890s, but were no longer able to keep pace. Getting National League stars meant overcoming the option clause that bound them to their teams, although that was under assault too.

The National League owners were getting edgy. A Philadelphia newspaper reported that the American League was wooing Philadelphia's Nap LaJoie. In Buffalo, where he lived, Collins denied rumors about him jumping leagues. "There is absolutely nothing in the story," he said.

"I don't know anything about it. I think the wise players will stick to the men who have paid them good money till they see something better. The American League is going to have a hard row to hoe in Boston, and I would look nice managing it, wouldn't I? They would have to show me a lot of money ... I have not signed yet, but I expect that this trouble will all be settled in a few days and then I will put my name to a contract in large letters," he said.

It was here that Johnson's alliance with the affluent Somers really paid off. On February 16, with spring training a month away and the building of the new baseball grounds at Huntington Avenue proving troublesome, Somers declared that the new Boston American League team would open on time despite problems.

Johnson would go at the National Leaguers in another way: money. With backing from well-to-do businessmen like Comiskey and Somers, Johnson was ready to offer the National League players more money to join his new American League. The National League owners would not budge from a ceiling salary of $2,400 a year, which made many of the players happy to talk to American League owners. That included the great LaJoie, one of the premier hitters and stars of the game. Johnson and the American League owners set their sights too on Cy Young, who had brought a blazing fastball to the game at a time when many pitchers were content to just let the ball be put into play. They thought they could get him out of St. Louis.

In late February of 1901, just two months before the start of the new season for the American League as a major league, Johnson said, "The National League has taken it for granted that no one had a right to expand without first getting its permission. We did not think that this was necessary, and have expanded without even asking for permission.... If we had waited for the National League to do something for us, we would have remained a minor league forever. The American League will be the principal organization of the country within a very short time. Mark my prediction."

Johnson said the American League would only go after those National League players not under contract, but with financial backing from some wealthy entrepreneurs, the American League was prepared to offer top stars some dazzling numbers for the day, with talk of salaries as high as $4000 to $5000 at a time when the average annual income in the country was only about $700, and that for as many as 60 hours a week. The National League desperately tried to stem the flight of its stars, especially LaJoie. In Pittsburg, Dreyfuss was fearful of losing his marquee player as well and was appealing to Wagner's loyalty and roots in the area.

The public was paying attention. "Baseball news and gossip is now flying fast over the land," Murnane wrote in his column. "The 'fan' is in his element and takes sides as if he was interested financially, while the magnate smiles to learn that folks are once more talking about the old game."

On March 4, the Boston Americans said they had signed two important National League players — from the rival Boston Beaneaters of the National League — outfielder Charles Sylvester "Chick" Stahl, and pitcher Big Bill Dinneen. Stahl, 28, had played four years for the Beaneaters, hitting .354, .308, and .351. and .295, while Dinneen, a 6–1, 190-pounder who threw hard and was tough-minded on the mound, had gone 20–14 and 15–18 for the Beaneaters the previous two years. He was only 24 and thought to be a mainstay on any pitching staff. But it was Collins, of course, that was the important man for Boston because he was a no-nonsense ball player and manager, and kept his own counsel.

Then he made his announcement: "I have signed to play with the Bostons and shall have a team that will be first-class in every particular. Boston is an ideal baseball town and I know the American League will make a complete success," he said after the Stahl and Dinneen signings. On March 9, he explained himself further and said "I have given the National League people my best efforts for several years past and often asked them for more money, knowing that I was worth it. But until now they have turned a deaf ear to all my requests, and so it is the same with many others. They come now when it is too late with their liberal offers," he said, adding he had no ill feelings toward the Beaneater owners.

While the jawboning between the leagues was going on, Somers was starting to move fast. On March 12, 1901, dirt was turned in Boston on the Huntington Avenue Grounds and work was begun on what would essentially be a wooden and light gray cement park. It would have grandstands by the first and third base lines, but no seats in the outfield, which was to be a high wooden fence right on Huntington Avenue, a major thoroughfare. The Americans hadn't played a game yet, but already the talk in Boston was about the newcomers.

Fight for Sheckles and Glory

The Beaneaters had already lost several of their stars and Johnson held a meeting in Philadelphia where it was expected many more signings of National League stars would be announced. There was a festive atmosphere in the city, and in the hotel, where plenty of players were milling about, talking about the birth of a new major league. The new American League owners were putting on their finest airs, and their finest suits. "The new magnates really looked prosperous compared to the modest-looking crowd who attend the meetings of the National League," Murnane wrote. "It is a meeting where player, magnate and fan meet on common ground, and the air was fairly blue with baseball talk," he added.

Somers was absolutely ebullient, and gave an order for 15,000 tickets to be ready for his new ballpark in Boston, where the foundations for the stands were nearly completed and steel pillars almost ready to be put into place.

And on March 21, it was revealed that the new league would open its first year on April 24. The Boston team, who would come to be called other nicknames, like the Plymouth Rocks, Pilgrims, and Somersets, would open at Baltimore, and would compete in Boston 25 times, on dates directly against the Beaneaters — 19 in May and June when fan interest in the new league was sure to be high. In a story headlined *Many a Clash*, Murnane wrote that while Johnson wanted direct competition, there was some worry it would cut into the gate to have fans trying to choose between two home teams playing the same days in the same city. In Boston, it would be worse because the ballparks were so close to each other. "Pres Johnson has forced Somers to take disagreeable medicine, for the backer of the club calls it burning money to play conflicting games," Murnane wrote.

"As May and June are the best months, both teams were anxious to play at home, and therefore the real fight for sheckles and glory will take place at the Hub," he said. Murnane said the scheduling was approved by Johnson, "who has stated that he would give the league people all the battle they wanted." The American Leaguers would also go at the National League at the box office, setting ticket prices at 25 cents, half that of the older league, and bring innovations such as a megaphone man who would loudly announce players changes on the field.

Brush, one of the most militant of the National Leaguers, said Johnson's decision to put a team in Boston meant a different kind of baseball war. "Only one club will survive this battle in Boston, and that will be the same old National League club," he said. He further derided Johnson's idea and said, "They are minor-league teams playing in major league cities. The public will know the difference."

Now the American League was a month away from playing and still Johnson had not given out the rosters of all the teams and who would be playing where. He was angered, however, that some who said they would join his league — and agreed to do so — had reneged and that the National League had taken away some American League ballplayers. It was good for the public and the newspapers, but this was a business as well as a baseball war and Johnson wanted to win. "I don't understand how players want to be classed with ... the past, who never were bettered by jumping contracts. The game is injured by these players and the American League will make no effort to bring these men back," he said. The men the American League was going after, he said, were not considered under contract with their teams when they were being wooed. But the Americans got Young, the big prize.

April 24 was opening day for the first season of rivalry between the two leagues of professional players at the major level. In Baltimore, the Orioles would host the Boston Americans and Cy Young — if the weather allowed. The weather in Baltimore was wretched, with a constant chilly rain. Baltimore fans were happy to get baseball back — and in a new park.

In Pittsburg, the playing field at Exposition Park, next to the river, was so bad from flooding and cold that Dreyfuss declared, "I have just let my order for snowshoes and ulsters for the members of my team. It does not help them if we were going to get any baseball weather for a couple of months and I want my men prepared to play in the snow and the cold. We've got to play some time, and I don't propose to let the snow stop us."

Johnson's big day didn't happen. Of the four games scheduled for April 24, only one took place. Chicago beat Cleveland before 8,000 fans, but bad weather forced postponements of the Baltimore-Boston, Washington-Philadelphia, and Milwaukee-Detroit games in the American League, so Johnson had no barometer by which to measure the initial popularity of his product. It didn't help that only two of the four National League games could be played, because Johnson wanted to know what fans thought. It was all gloom and doom in Baltimore, even though a spectacle had been planned. The mayor was going to throw out the first ball. There were cut flowers everywhere bearing all sorts of monograms and congratulations, and telegrams aplenty. But a heavy rain fell all the night before and it was still raining slightly by noon on the 24th only a few hours before the scheduled first pitch.

Despite the late spring start, the weather in many cities had been unplayable. And Boston, Johnson's heartfelt hope to be the centerpiece of his league until he could find a way to get into New York and challenge the Giants, hadn't played yet. Worse, the Beaneaters Dinneen stayed with his National League club.

Finally, on April 26, two days late, the Boston Americans opened in Baltimore before a crowd of 10,371, second only to the 10,547 that turned out in Philadelphia to see Connie Mack's Athletics take on Washington.

It wasn't an artistic success for Collins and his Americans, who lost 10–6, as Young, complaining he didn't feel well, was far off his game, but the Boston manager promised better days for fans who stuck by him and his new team.

The Boston hitters couldn't handle Baltimore pitcher Iron Man Joe McGinnity, but the work of catcher Lou Criger showed such sterling effort that Boston sportswriters wrote that "His all around work was grand and in him Boston has a rare jewel." And, true to his word to keep the game clean, the umpires followed Johnson's edict and had his backing, and waited only three innings in the Washington-Philadelphia game to eject a player who was too argumentative. What Johnson must have liked the most, however, was the attendance at the opening in Philadelphia of the Phillies game against the Boston Beaneaters. It was only 779.

The Globe explained that "Because of the counter attraction, the American League opening, the attendance was not all it should have been and was not at all flattering to the players and managers ... it was very dreary, and there is little hope of improvement tomorrow for the New Yorkers play." *The Globe* wrote *American League Begins Business with Warmest Encouragement*, and the results were similar in other papers where there were suddenly American League teams and new fans to attend games — and buy newspapers.

The Boston Americans lost their first three games, before beating Philadelphia there, with a crowd of 2,994 watching. Then finally came the day Johnson and a lot of Bostonians were really waiting fn: May 8, opening day in Boston for the new legion of fans of the American League team, including McGreevey and his Royal Rooters. It was big news in the papers and, typically, the mood of the city was captured by Murnane who wrote about the scene at the new baseball grounds, the wooden grandstands with flags on top of spires, the 12-foot high wooden fences surrounding the park, the long left field to center field wall along the expanse of Huntington Avenue, the big brick warehouses just past the left field fence, and the anticipation in the air for the start of baseball, for spring, and for a new league. The attendance was listed as 11,500, far above the capacity of 9,000, the fans there to see the birth of a major league baseball club for Boston.

"Everything inside the high fence was as new as this spring's tulip. The diamond shone in the sun like a great canvas of freshly spread green paint, the uniforms of the home team were as spotless as a just-from-the-wrapper ball and the great crowd seethed with good nature," Murnane wrote. And hope, always high with spring and the start of a new baseball season, filled the stands. The weather was ideal too, a shiny spring day in the city that brought out a holiday-sized attendance and kept the peanut man busy as he sailed his paper bags full of peanuts to people yelling for him in the stands, even before the game against the Philadelphia Athletics began.

Two tally-ho coaches drove in through the centerfield gate more than 500 feet from home plate, and marched across the bright new field under the warm May sun. The Boston cadet band played loudly and small American flags were passed out to the fans.

Boston hammered the A's 12–4, as Young easily put down the Philadelphians and the Americans hit with regularity against the visiting pitching. Young even contributed at the plate with a triple and single, and with a stolen base. There was mixed success for Johnson, because there were only 2,310 spectators for the Baltimore-Washington game and only 600 for the Chicago-Cleveland contest. It was a sign that Johnson couldn't rest easily yet.

The Americans didn't win the pennant, but Johnson won where it counted: at the box office, where the Americans outdrew the Beaneaters by more than 2–1, drawing 289,000 fans, the second highest in the league and fourth highest in both leagues. Throughout the American League cities, including where the competition was head-to-head against the National League entry, Johnson had been proved right.

And Murnane, whose heart had been with the National League, acknowledged that the new Boston team had surprised even him. In a column at the end of the year, he quoted Arthur Irwin's begrudging acceptance of the American League's success: "The National League has made a poor fight with the American League; in fact it has laid down as far as I can learn. Their game has always been to make the opposition lose money and quit. In this case, the American League came in under full sail and has won out on every end, and is going after the old fellows in better shape than ever."

THREE

Barney Builds His Dynasty

While Johnson was busy building the American League, Dreyfuss was trying to build a baseball juggernaut in Pittsburg, which had been a hotbed for baseball since shortly after the end of the Civil War. His 1903 Pirates were a dynasty and in mid-July were en route to capturing their third consecutive National League pennant in a league with other powerhouses. The Pirates were coming off a 1902 season that was at that time the greatest in baseball history. They had gone 103–36 and finished 27½ games ahead of Brooklyn, which had a record of 75–63, and the Pirates never went out of first place after May 4. It was the kind of showing which intimidated other teams and Dreyfuss was sure his men could beat the Boston Americans in a World Series. He wanted to further ensure the financial success of his investment, and gain a measure of victory over Johnson too.

If Pittsburg fans were delighted with their 1901 pennant winners, they were in for a historic season in 1902, even as the American League had established itself in the eyes of the public. After all, the Pirate fans felt, who could match the greatest team in baseball history? And that's what the Pirates set out to prove with an unparalleled resolution of spirit. They took over first place in April and simply ran away from the competition, aided, no doubt, by the American League raids that had decimated other National League teams but left the Pirates nearly intact and hadn't touched the pitching staff— Deacon Phillippe, Jack Chesbro, Jesse Tannehill, and the brilliant, eccentric Doheny. For that glorious season of 1902, the Pittsburg Pirates would establish themselves as a team of destiny and a team of the new century.

The prestigious *Reach's Guide*, which followed baseball, had a preview of the team before the season began that predicted the 1901 National League pennant winners would be even better in 1902. "The Pittsburgs owed their wonderful success to the fact that their team entered the race unbroken — and even strengthened, over the previous year. The team was superior to any club in the country in the matter of pitchers, strong in batting, fast in fielding and mater of a superb system of team play which its rival could not fathom, let alone break through," the magazine reported.

The Pirates team was close-knit. Wagner adored infielder Claude Ritchey, with whom he had broken into baseball and they were sometimes called the "cheese sandwich brothers" because they liked that peculiar delicacy so much. It was the kind of camaraderie that paid off for the whole team though and they roared through the schedule, even though Wagner broke a bone in his hand sliding into a base in Philadelphia late in the season. Going into the last day of the season, the Pirates stood at 102–36, tying the National League record for wins set by the Boston Beaneaters in 1892 and 1898, when the schedules were longer. But on the last day, October 4, following ferocious rainstorms, they beat the Reds, 11–2, to go 103–36 and set a new record, finishing the 1902 season with a 27½ game margin over the rest of the league, an almost unbelievable difference, and the pitching staff took five of the top seven positions for the year, including the remarkable 16–4 put up by Doheny. Beaumont hit .357 while Wagner hit .329, Clarke, .321 and Bransfield, .308, and the pitching was unparalleled. This was the greatest collection of talent ever put on a baseball field to the time. The only challenge left was in the American League, but no one was talking about taking on the champions there yet.

Instead of taking on the champions, the Pirates played a group of American League All-Stars in what was supposed to be a three-game series. The American Leaguers were a formidable group, led by Young and LaJoie, although LaJoie still couldn't play in Pennsylvania because of the restrictions caused by his jumping clubs. In the first game, Leever out-pitched Young and the Pirates won 4–3. In the next game, Wagner had two hits and the Pirates shut out the American Leaguers 2–0. The clubs then traveled to Cleveland for the next game, which was a sensational 11-inning scoreless tie, one of the most peerless games in baseball history. The teams then decided to play another game, which Young won, 1–0 over Phillippe, the big American League fireballer out-dueling the crafty National Leaguer. But the Pirates still won the series and their superiority seemed certain in both leagues.

But the Pirates' success was almost their undoing, as Johnson wanted to break up the Pittsburgers in a different way — by stealing away their best talent. At the end of 1902, the American Leaguers got Chesbro and Tannehill to jump to a new team — the New York Highlanders — and went after Wagner again.

In December, a three-man executive board, a new President replaced which had been running the National League: Pittsburgh's Harry Pulliam. Dreyfuss supported his man and said Pulliam would show no favor to the Pirates, and Pulliam would play an integral part in the peace compact between the two leagues in January of 1903. Pulliam, learning from Johnson's rule in the American League, tried to clean up the National League during the 1903 season.

Early that season, Dreyfuss told the Pirate Clarke about Pulliam's aims. "He's going after the roughnecks, the rowdies, the umpire baiters, and the men who swear so you can hear them all over the stands. I told him I'm all in favor of it. Now I want you to fight as hard for games as you ever did. I don't want a ball club that will let anyone push it around, but if we lay off Harry's umpires, we make it easier for him."

The two-time defending champions came into 1903 brimming with confidence and poise despite the loss of Chesbro and Tannehill. But there were some signs of trouble right away, starting in spring training which got off to a bad start for outfielder Jimmy Sebring when he was bitten on the right hand middle finger by a monster centipede while taking a bath on April 3, and Pittsburg sportswriters thought the loss of Chesbro and Tannehill from 1902's record-breaking pennant winners had hurt.

By April 13, the start of the regular season just a week off now, Dreyfuss was feeling good about his two-time defending National League pennant winners and figured the Pirates were going to do it again. "The team is as strong as ever and looks to me like a sure pennant winner," he said, discounting so-so spring training. "The poor work in some of the games was due to bad grounds on which the men were ordered to take no chances that might lead to injuries. We are strong just where some of the wise ones think we are weak — in the pitching department. As to the unfavorable outside criticism, I could ask for nothing more pleasing, as I prefer to have the team underrated than overrated," he said, ever the smart businessman.

Pittsburg was growing fast now too, expanding across the rivers to its western territory with the help of the Fort Pitt tunnel being built under Mount Washington. This new access would lure thousands of people out to buy homes on cheaper land outside the city, but they would still be close enough to come in for baseball games, Dreyfuss knew.

Even with the loss of Chesbro and Tannehill, Clarke was feeling a little better with the growing improvement of left-hander Doheny, who had a nasty assortment of pitches that were especially difficult for right-handed batters.

On April 18, 1903, Doheny won easily over Cincinnati, and the Pirates opened the season with four straight wins over the Red Stockings in Cincinnati. On April 22, they came home to a huge opening day crowd, but lost. Two days later, Sebring, the team's leadoff hitter whacked two home runs, a rarity, although the second was inside the park. The last Pirate player to hit two in one game was Wagner four years earlier when the team was in Louisville.

The team continued to roll along. On May 1, Tommy Leach hit a grand slam home run, and on May 5, Wagner's running catch in the ninth inning with two out preserved a 2–1 win over the Chicago Colts. Again, it was Doheny on the mound, and John Gruber in the *Pittsburg Post* reported that "Doheny pitched a masterly game from first to last and also fielded his position superbly ... Doheny never lost his steadiness." At least not on the mound. Doheny was constantly suspicious of his surroundings. He and his wife had decided to rent an apartment in a house in Andover, about 20 miles north of Boston, and she stayed there with their infant.

On May 7, Phillippe was cruising along easily against the Cubs, taking a 4–2 lead into the ninth — before Chicago erupted for nine runs to beat the Bucs and keep Pittsburg in second place with a 12–6 mark, three games behind John McGraw's New York Giants. "FIERCE SLAUGHTER IN NINTH INNING," the *Pittsburg Post* reported, saying the Giants had beaten Phillippe so bad that "What they did won't be found on the record page of the Deacon's bible."

And while Johnson was vowing to end rowdyism in the American League, and the National League owners were worried the past brand of rough-and-tumble baseball was a deterrent to attracting some fans, the *Post* reported on May 9 that some older fans found the current version too tame, talking to them at the city's produce market and finding after its interviews that the consensus was the game was too mild.

"The good old riotous and happy days of baseball seem to have been shoved off to the ash dumps and vacant squares. There is really more good, live fun to be derived from reading the signs on the fence at the ballpark than in watching the game. No more does a player rush up to the umpire and call him a pink lobster and inform him that he isn't fit to judge a game of craps, and never again will a policeman be compelled to escort the umpire from the field and put him to bed. Of course the bleacherites still have the privilege of roasting the umpire and throwing bad eggs at him, but even that is discouraged since the players are not permitted to bang him about as they please. The great game has become so orderly and placid that it might be taken for an Allegheny society function. So mild is it this year excitable people doze in the grandstand and in the bleachers and leave the field without asking for rain checks on wet days. There must be no restrictions on the players. People want to see a scrappy game and they want to hear the umpire called all sorts of names, for that is what he is hired for. It is okay to set rules but patrons of the game don't appreciate the fact that players are cussing the umpire in their minds, they want to hear him cussed. That's what they pay their money for and if they don't get it they'll save it for the saloons."

The Pirates' fans had more to worry about, though, when Harry Pulliam, the team's former treasurer, suspended Wagner on May 9 for three days. In the fifth inning of a game against the Reds at Exposition Park, Wagner hit a ground ball that forced Clarke out at third base, but the Reds' third baseman said Clarke had run into him too hard. On the next play, Wagner broke to steal second and slid hard into the Reds' second baseman, who said Wagner had tried to spike him, and the Reds players converged on Wagner, who was ordered out of the game by umpire Bugs Holliday as Wagner approached him. It was a bold move but one which did not sit right with the fans, even if Clarke and Wagner accepted it.

A major league record crowd of 31,500 fans turned out on May 16 at the Polo Grounds in New York for the opener of a four-game series between the Giants and Pirates. On May 18, the Pirates beat the Giants 3–2, but the game was marked by a bizarre incident when Doheny incensed the spectators in New York by throwing his bat up into the air when Giants catcher Frank Bowerman was about to catch his pop fly in the seventh inning. Doheny's behavior seemed increasingly erratic to his teammates and Dreyfuss was worried something was wrong with his mind. The Pirate pitcher was starting to seem distant and moody. Doheny, in mock derision, bowed to the fans booing him.

It was a rough game that created a lot of bad blood between the teams, especially when Clarke was called out for interfering with Bowerman in the ninth, and Wagner was rough on the sliding Giants pitcher Iron Joe McGinnity during a play at second base in the seventh inning, and Wagner grabbed the Giants' third baseman around the neck. After the game nearly 1,000 fans tried to converge on the Pirates and some stones were thrown before order was restored. But the trouble between the teams wouldn't end there that season, and this time Pulliam suspended Doheny for three games, even though Bowerman said he didn't think Doheny had tried to hit him with the bat. A bitter Doheny protested the decision. The Giants took three of four games from the Pirates and were now a game behind them.

On May 20, Clarke had to emphatically deny that his health was breaking down, but six days later admitted he was not feeling well. He didn't want to rest. "If I drop out, I will set a bad example for the others, and a headache will furnish an excuse for a day's rest," he said. Coming off their great record-breaking season of a year before, the Pirates were feisty and playing well, but there were signs of fray everywhere, from Clarke's health to Wagner's uncommon ire, to Doheny. And half a dozen Pirates were hurting or tending to personal problems.

On June 2, the Pirate team, which had lost Chesbro and Tannehill, began an incredible scoreless streak that would last all week, and at home in

Exposition Park. Phillippe started it with a 7–0 whitewashing against John McGraw's New York Giants, and the next day Sam Leever shut out the Giants again, 5–0. On June 4, the Boston Beaneaters went down 5–0, and the Pirates' incredible shutout streak reached four games and 36 innings on June 5 when they again blanked the Beaneaters, 9–0, establishing what newspapers called a new world's record for baseball. Only four runners got as far as second base during the shutout run. The record-breaking win came through the arm of Doheny, who gave up seven hits but kept Boston batters baffled all afternoon in Exposition Park as the Pirates wowed a home crowd. The next day, Phillippe won again, 4–0, and on June 8, Leever blanked the Phillies 2–0. The scoreless inning streak reached 56 and the Pirates were on a 15-game winning spree, surpassing the winning streak in the American League of the Boston Americans. But Pittsburg still remained in third place, close behind league-leading Chicago and the second place New York Giants. The shutout string would disguise a pitching staff that, despite the brilliance of Phillippe and the erratic wonder of Doheny, would labor toward the end of the season.

As they had all season, the Pirates beat up on the Boston Beaneaters again, this time gaining their 12th straight victory on June 18 with a 7–2 win in Boston to run their record to 37–17, now just a percentage point behind New York for the lead in the National League. Again it was Doheny who dominated the Boston boys in a game in which the Boston infield played so badly that *The Globe* said "a man playing the mandolin with a crowbar would have been aces up compared with the side show" Boston put on. The Beaneaters also had been shut out more than any other team in the major leagues in 1903, and even the appearance of the pennant-winning Pirates wasn't enough to draw more than 1487 to the South End Grounds.

When the Pirates won again the next day against Boston, the Pittsburg winning streak reached 13, this time behind Leever. It was another example of the sad demise of the once-proud Boston franchise in the National League, when the team ruled in the 1890s, cause enough for *The Globe* to write that "The home team was outclassed as much as a tin whistle is outclassed by a German flute, and the spectators who sat through the performance found themselves wandering back to the time when battles royal were fought and won on the same turf. The Pittsburg boys are playing ball, while the home team is still drawing salaries for fast work."

On June 22, after a game in Boston was put off because of heavy rains and wet grounds, Clarke said he was confident the team could win the title again, despite the obstacles. "Well, you know the proverbial uncertainty of baseball, but I am very hopeful of being able to hoist the flag again for the third straight time next season. One reason why is that our team is working together as one man. All heart and soul devoted to the one object of winning as many games as possible. That is what gives us the advantage over the 'All-Star' aggregations which are torn with dissensions and jealousies," he said.

On June 25, Doheny beat the Phillies 4–3, and by June 26, the Pirates had opened a 2½ game lead over John McGraw's hated Giants, their fiercest rival, but that day trouble erupted again between the teams when Giant catcher Frank Bowerman attacked Clarke before the game. Bowerman would later say he thought Clarke had repeated a criticism. *The Pittsburg Post* said three Giant players were waiting for Clarke and called the attack a "disgraceful affair ... was carefully planned and designed to put the Pittsburg leader out of the game."

Bowerman, standing near the gate into the park walked up to Clarke and said, "Hello, Fred," stuck out his hand to shake Clarke's and said to him, "May I speak to you for a few minutes?"

"Certainly," said Clarke, smiling as he said it while the traveling secretaries for both teams watched. The two men walked into a ticket seller's office and, after Clarke came in, Bowerman snapped shut a door behind them, and Bowerman accused Clarke of repeating that Bowerman said another Giant player, John Warner, could not catch a certain pitcher.

"You are wrong, Frank. I know you made that statement, but I did not tell Warner," Clarke said.

"You lie!" shouted Bowerman, uttering a profanity, and then he landed a blow to Clarke's face in a tiny room filled with desks. Clarke fell backward, his arms wedged to his sides, unable to protect himself after Bowerman's assault. Bowerman stuck his knee into Clarke's chest and continued to wail away at the defenseless Pirate. A police officer came but was momentarily barred by a Giant player, and then Bowerman came out himself. It didn't keep Clarke from playing, but the attack drew the wrath of the Pirate media and fans. The Giants won, 8–2 that day, and New York Club Secretary Fred Knowles said, "We regret that the trouble should have occurred in our private office, but Clarke got what he deserved." Dreyfuss demanded action against the Giants from Pulliam, but Clarke refused.

The publicity drew another record crowd in New York the next day of 32,240 fans, but the Pirates prevailed in 11 innings behind Phillippe and had a 3½ game lead over the Giants. Clarke scored the winning run and, the next day, Bowerman was badly spiked in an exhibition game, setting Pirate fans to utter no sympathy for the man.

By July 4, in the middle of an intense heat wave, the Pirates were still rolling, taking a doubleheader from the Phillies 7–0 and 7–1, to go to 46–20. But Clarke was injured when he made a sensational catch in the ninth inning on a short fly to left that he chased, snaring it only a foot from the ground as he lost his balance and took a tumble onto his shoulder. Two days later, he would find out it was dislocated, but that hadn't stopped him from firing to Ritchey at second base to catch a runner for a double play that ended the game. Clarke had rubbed his sore shoulder and tried to shrug it off until it hurt so much he could not. It would be a harbinger for the rest of the Pirates' season.

On July 6, Doheny showed signs of his occasional erratic brilliance, striking out nine batters in a 5–2 victory over Brooklyn, boosting the Pirates' lead over the Giants to four full games. By July 15, the Pirates still held that lead over the Giants, who were coming to Pittsburg that day to play the Pirates. A dozen police officers were put into position in case the crowd tried to react against Bowerman. Clarke, his shoulder still hurting, insisted on returning to the lineup to face his nemesis. There was more satisfaction in that than the $100 fine that had been levied on Bowerman by Pulliam. Bowerman received a shower of boos when he appeared.

The Giants, behind the great pitcher Christy Mathewson, took the first game of the crucial series, but in the next game the Pirates beat back McGinnity for the fourth time that year, a season during which the Iron Man had already won 18 games and seemed invincible as far as the other teams were concerned.

McGinnity's defeat kept the Pirates lead at four games and then the Pittsburgs won the next two games to open some distance over the New Yorkers. But they didn't know that their greatest challenge was yet to come, and that it wouldn't come from any teams in the National League.

FOUR

Murnane's Baseball

Of all the baseball writers of the time, the dean was perhaps Timothy Hayes "Tim" Murnane of the *Boston Globe*, both because of his erudite knowledge of the game and because he had been a player in the major leagues. He was born in Naugatuck, Connecticut, on June 4, 1851, and began to play baseball as a schoolboy. His first professional play came with a team in Stratford, Connecticut, when he was 18.

The next year he went south and joined a team in Savannah, Georgia, as a catcher. There were only nine men on the team and no substitutes, and Murnane took to writing about their exploits, displaying a deft style with the jargon of the game and a keen eye for observation. He had an engaging writing style that made the events seem real and close to the reader.

He combined his writing ability with baseball and started a small newspaper in Boston, which lasted for a couple of years, catching the attention of editors at the established *Boston Globe* who offered him a job covering baseball. He became the paper's baseball editor, following Boston National League teams through their glory years in the 1890s, when they won four pennants, and establishing a unique rapport with players, owners, managers and fans, creating a niche as a really professional baseball writer who knew the game integrally and how it operated off the field too.

He had a prominent nose, curly hair and a large mustache and an earnest, stolid look, and Murnane was always ready to help a colleague or a new reporter learn the nuances of the game and how to dig for information. For a time, he also served as president of the New England League, learning first hand about the intricacies of running a baseball operation and not just how a player sees the game. He became a member of the National Board of Arbitration and helped several times to stem quarrels that threatened the existence of the game during its rowdy period. Another colleague described him as a consummate baseball man who lived the game. Murnane could be critical, but of the game and policy matters, and not be personal.

"After all," he told colleagues, "They're human beings and you know we're none of us perfect, boy."

It was that understanding, and his knowledge of the game that let him get close to players and everyone in the game and helped enlighten fans and earn the respect of other learned writers of the game. His habit was to go directly from his home to the ball game and then, after finding out news from the players, to head back home and dictate his stories to his daughter, who was his personal secretary.

His Sunday column in the *Globe*, called "Murnane's Baseball," was essential reading for all fans, and for writers, players, owners and administrators in the game, because Murnane was able to give them information too, ferreted out from his many contacts and delivered in a straight, no-nonsense fashion that showed he knew his business. If it was from Murnane, it was gospel.

As fair as he was, Murnane was slow to warm to the new Boston Americans, although he had a good rapport with Jimmy Collins and knew the Beaneaters players who'd jumped, as well as other National Leaguers who'd gone over to the new league. But he knew a good story when he saw one, and the new team was providing a lot of fodder for his baseball column. He loved the competition between the leagues and the news it created. After the Americans' strong 1901 season, Murnane found plenty to write about in the off-season too as the two leagues prepared for the next year, when it seemed like the intensity could only increase.

After the December, 1901 meeting in which the National Leaguers set up a three-man committee, partially because their president, Nick Young, had so badly been outsmarted by Johnson, the American League president succeeded in upstaging the National Leaguers again, saying he was going to transfer the Milwaukee franchise to a former National League city, St. Louis.

Seizing on the confusion, the American League stepped up its raids in 1902, with only the Pirates avoiding any real losses in the National League. And Bill Dinneen finally left the Beaneaters to come to the Americans, without any of the enmity he'd earned the previous year when he'd flip-flopped on jumping. The Americans also picked up a player from Cleveland, George "Candy" LaChance, a big, burly French-Canadian from Connecticut who liked eating candy, to play first base, and Patsy Dougherty, a curly-haired lad with a constant quizzical look on his face, but who could hit and run, to play left field. It looked like the team had improved itself considerably, especially in pitching, where Dinneen was counted on to be the number two man behind Young.

But at the box office, the Americans again trumped their National League rivals, outdrawing them in 1902 by 348,567 to a paltry 116,960.

And there was growing talk of an American League team being placed in New York. In the July 17, 1902 edition of *The Sporting News*, sportswriter George Geer said he didn't like that talk—not because it wasn't a shrewd move—but because he thought Dreyfuss would sell out his fellow National League owners to prevent Johnson from putting another team in Pittsburg to compete with the Pirates.

"If Dreyfuss wasn't a Benedict Arnold, why didn't the American League go after him," Geer wrote. "He must have played his own associates false. There is no other way to account for the fact that Benedict Dreyfuss was handled with gloves," he said. He didn't know how right he would be and how soon that would come. The first two seasons of the American League had set up an inevitable evolution for the game, and it was changing even more rapidly now.

Peace Comes to Baseball

In August of 1902, Johnson announced the American League would have a team in New York for the 1903 season, and in December he said grounds had been purchased for construction of a new ballpark. That was the final salvo for most National League owners already weary of battling him. By January of 1903, they were under siege from Johnson's league—where prices now had risen from 25 to 50 cents and where Johnson had succeeded in gaining the public's attention so much that even Spalding's *Guide To Baseball* said, "The American League has more star players and can furnish a better article of baseball than the National League."

The approaching 1903 season would be the most critical in the history of the game so far. Two major leagues were at peace, at least temporarily, and working together to set rules and regulations that would make each equal. They did everything except set up a post-season series between the champions of each league. The final series idea had been bandied about briefly at the end of the 1902 season with talk of playoffs between the Pirates and the formidable Philadelphia Athletics, but it had failed to get enough notice or acceptance among owners and sportswriters, as tension remained high between the leagues.

Two committees met in Cincinnati in January of 1903. On January 9, only two days after they started talking, they reached an agreement. The National Leaguers agreed not to fight Johnson's move into New York as long as he stayed out of Pittsburg, a Dreyfuss victory, and lists were drawn up showing which players would belong to which club, and the reserve rights of the teams would be honored. Uniform contracts were established and the leagues were to stay intact unless there was further agreement. A new National Agreement would be drawn up to handle details such as scheduling of games, and only Giants' owner John Brush, who didn't want competition in New York, resisted to the last.

On March 14, 1903, in a story headlined "Critical Period: Game's Future Hinges on 1903 Attendance," *The Sporting News* reported: "The newly formed peace agreement will have its real test, and it will require only a few weeks, perhaps days, to show if it is strong enough, the existence of two major leagues working in harmony will have its success or failure demonstrated before the year is over, and in five of the leading cities it is to be decided whether they will support two teams or one." A week later, H.G. Merrill said in the same paper, "We are now away from the monopolistic tendency which nearly caused the ruination of the sport, and common sense dictates that there should be no attempt to return to this line of business. It is the demand of the public that there be two leagues."

After the disappointments of 1901 and 1902, Collins wanted to push his team to do better in 1903. There were changes made, too, in the front office. The peace pact enabled Somers to sell the team to a trusted Johnson ally, Henry Killilea of Milwaukee, who made fellow Milwaukeean Joseph Smart the business manager. Murnane wrote, "The choice is a good one as Smart is known as one of the most enterprising business men of the city's younger set." Killilea was handing over the financial operations to Smart, who said he never missed a ball game in Milwaukee.

And, following Johnson's tough stance against trouble in the American League by players, President Pulliam on April 12 issued an edict against rowdyism in the National League. "It is not my intention to rob the game of any of its enthusiasm or interest, but instead of that I wish to increase the enthusiasm of the players and the interest of the spectators at the expense of the so-called 'rowdyism,'" he stated.

On April 20, Patriots' Day and opening day in Boston for the Americans, it was evident they had overtaken the Beaneaters for the hearts and souls of the city's fans. Killilea had raised and re-sodded the field, improving its drainage. A record-breaking crowd of 27,658 showed up at the Huntington Avenue Grounds for a doubleheader that included a showdown between Cy Young and the great and crazy Rube Waddell of the defending pennant winning Philadelphia A's. The Beaneaters, meanwhile, were playing the Philadelphia National Team at the South End Grounds at the same time. The morning game for the Beaneaters drew 1827 fans, and the afternoon game brought in only 4000 and the *Globe* reported, "Neither crowd, however, was especially enthusiastic."

Meanwhile, there were 8,376 fans for the Americans morning game and 19,282 for the afternoon game. "Before the game was started, the grounds were completely surrounded by a wall of humanity, many women in the field being unable to get into the pavilion," the *Globe* reported. The stands could not hold the crowds, which were allowed to stand in the outfield, as far back as they could get. "The crowd was held well back against the bank in left field and close to the fence, and yet ground rules were made allowing only three bases when the ball was hit into the ground." There was little confusion though, thanks to Smart, who had plenty of police present, "although one of the bluecoats received a bad roast for taking a schoolboy from deep center past the crowd to the entrance," it was reported.

Boston then went to Philadelphia to take on the defending champions there, and was treated to a show they wanted for themselves: ceremonies honoring the pennant-winners that included a raising of the banner. "The bunting unfolded gracefully, and hundreds of tiny reproductions of Old Glory were wafted by the breeze outside the grounds," Murnane wrote. Standing by the flagpole, Collins and his men were watching.

But they still couldn't handle the offerings of Rube Waddell, who could be brilliant when he wasn't being wacky, and the Americans fell 6–1 before a crowd of more than 13,500 spectators. The next day, the A's beat Boston again, for the third straight time, but the crowd this time was only about 1500 people. Collins though was concerned only with not letting Philadelphia get too far ahead of Boston so early in the season, and in the next game sent Cy Young out. Young stopped the A's, 3–1.

But the big news was in New York, where the Highlanders, the new American League entry which had angered New York Giants owner John Brush and manager John McGraw were finishing their new ballpark for their official home opening. It was reported that an army of workingmen was trying to get the field ready for the opener on April 30, when Ban Johnson would take part in the ceremonies.

Only nine games into the season, the Highlanders were in sixth place, just a game behind the Americans, who were playing erratically. On April 29, Boston lost to Washington, 9–5, to slip to 4–5 on the season, with no indication they would become the pennant-contenders Collins had thought. A double showdown of sorts would take place in Boston the next few days as the Beaneaters were hosting John McGraw's Giants, while the Americans hosted Philadelphia for a three-game series, important even so early in the season, and they split the first two games. And on May 2, came the feature game in the showdown series, Young going to the mound against Philly's ace, Eddie Plank. It was an extraordinarily chilly day, but the battle of pitching stars still brought out 4,610 fans. "A cold wind whistled across the field and through the grandstand, until the mustard refused to work in the cheese sandwiches and most of those in the crowd, wrapped up in winter ulsters, wished they were playing ping pong at some fireplace," Murnane wrote.

The weather made the players move with alacrity and Murnane noted, "Old Cy was on the rubber for the home team and pitched for all he was worth. He had speed to burn and curves galore. Plank, a lefthander, was shying up a variety of twisters for the Quakers, and the locals were unequal to the occasion when a hit would put them in the game." It took only 1 hour and 15 minutes for Athletics to win, 3–0, with one of the runs a homer from Plank. But at least the Americans were still winning the attendance war against the Beaneaters, who drew only 910 fans for their game against the Giants, even though the rival Beaneaters wound up winning 5–2 and were now doing nearly as well in the standings in the National League as the Americans were doing in the American League.

The 1903 season was beginning to engage the fans. The next day in Chicago, nearly 36,000 turned out to see the Windy City's two major league teams — 19,000 for the American Leaguers and 17,000 for the National League Cubs, prompting the *Globe* to run a headline that said: "Baseball Crazy." It was the first time the two rivals would play in Chicago on the same day — and on a Sunday, when religious groups had so staunchly opposed the idea of baseball being played at all. The *Globe* published a chart comparing the Americans' and Beaneaters' players statistically and said, "Neither appears to have struck a gait from which its season's work should be judged, but the figures are interesting."

'Twas All Cy

Cy Young brought the talk back to baseball in a hurry. On May 6, he pitched and batted the Americans to a 6–3 win over Washington, hitting a home run in a performance that was described thusly by Murnane: "Nothing more symmetrical and better gaged has even been offered to the patrons of baseball in this city. As a dispenser of the curve and shoot, Cyrus has a record of even time on many a slow track, and as a repeater he has no opposition in the great American game at the present time."

The Americans responded and went on a winning streak, including a six-game road trip that began in New York where they beat the Highlanders, 8–2, and moved into first place, prompting a big headline in the *Globe* which said *Boston American Team Is Now the Pacemaker*. The next day, June 3, Young beat New York again to give Boston a sweep and nine victories in their last 10 games, including seven in a row. The Americans pleased more than 5,000 fans who turned out to watch them defeat Chicago, 10–3, as all the regulars except Criger got at least one hit, keeping up the hitting spree that had propelled the team into first place. The next day, Boston beat Chicago again for its ninth straight victory, a streak that was overshadowed only by the phenomenal play in the National League of the Pirates, who shut out the visiting Boston Beaneaters for the second time, to give Pittsburg its fourth consecutive shutout — this one behind the eccentric left-hander Doheny. *Pittsburg Makes a World's Record — In 36 Innings Only Four Men Get as Far as Third,* the *Globe* reported. The Americans and Pirates were now looking at each other on top of their leagues.

A duality of brilliance was beginning, and when Boston beat Chicago again the next day for a 10th straight victory, 10–2, continuing to hammer the ball all over the South End Grounds, there were 10,278 people in attendance, several thousand alone the sidelines and deep in the outfield because all the seats had been taken early. Despite the streak, the defending champion A's were only a game behind, but the Americans were playing with an easy confidence now, swatting the ball with pepper, and its pitching staff, behind Young and Dinneen, was rivaling any in either league — except perhaps for the Pirates, who, the next day, shut out the Beaneaters again to give Pittsburg five consecutive shutouts.

Meanwhile, the Americans won another before their 11-game winning streak ended on June 9, when they lost, 7–3, to their growing nemesis, Detroit, despite six strong innings of relief by Young.

The fans were pouring through the turnstiles now to watch the Americans, and a double-header the next day drew 19,000 fans for the two games, Cleveland winning the opener 3–1, and Boston winning the second 6–1. The split put Philadelphia back into the lead and kept Cleveland close on Boston's heels. By now it appeared that the Americans and Pirates were, as much as in a pennant race in their own leagues, chasing each other along parallel lines: winning streaks and sensational play in the first surge of the still-early season of 1903.

When Boston rebounded to take the second game of a series against Cleveland 5–2, in weather on June 19 that was still chilly and raining and bleak in Cleveland, the Pirates got almost as much attention in the Boston newspapers. They beat the Beaneaters for their 13th consecutive win, including the string of whitewashes.

The Americans came home for a July 4 doubleheader against the Browns before crowds totaling more than 15,000 people "who were as full of enthusiasm as a young boy with his first pistol," Murnane noted with good reason, because in the stands, gaily decorated with flags and red, white, and blue bunting, the fans got very worked up. "The spectators had a lot of satisfaction shooting off revolvers and firecrackers when the home team made a good play, and they gave the home team a hearty welcome as they came to the plate in the morning game," he said. The Americans didn't let their fans down, winning both ends, 4–1 and 2–0. Pennant fever was already starting to grip the Hub.

While Johnson and Pulliam and the executives and the owners wrangled over the present and the future of the game from their vantage points, the Americans had an important home stand series against third-place Cleveland. After yet another day of rain set the series back a day, they played a doubleheader and split, Boston taking the first 4–3, behind Young, and dropping the second, 4–2. Besides yet another brilliant pitching performance, Young won his own game at the plate, his 10th inning triple bringing home his battery mate Criger with the winning run. The games drew more than 11,500 people, and the next day, July 17, the Americans routed Cleveland, 11–4, opening a four-game lead on Philadelphia, which lost to Washington.

All that was missing in Boston, it seemed, was for the Beaneaters, who were falling toward the cellar just ahead of the Philadelphians there, to give their fans some reason to come to the South End Grounds to see them, and not jump to the Americans, as so many of their players had. "The local Americans are going along nicely for the pennant, while the local National League boys are working gamely with a small force in what may be a vain endeavor to keep out of last place," Murnane wrote in his Sunday column on July 19.

On July 22, the Pirates lost their third straight game, still feeling the absence of the injured Clarke, who was having a rough season trying to keep himself and his team together. They even lost an exhibition game against Homestead, as Doheny threw wild on a bunt attempt and let in three runs, although he had pitched a strong game. Next they lost another exhibition, this one to Altoona.

Then, on July 26, 1903, in Cincinnati, Clarke got troubling news. Doheny was having delusions that detectives were following him. During the road trip to Cincinnati, he came back from a cobbler's shop screaming that the shoemaker was after him too and had tried to kill him. It was unnerving to the rest of the team. The next night at dinner, Doheny threw a plate at a policeman only he could see as his imagination and mental illness made him begin to unravel right before his teammates' eyes. In the incident with the imaginary detective, he said he was going to "give the detectives the slip and go home."

A worried Clarke went to Doheny's hotel room to talk. Doheny had been high-strung and intensely competitive and his nerves seemed to be in trouble these days, the manager knew.

"What's wrong, Eddie?" Clarke asked. The pitcher looked downcast and reluctant to talk. "I know I'm not right. I guess I need a rest," Doheny told him.

Clarke thought it over. "Why don't you go home to your wife in Andover," Clarke suggested, thinking Doheny might find some solace in the peaceful little Massachusetts farm. The Pirate manager knew he needed Doheny to win a third successive pennant. He didn't know there was even a real possibility of a series once the season ended, and there was still some talk of the two leagues going at each other again.

As usual, there was a photograph of a ballplayer accompanying Murnane's Sunday column. This time he was in civilian clothes, a suit with a tightly knitted collar under a stern, handsome face that seemed almost serene in its detachment and earnestness. The visage was recognizable in both leagues and to baseball fans across the country. It was a Pittsburg Pirate.

"Hans Wagner."

FIVE

Play Them, but You Must Beat Them

With the end of the war between the leagues in 1903, it seemed natural to have a series between their champions, one that probably would benefit the American League more if its winner were to prevail. So it was surprising when Dreyfuss wrote Killilea suggesting the series. But Dreyfuss was supremely confident in his team because he had paid the players better than other clubs had, and he thought a victory over the American League champions would add more prestige to his team. Killilea, seeing the revenue potential, liked the idea and took it to Johnson, who had crafted the league and infuriated some of his old rivals, most notably McGraw, who had been an American Leaguer but now hated what he called the "inferior" league.

Johnson saw the possibilities too, if the American league would win: public acceptance of the parity of the leagues and a long-term structure that would ensure financial success. It could even promote the notion that the American League had already caught the old league in ability and talent, something critical to survival and staying power.

Johnson had a simple message for Killilea: "Play them, but you must beat them."

A single paragraph on the inside pages of the newspapers in Pittsburg and Boston on July 29 first told of the idea of a post-season series between the champions of the two leagues, with little fanfare: "Pres. Dreyfuss of the Pittsburg team of the National baseball league announces that if Pittsburg wins the National league pennant, the winner of the American league pennant will be challenged to a series of 11 games to decide the championship of the world, the conditions being that the winner receive 75 percent of the gate receipts and the loser 25 percent, the winner also to visit the west and the Pacific coast as world's champions, the loser to remain home."

And for a few days, there was little else to it, as if the sportswriters and fans had to absorb the possibilities. The Americans and the Pirates were opening leads in their leagues and seemed certain to collide if such a series was held. No one knew that Johnson, Killilea and Dreyfuss had been talking about the possibility.

But Murnane found out. A few days later, Murnane talked about the upcoming series and said it hadn't impressed the Boston team. "Boston has set out for the bunting this season, but is not advertising the fact. Capt. Collins had paid no attention to the offer of Barney Dreyfuss," he said. And, he said, "Mr. Dreyfuss may depend on it that Pittsburg would have to play much better ball than they have played so far this season to win the series from the Boston Americans. In fact, I do not think Pittsburg would hardly have a look in, and I say this after having witnessed the work of both teams and knowing the men on both clubs."

Murnane picked up on the growing buzz about the post-season series and said, "Now that the magnates have been relegated to the background once more, the chances for championships is interesting gossip for the fans." He said Boston and Pittsburg were best suited for the matchup because of the way they were playing as teams, but for other reasons as well. "To win a championship at the present time the players must have the respect of the management and the captain of the team. This state of affairs exists in both Boston and Pittsburg at the present time, and this is what makes them great factors in their respective leagues," he wrote in his Sunday column. In the same column he criticized Collins. "Collins has the best bunch of pitchers in the business, and the loss of the championship would simply mean he lacked judgment in working his box artists," he wrote.

But overall, Collins was doing a good job of getting his team to play together, especially given the high salaries some were drawing. The Americans' payroll was more than $60,000 for the team, a sizeable amount, and they were locked into two and three year contracts. But Killilea's decision to take over the team from Somers had paid off well, even given what he was paying the players, because business was up 33 percent from 1902, and the rivalries with Philadelphia and Cleveland were helping that.

On August 2, the Pirates easily handled St. Louis, 13–4, as Wagner handled 13 chances cleanly, and two days later the champions sat alone in first place with a mark of 60–29, leading the hated New York Giants by nine games, and with five more wins than the Americans. On the field, the Americans were playing well.

They still hadn't been able to put any real distance between themselves and the pesky Philadelphia A's though, and a losing streak could put the 1903 post-season series in jeopardy if Boston were overtaken. The Americans had only a three-game lead over Philadelphia, with 50 games remaining in the season, and were to play them in Philadelphia after a brief series in Washington against the Senators. There followed a rainout though and the Americans went on to Philadelphia for a crucial series that would include three games there and then three in Boston against the A's. It seemed the season — and the possible first World Series — was on the line. Boston was 55–33, Philadelphia 53–36.

Leaders Clash

The atmosphere was tense in Philadelphia on August 5, when the Americans opened the series there. Collins was in a feisty mood from the get-go, and the crowd of nearly 11,000 was behind their A's all the way, making a good amount of noise as the game started with what was expected to be a pitchers duel between Dinneen and the A's erratic and eccentric ace, Waddell. The Philly hurler had the ability to make batters daffy too, with his dancing array of pitches. The A's had a formidable team as defending champions and they were playing for all they were worth too. But today, Dinneen would not be denied. He was masterful in shutting out the A's, 3–0, behind defensive work that was at once faultless and phenomenal.

But the next day, nearly another 10,000 fans showed up at Columbia Park for a showdown between A's pitcher Chief Bender, and Young, who was not in good form, giving up 12 hits. The Philadelphia fans were curiously quiet for the first three innings, especially when Boston scored in the first inning, but raised their cries when their team came to life. Boston was behind 4–3 after 7½ innings when the umpires called the game for darkness, sending Collins into a tirade again. The series was now 1–1, but the Athletics' hopes to overtake the Americans in the standings were short-lived. The next day they fell easily, 11–3, before 11,291 fans.

The A's couldn't handle the offerings of Hughes, who was getting even for being tossed in the first game. Boston had gained a game on their rivals as the series headed back to Boston, where even bigger crowds were expected for the Saturday, August 8, opener. More than 14,500 fans turned out to see if the Americans could finish off the A's in a three-game series in the Hub. They wanted Boston to win, but they wanted a good game too.

They didn't get it. Boston won the opener easily, 11–6, behind Dinneen again. "Never was a crowd more eager for great sport, and it was disappointed in the easy manner in which Jimmie Collins' boys wiped up the earth with the Quaker champions," Murnane wrote. After losing the first game in Philadelphia, Boston had now taken three in a row from the A's, who had come to Boston without Waddell, who had disappeared again.

Connie Mack had to do something to rally his team, and before the next game in Boston he said he was confident because he was going with Eddie Plank on the mound, who had given Boston trouble before. He thought he had a good sign when Waddell finally showed up, but again there were more than 10,000 people ready to root for the home team, and Young was back seeking revenge from his poor performance in Philadelphia.

There was a special spectator in the stands: Ban Johnson, who said he wanted to see the Americans before heading west to watch games. "He had faith in the Boston boys holding their own with Pittsburg in a series for the world's championship," Murnane reported. But first, they had to beat the A's.

With Waddell sitting out to pitch the next day, August 11, Boston won easily, 7–2. Murnane said the champion Athletics made "another unsuccessful effort to stop the steady march of the Collins brigade toward the championship. Their effort was like running a baby carriage against a locomotive." Young had a perfect game for seven innings. Murnane elaborated, "This feat was accomplished without the turning of a hair, and Cy worked all styles of delivery and had perfect command." The Americans had now taken four out of five from the A's and could put a hard crimp in their chances by taking the last game of the series.

Mack brought out his last hope, Waddell, to try to stop Boston before yet another crowd of more than 10,000 fans. Even Waddell couldn't slow the Boston run toward the pennant, losing 5–1, again to Hughes. More than 70,000 fans had seen the six games in the series, 36,000 in Boston, in what was believed a record for a six-game set, and further establishing the strength of the American Leaguers in drawing crowds.

Murnane still thought Philadelphia might catch the Americans, who were leading the league in shutouts, but in his Sunday column on August 16, he wrote: "It looks very much like Pittsburg and Boston for the honors this season," although he thought Pittsburg's pitching was suspect, with Doheny's uncertainty. And, he said, "A series of games between these clubs, played at Boston, New York, Philadelphia and Pittsburg would be a big money-winner and help the game, for the contests would bring out some grand good baseball."

The Americans had 21 remaining home games and he thought that, too, was enough to give them the edge over Philadelphia and Cleveland and set up the World Series that had started to take hold of the public imagination. Murnane wrote:

> It is practically settled that Boston and Pittsburg will play the best in 11 games for the 1903 national championship if they are lucky enough to win out in their respective leagues, and this would give the public a good chance to see a couple of great ball teams out for business. Down this

way the Boston club is a favorite and Barney Dreyfuss will have no trouble in placing a good big sum on the team that he declares can beat the world ... Boston people will back their club stronger than any other city in the land, and this will be proven to the satisfaction of anyone looking for the Pittsburg end of the series.

There would be great stakes too, although Murnane remained cautiously conservative in his estimation of the worth of the games. "I look for more betting on the series between the leaders this fall than was ever known in baseball before, and the games will be for blood," he wrote, and it was a phrase that would echo again before too long.

The Pirates had split a doubleheader with the second-place Giants, losing 13–7 and then winning 4–1 on August 20, but their lead had slipped to five games; their play had been as erratic as Doheny's demeanor. On August 22, the Pirates swept the last place Philadelphians, who were reeling all year after the raids on their club by the American Leaguers. Doheny won the first game and showed he had rebounded from the loss to the Giants, but two days later an 11-inning game that was tied at 2–2 with Philadelphia was suspended because of darkness.

The next day, Pittsburg swept Philly again, with Doheny winning another game. The Pirates had a seven-game lead over the fading Giants, although they got a scare when Wagner keeled over in intense heat in a game against Philadelphia during the doubleheader victory. On August 29, the Pirates rolled again, sweeping a pair from St. Louis to increase their lead over New York by eight games for a standing of 75–37. The next day, Doheny threw a six-hit shutout, 3–0, against St. Louis, and the following day the Pittsburgs finished a five-game sweep at home against the Cardinals. Clarke could feel better about the prospect of games against the Americans if Doheny could keep it up. He felt the left-hander could bedevil Boston's hitters.

Late in August, Frank McQuiston of the *Pittsburg Daily Dispatch* gave what the paper called "A Pittsburg View Of It," and said that Boston fans and gamblers were being too cocky for an upstart new league that would be taking on one of the greatest baseball teams ever put together. "This is lovely. If a book should happen to fall off the center table now and wake them up they would immediately begin blessing the man who invented headache powders. These dreams are nice while you are at them, but things don't look so good about the time one gets up to reach for the pitcher only to find that the ice is melted," he put it sarcastically. The story also ran in the *Boston Evening Record*. It didn't slow the Americans, who went to St. Louis and beat the Browns in a double-header seen by more than 21,000 fans, bolstered by a triple play started by Ferris.

The next day, Hughes threw for the Americans for a 4–2 win over Philadelphia. He added insult to injury, winning the game himself not just with his pitching, but also with a ninth-inning home run. Two days later, Boston swept Washington and had a 10-game lead over Cleveland, and a 71–39 mark, rivaling the Pirates.

On September 1, 1903, it was reported that Killilea would soon be talking with his Pirate counterpart about the idea of the World Series and the terms. Killilea wouldn't talk to the writers about it, though, because he wanted to hear from Dreyfuss first, although the talk was that the series might be popular enough to take some of the games to other cites such as Chicago or New York.

Two days later, Collins said his team was ready for it. Collins was a sagacious man as well, and he could see the ramifications for baseball beyond the significance to his own team. "I really do not know if the series has been definitely arranged. So far as I understand it Pittsburg wants to play a series of 11 games with the leaders of the American League. Well, that question remains to be settled. Personally, I am confident that neither Cleveland nor the Athletics will beat us out, but you can never tell. Provided we do win the championship I am ready for such a series and am sure that they will draw tremendous crowds from all over the country."

He fired a shot across the Pirates' bow too. "Boston is ready for such a series. I am confident that if we played those games now Pittsburg would never get a look in. I won't say how many of the 11 games we will win if we play, but you can put it down in black and white that we will get the majority," he said. "I think we have the better team in every branch. We have three pitchers, Young, Hughes and Dinneen, and if you find their equal in any club I shall be a sadly disappointed man," he said.

But first, the Americans still had to deal with the A's, who, without Waddell, had fallen to third place behind Cleveland, and who were in Boston for a series. In the first game, they beat the A's again 6–5 in 12 innings before nearly 7,000 fans. The Americans were given a loud ovation — led by the Royal Rooters — when they came out on the field.

The weather was damp and cold and the Americans played listlessly at first, before rallying to tie the game in the seventh, as Young, who was shaky at the start, shut down the A's the last six innings. Boston should have won the game in nine innings, but for a run taken away on an interference call at the plate, a call that had Collins fuming. Boston was still far ahead in the American League, with a record of 75–40, Cleveland in second at 65–53, and the A's in third at 60–54. While people were still marveling at the feat of the New York Highlander's Iron man McGinnity, who on August 31 won his third doubleheader of the year, beating Philadelphia, 4–1 and 9–2, the Americans were getting ready for another series with the American League Philadelphians, hoping to finish them off.

By September 3, the Pirates were 79–37 with the Giants in second at

71–47 and Clarke wanted his charges to finish hard. That day was especially important for Clarke because it marked the return of Doheny, back from his home in Andover, presumably recovered from the delusions and mental depression that had struck in July.

Doheny was masterful in shutting down the Cincinnati Reds, 6–3, winning his fourth straight, aided by a sensational catch in the outfield by Beaumont. Clarke continued to fret over the psychological health of his star left-hander, who was vexing batters and his teammates alike. If there was going to be a series between the two leagues after the season ended, Clarke knew he had to count on his cagey left-hander and was hoping he could stay balanced. The Pirates won again the next day and had 81 wins now, eight games ahead of the New York Giants.

On September 3, the Americans beat Philadelphia 6–5 in 11 innings. The pennant races had turned into a two-team race for greatness, like a match race between two horses almost oblivious to the other, tearing down the stretch at their own torrid pace. But a few days later, Doheny began to self-destruct on the mound. He walked four and threw wild as the Pirates split a doubleheader with Cincinnati. Doheny complained that he was ill again.

On September 4, Murnane wrote about the prospects of a World Series and how the public was taken with it. "The interest taken in the Boston-Pittsburg series for the championship of the world is greater than has ever before been shown in baseball. The long, bitter war between the two big leagues caused people to take sides and often their judgment was influenced by prejudice," he wrote in his weekly column that Sunday. Murnane said some caution was needed, however, because of Pittsburg's reputation for toughness, what he called the "win, tie or wrangle disposition." And Murnane said a warning by the Boston players that they wouldn't play unless they got paid properly was no idle threat and that the series might be cancelled otherwise.

In his Sunday column on September 6, Murnane said interest in the proposed series indeed was picking up, but he wasn't sure how the betting line or odds would be. "Championship honors this season will go to Boston and Pittsburg without a doubt, as both clubs have a big lead and are playing the best ball," he said. Despite some pressure from other owners, such as in New York, to host a couple of the games, they would all be played in Boston and Pittsburg. "It was expected that the Pittsburg sports would have all kinds of money to back up their team's chances on the strength of Barney Dreyfuss saying some time ago that his team would play for all the gate money. It looked as if Pittsburg would be even money, at least, and I cannot say why one team has not as good a show as the other," he said.

When the Bostons destroyed Philadelphia 12–1 on September 5 in a game stopped after eight innings because of mist that turned into rain, it was the ninth win in 10 tries against the pennant defenders and it put the Philadelphians far behind. The Pirates were losing two in a row to Chicago, and Clarke, still trying to recover from his injuries, was worried about the physical condition of his team, with Wagner still hurting from a sore leg and Doheny coming apart mentally.

Murnane said baseball was the country's game now, the American League having provided new venues and competition. Attendance had passed the 2 million mark for the year. That included a large and happy crowd of more than 8,400 on September 11 in Boston to see the Americans batter New York 10–3, a win that gave them the American League pennant. "Jimmie Collins was full of dash," Murnane wrote. "In fact, a big load has been lifted off the manager's shoulders, and he can now see Ban Johnson handing over that pennant," he added. "The crowd was a very large one for this season of the year, and all were delighted at the grand good playing of the coming champions."

The Pirates were still banged up, hampered especially by a leg injury to Wagner five days earlier. He made a dramatic appearance in a game on September 12 that was described by Frank McQuiston, a sportswriter for the *Pittsburg Daily Dispatch*: "A great big fellow with shoulders like a safe mover and whose legs plainly said that his uniform had been cut out by a circular saw strode or rather limped from the bench at the opening of the game yesterday with the gang following. One-tenth part of a second later everybody was on edge yelling approval. It was Hans the Hitter, Hans the bruised and maimed, who should be in the hospital, but who couldn't lie by in a sling and see the boys lose all the time. He was there to lead us to victory once more and he did."

Murnane said even the Boston players didn't like the specter of an injured Wagner. "Capt. Collins and the Boston players are in hopes that Hans Wagner is in shape to do his best work in the coming series. Queer, but a fact nevertheless, the Boston Americans this season have shown the greatest ball playing when up against the strongest teams, and when the games were put down as difficult," Murnane wrote.

But there was, it was reported, yet another chance the games might not come off. It was a little paragraph in the paper which read, "It is possible that there may not be a post-series between the Pittsburg and Boston clubs for the world's championship." The reason? The banged-up condition of the Pirates and what was described as "the peculiar actions of pitcher Eddie Doheny ... said to make it doubtful whether the series will be played." Doheny still hadn't settled down with Pittsburg after his recovery period at home from July to September.

The *Pittsburg Daily Dispatch* reported the same and said Doheny had

had a quarrel with Dreyfuss, prompting the Pirates owner to think about canceling the prospective series. The fallout remained from the game five days earlier in which Doheny had bitterly complained about a lack of defensive support from his teammates.

McQuiston questioned Dreyfuss about the trouble with Doheny and whether it would affect the possibility of a World Series.

A tense Dreyfuss replied, "Doheny did not pitch a good game Monday morning. He was accused of not having kept himself in shape. This he denied. The next day Mrs. Doheny came to my office and told me that he was sick. On Friday he made his first appearance since Monday at the ballpark. This is all I will say on the matter." He wanted to be fair and compassionate with Doheny, but the Pirates owner had no idea what was happening and whether Doheny was just slacking off. The owner was worried now too about Wagner, whose leg was hurting him so much the Pirate great was thinking about checking into a hospital to have it looked at.

McQuiston asked Dreyfuss, "You will not try the post series games unless Wagner at least is well?"

"I don't like to try any games without that fellow," Dreyfuss said. "Our chances would be lessened greatly if he was out. We shall see. The American League is waiting now to hear from me. If our team is not in the best of shape, and it is now, we will not play the games. If we are in good shape, we will play them. This will be decided next week. I surely do not want to go into any such series with half a team," he added.

Dreyfuss knew the World Series games were too important. Unbeknownst to the players, Killilea went to Pittsburg to try to arrange the details of the series with Dreyfuss. Both men knew the significance, financial and otherwise, and wanted to work out something suitable for each side, while insuring the revenues would be satisfactory. The two men agreed on a best-of-nine affair with the first three games in Boston on October 1, 2, and 3, with four in Pittsburg scheduled for October 5, 6, 7, and 8 and, if necessary, in Boston on October 10 and 12. The admission price would be doubled to 50 cents from the regular season's 25 cents, and there would be one umpire from each league chosen. There was also a little proviso that the home team could postpone games because of inclement weather, a caveat no one thought much about at the time because there was so much interest in the upcoming games. It was an unremarkable document, a single typed page with little fanfare or formality to it, except the players didn't know it yet.

They soon would.

The Greatest Aggregation of Ballplayers

Collins and his men were closing the season with a flourish, sweeping Cleveland in a three-game series in Boston, including a sensational rally from a 6–0 deficit to win 7–6, when Parent hit a two-out two-run homer in the bottom of the ninth. Boston's record who lifted to 85–43. Even with their injuries, the Pirates clinched the pennant on September 18, sweeping a doubleheader from the Boston Beaneaters in near wintry conditions in Pittsburg's Exposition Park. It was reported that "over 3,000 half frozen fans stood on chairs in the gathering gloom and cheered Fred Clarke madly as the little captain and manager tore over the plate with the run which clinched the pennant" in the second game in the bottom of the ninth. He had tripled and scored on Sebring's single. Now he could think about trying to rest some of his players to get ready for the series against Boston.

The same day, Collins even got a congratulatory telegram from the Beaneaters players who had faced the Pirates so many times. And Smart, the team's business manager, finally got a telegram from Killilea outlining the details of the series, but the players weren't sure about the financial end. And while the Pirates were under contract until October 15, Collins and his men were signed only through the end of September and couldn't be forced into playing if they didn't like what they would get.

Curiously, it was Murnane who was immediately skeptical and his word was heavily weighed both because of his standing as a former player and because he had such good contacts within the leagues. On September 20, in his Sunday column, he wrote that he didn't think that post-season games, including the matchup between Boston and Pittsburg, would be successful. The owners of other teams had also proposed a series of games between American and National League teams at the same time the World Series would be going on, as a way to keep interest in those cities as well.

"This fall we are to have a lot of exhibition games, and I predict nine-tenths of them will be failures. In most cases the players are not under contract and will be unmanageable," Murnane wrote. "Even the series between Boston and Pittsburg will fail to attract the crowds anticipated. Here in Boston the baseball season will be over, and the football season well on. The public may go out to see the games, but will hardly enthuse unless the games start off with close scores," he added. "Two ball teams were never more evenly matched than Boston and Pittsburg, and yet you will hear people tell how much stronger one club is than the other. Most of those who pick Pittsburg as the winner have yet to see the Boston team at work, and therefore their judgment is useless," he said.

The attendance for the team had hit 100,000, and for the American League it was now over 500,000. Baseball's popularity, with two organized leagues competing with each other, was on the rise. It was perfect timing, Johnson, Killilea and Dreyfuss thought, to capitalize on fan interest.

Collins and the Boston boys were scrapping for a fight with Pittsburg, unhappy that they and the American League had been demeaned for three years, and with the names they'd been called for jumping leagues. But there would be a price. The players knew the strong attendance the Americans had enjoyed had profited the team's two owners in two years and that a championship series had the potential to be a financial bonanza, and they wanted to share in it.

But the team got more bad news on September 22 when Clarke, who was sitting out the game against Brooklyn, hurt himself as a pinch hitter in the ninth inning. He had cracked a two-run homer to center to tie the game, but in rounding second base had wrenched his right leg badly and limped home while the crowd was cheering his feat, unaware of the cost to the team.

Meanwhile, Doheny's wife and his brother, who was a priest, took Doheny, who hadn't played since his a blowup on September 7, home to Andover. He was going to be cared for again at home in hopes that he could return the following week for the series, but the aid "The chances are that he will not work again this year, and that Pittsburg will go into the world's championship series minus the services of one of its best pitchers. Clarke will depend upon Phillippe, Kennedy, and Leever."

On September 21, with Otto Krueger added to the list of the injured when a pitched ball hit him, the Pirates tried a jury-rigged lineup of substitutes, but dropped two games to Brooklyn, and lost again the next day to the Brooklynites, 5–4, in 10 innings. "Pittsburg's new players could not win," it was reported.

On September 22, National League President Harry Pulliam said the Pirates would win because they came from a stronger league, a shot at his American League counterpart, Ban Johnson:

> While the Bostons have a good team, the Pirates outclass them at every point, I think. They are the greatest aggregation of ballplayers that ever stepped on a field. When it is necessary they can do with a ball just about as they please in a batting way, while in the matter of fielding, they are far superior to any team now doing business in either league. I look for a large attendance in the series, and, as I have already said, I believe the Pittsburgs will win a majority of the games.

Murnane, getting wind of a problem, reported that Smart and Collins weren't talking about too much about the arrangements for the post-season series but said "the fact is that some of the players have protested against the business manager being counted in the division," how the revenues would be shared after the series. "Mr. Smart has in no way signified his desire to share in the rake off, but Pres. Killilea thought he was entitled to do so the same as the other salaried men," Murnane wrote. There was trouble brewing for Killilea, who was often absent from Boston. Murnane said he thought Killilea would have to come to Boston quickly to save the series.

"Mr. Killilea may have to come up here and fix up matters, as Lou Criger has informed friends that he will leave for home at the close of his contract, and one or two other men have hinted that they will do the same," he said, although still believing the games would be played and the difficulties settled. It didn't look that way a couple of days later. With the regular season winding down, there were rumors that the series might not be held after all because the agreement had been reached without the players being involved.

The sportswriters pigeonholed Collins. "How about it, Jimmy?" he was asked. "Are you going to play."

Collins didn't seem happy with the question but he answered snappily. "The games will be played." Some of the Boston sportswriters thought his answer was disingenuous and said the Boston manager's manner didn't fit his words. The players were upset too that Smart was apparently going to share in the proceeds of the series. Smart tried to dance away from reporter's questions and said he would not talk about the arrangement that Killilea wanted. Several players said they would quit playing before they'd lose a part of their share to non-players and one writer glumly predicted, "Unless the temper of the players is different than it was yesterday, there will be no games here or in Pittsburg."

The Boston players weren't bluffing, despite their desire to take on the Pirates, who were just as eager to show the baseball world that the Americans were pretenders to the championship throne who couldn't stand up to the National League winners. The Pirates players, under contract until October 15, had to take whatever was decided, but the Boston players did not. They could walk away after October 1 without risk of reprisal or even losing their jobs, unless Killilea directed a vendetta in which they would not be brought back in 1904. The Pirates were willing to take whatever terms Dreyfuss decided, but the Bostonians were not willing to take whatever Killilea proposed.

Some of the Boston players were grousing openly in the dugout and to a few of the writers, who were eagerly reporting the dissension, even though the players were warned precipitous action against a series that the public wanted would bring them disfavor. "Any player who would do anything rash just at this time would place himself in a most unenviable light," the *Globe* reported. "It is too bad that at the very outset anything like disaffection should be brought to light," the paper stated. And with so many papers in the city following every game now, the players were subject to growing scrutiny.

Killilea was offering the players a split of 50 percent of the receipts from the series, but they didn't take to that offer very kindly at all. They wanted all the money to go to them, a view which earned them a reprimand from *The Sporting News*, in a column in which the paper stated the players' demands were "unreasonable and showed a spirit of greed which will go a long way toward disillusioning the public which thinks the players sole dreams all season long are of victories and pennants instead of eagles and ducats."

While the Pirates were looking forward to the series without grousing, on September 25, the Boston papers reported that the series would not be played without some resolution to the financial bickering. "Boston Team Calls It Off," a *Globe* headline read. Collins said the players were not satisfied with Killilea's decision to let them share in only half the gate receipts. He said he had gotten the players together to talk about it and they unanimously rejected the proposal unless the revenues were split evenly among everyone, and not half to Killilea and half to the club. Killilea had sent Collins the terms and asked for a response by telegram, which he pointedly got: the players refused to accept the proposition and would not play. It was an answer for which he was not prepared, because more than money was at stake now.

Reporters from the many newspapers in the city were now running back and forth from the players to the management trying to find out what had happened. Collins was in a dilemma because he was not only a player, but also the manager, but he had told the reporters bluntly, in an answer that was partly contradictory to the management's view:

> The series is off. No one feels worse about it than I do. Mr. Killilea wired me this afternoon that everything was off, as he and the players could come to no understanding. I am inclined to side with the players. We have the greatest team in the country and delighted the Boston public by winning the pennant. It seems hardly right that after making big money for the club owners Mr. Killilea should ask for one-half the total receipts. The players wanted to give him one-half provided he pay their salaries for two more weeks. It is too bad that the Boston public, which has given us such loyal support, cannot see us play for the world's championship. However, there is not one chance in a hundred of the games being played.

At first, Smart didn't want to talk about it. "I have nothing to say. Mr. Killilea thinks he is right, so do the players," he said sharply to reporters. Smart said Killilea met with the Boston team while they were playing a midwestern swing and offered them two weeks' salary for the series, even though it might not last that long. "I know that Mr. Killilea intended to treat the boys handsomely, but he naturally felt he was interested in the outcome of a series where he had made it possible to have a champion team," Smart said. It was an argument the players weren't buying. They not have had many rights, and the chances of reprisal were great, but they too sensed the significance of the series and they didn't want to be left out of the rewards.

Even with limited rights, the players were standing their ground and the public was with them, because people wanted to see the games. One told the *Boston Post* that while fans were happy Killilea had provided the city with a team that had won, they were upset he was so insistent on sharing so heavily in the financial gain they felt should rightly mostly go to the players. "Throughout the city last evening nothing but the deepest regret and disgust was expressed over the calling off of the games," the *Boston Post* reported on September 25. Killilea wasn't helping himself by staying in Milwaukee and Chicago, illustrating his absentee ownership.

Collins tried to force Killilea's hand by saying the pennant winners would make their own barnstorming tour throughout New England and New York State, but the *Post* thought he was bluffing because there was too much money to be made by playing against the Pirates. "There is yet a remote chance that the Pittsburg series will yet be played," the paper reported. "A long, cold winter is expected. Each player, at the least, would net $500 on the series. This is a lot of money during the off-season and would more than pay for the winter's coal. In a few days, possibly, the men will come down from their high seats and be willing to play at any old agreement."

Killilea, though, wired a friend in Boston that he would rather lose every dollar he had in the team than submit to players dictating terms to him. The series, it seemed, was unraveling before it could even be played, as financial matters began to take on new importance and the players felt themselves gaining if they could stand their ground against the powerful owners. It was a big gamble because most of the players had no contracts yet for the following year. An irate Killilea thought if he could get public opinion on his side he could say the players scuttled the series, and then sign them for less than he had paid for the 1903 season and they would have no other place to go. The players said they would not stand for it, but they had little alternative.

In Pittsburg, Dreyfuss was gotten out of the bed to hear the news and he was unhappy, saying he expected to hold the players to the contract he had reached with Killilea. "Until I hear something from Mr. Killilea myself, I will expect that the owners of the Boston club will make good their contract with me. I signed the contract in good faith and expect to fulfill it. I will hold them to the same. A contract is a contract and must be respected. I have heard, not officially, that some of the Boston players have kicked. I know what I should do, should any of my players kick and fuss. I should at once declare out of the deal," he said.

And then Dreyfuss rubbed it in a little. "We will go into the games with several badly crippled men, but will go in. We will do the best we can and will beat Boston badly at that," he said, challenging the Boston players. "That is, if the boys are not too badly frightened there to let us have a crack at them," he added.

Killilea was under tremendous pressure to reach an agreement with his players, but instead said he felt their action left him no decision but to call off the first World Series, no matter how much it meant. The next day Boston went out and beat Detroit 8–2. But the same day the public was reading about the trouble, September 25, Smart summoned Collins into his office and made a long-distance telephone call to Killilea, and told him that the public had demanded the series. He urged that the parties try to find a resolution or else risk the public wrath, and lose the potential for a lot of revenues. It was a persuasive argument for the businessman Killilea, who didn't want pride to get in the way of moneymaking matters.

The two sides talked on the telephone for 30 minutes and an agreement was reached at 5:45 P.M. When Killilea agreed, so did Collins, the proposal being that the players would split 75 percent of the pot and 25 percent would go to the club and Killilea.

Collins had received a lot of pressure as well for the players' refusal to play. Johnson had sent him a lengthy telegram, chastising him and the Americans for their action. "The press and the public demand these games and you should impress this fact upon your players," said Johnson. He had enormous power in the league, and the players, many of whom had jumped from the National League and wanted a secure setting to finish their careers, were reluctant to balk now because of what might happen in 1904 and beyond. Collins had said he thought the players were entitled to more than half the profits and said they would agree to play now that Killilea had softened his hard line.

And then he took a shot back at Dreyfuss and Pittsburg. "It looks as if those stories from Pittsburg about the poor condition of the team were for the purpose of letting the Dreyfuss boys down easy," he sneered. First, there was a lot of making up to do. Collins said "I know how the Boston public felt on the matter, and Mr. Killilea deserves much praise for the liberal terms he now offers. I am confident that our team will beat the Pirates ... the trouble was unfortunate and at the same time unavoidable."

Smart was businesslike. "Mr. Killilea offered new terms and Manager Collins accepted for the players. The public will now be able to see the two teams battle for the world's championship. To say I am happy is putting it mildly," he said, although joy was not a quality he publicly offered much. What the public didn't know is that Dreyfuss had set a deadline for 6 P.M. that Killilea barely met. The first World Series had come within 15 minutes of being cancelled.

Charley Lavis, one of the leaders of the Royal Rooters, said relief was the feeling most in order at McGreevey's saloon. "It is a good thing for the game. It would have been a sad state of affairs when a series for the world's championship would have to go by the board on account of a disagreement between the players and owner," he said. That was enough for the gamblers in both cities. They were already trying to get their money down and the odds set on what they figured would be the biggest take in baseball history.

Johnson wasn't satisfied with a telegram and although he was in Chicago when he heard about the trouble, he immediately set off for Boston. When he arrived the next morning, September 26, he found out the matter had been settled and just in time. "The baseball public demanded the games and the American League is trying to please the public," he said. He also said he and Killilea expected to attend the games, although the Boston owner was frequently absent during the season. Johnson tried to buoy up the Boston public and promoted the series at the same time.

"From April 16 Collins and his men have played great ball. In Pittsburg they will find opponents worthy of their steel. Boston should win," he said. "We want to make good our contention that the American League is and has been playing the faster article of ball."

Both Ready for the Great Test

For all the talk about the World Series, the regular season had to go on. And on September 26, with Ban Johnson in the stands in Boston, the Americans split a double-header with St. Louis, resting some of their regulars, although Young lost the first game 6–2. The next day the Americans finished with a doubleheader sweep of St. Louis to finish at 91–47. They were tied in victories with the National League champions. Pittsburg had finished its season at 91–49, seven games ahead of New York.

That day was closing day for the Americans, but the city was looking ahead to the series only two days off with the *Post* saying, "the games will be for blood." The papers were talking openly of rumors that there was so much money involved that the series would be influenced or even rigged, stories, which had the players spouting, mad in public. As the *Post* said, "The management of both teams indignantly deny that the games will be 'fixed' in order to enlarge the gate receipts. There is too much at stake and it is only the 'croakers' who are claiming that the full nine games will be played." Johnson knew that money for generations was at stake too, with a future of expanding interest and revenues if a great series was played, and especially if the Bostons could beat the invincible Pirates. With the National League Beaneaters finishing in sixth place, the Americans had the baseball fans to themselves in Boston.

Honus Wagner, the "Flying Dutchman," follows Fred Clarke over home plate in a practice session at Hot Springs, Arkansas. George Gibson is the catcher in the picture (courtesy Carnegie Library, Pittsburgh).

The Pittsburg money people were ready to back their boys too, though. Col. Alec Moore, a renowned Smoky City gambler, telegraphed a friend in Boston: "Hear that you have money in Boston to put up at two to one on your favorites. If so, let me know and I will furnish you all you want." Moore, a warm friend of the Pirates players, got this back from his friend: "Stop squealing: be a good sport and bring all your money to Boston, where you can place it at even up, which should be good betting."

That same day, an estimated $25,000 was bet on the series and Collins predicted that 40,000 fans would turn out for the three games in Boston. With Boston still curiously the favorite because of the injuries to key Pirates players, a lot of money was sure to be put down, especially with 14-year veteran Cy Young to take the mound for the Americans on Thursday, October 1.

"I will do my best and that is all any man can do. The other boys will also do their best. If defeated, I don't think we will be making any excuses. I never felt better in my life," the 36-year-old Young said. The *Boston Post* ran a cartoon of him showing a caricature even more portly than he was, but those looks had fooled many a batter who wasn't ready for the blistering fastball he threw in a time when many pitchers did not have such speed.

On Tuesday, September 29, just two days before the start of the series, the *Globe* put an across-the-paper photograph of the hatless Pirates, in uniform, on the sports page under the title *Three Time Winners,* showing a grim and determined bunch of ballplayers, their arms folded tightly across their chests, eyes straight ahead, a fighting demeanor in the eyes. They looked formidable. The Pirates were bringing a 15-man roster, Doheny and Krueger still out, and many of those set to play nursing injuries that Clarke thought would affect his lineup. He was especially worried about the Boston pitching, with three 20-game winners. Besides Cy Young, he knew that Big Bill Dinneen was difficult to hit when on. Young had won 28 games, Dinneen 21, and Tom Hughes gave them depth and had won 20.

The Pirates had himself, Ginger Beaumont and Jimmy Sebring batting left to confound the big right-handers, and Claude "Little All Right" Ritchey was a switch-hitter, but he knew Young and Dinneen could be death on any hitters when they were on to their twirl because they threw hard and had sharp curves to throw off any batter from either side.

On Wednesday, September 30, the day before the series was to start, the *Globe* did a comparison of the two teams for its readers that showed how even the test would be, and its headline put it this way: *Man For Man, It Would Appear That Boston Does Not Suffer By It.*

The *Boston Post* said, "Tomorrow at Huntington Avenue, what is expected to be the greatest series in the history of baseball will begin," adding that 16,000 people were expected. "Interest all over the city and by all classes is at fever heat. In the downtown hotels and sporting resorts last evening nothing else was talked of."

Boston was going to rely on its pitching and slugging, while the Pirates, with the best base-stealer in the game in Wagner, the fastest man in Beaumont, and their heavily left-handed hitting lineup, thought they could counter, although Clarke was seriously worried about his hurlers. The Americans remained 10-to-8 favorites among the bettors because of the uncertainties about the Pirates' injuries.

The *Post* thought Criger was a key element for the Americans to keep the Pirates from running amok on the bases and said he "can be depended upon to keep his head even if 50,000 people are watching him." The load on the little catcher would be heavy indeed because he was counted on for his defense and pitch calling and was Young's favorite behind the plate. The teams had similar managers in many respects. The tempestuous Collins was called the "king of third basemen" for his ability and had shown his managerial skills in molding the pennant winners, while Clarke had a long history of winning and was close to his players. He was a good man in a storm, levelheaded, cunning and fiercely competitive.

Murnane was keying on the match-ups of the two teams now, his waffling diminishing rapidly as the excitement of the series was upon the city. Throughout Boston the nights before the games, baseball had become the *lingua franca* in restaurants, stores, pool halls, saloons, offices, street corners and wherever people gathered. It was becoming evident that there might be a great crowd for the first games on Thursday and Friday, and perhaps more for the third game on Saturday, when more people were not working. Murnane pondered in his column, "At the beginning of this series the determination to win, team work and ability to hit will be evident in both teams. But the boys of the Smoky City are in a rut, and the question is how long will it take in these games to key them up to a standard of play equal to that of Collins' team?"

Still, the residents of Boston and Pittsburg loved the idea of a series and the *Boston Daily News* even wrote about the admiration in Beantown for Wagner and his great skills and unassuming demeanor, attributes that sat well with the Irish-American immigrants too. The paper called Wagner "The Hercules Of The Diamond," and applauded his "simple, direct nature and the fact that he is so modest he does not appreciate his own worth."

There were logistics to think about too. Smart had the job of getting the field ready and the preparations set for the opening game on Thursday, October 1, including trying to estimate just how high the public interest would be and how many police officers he would need for crowd control, and how many tickets would sell at the ballpark and at downtown outlets where fans could go. The only communication on which all could rely was the many newspapers in both cities and throughout the country, and scoreboards that would be set up in common places throughout cities where fans could go to watch the inning-by-inning postings of the score and highlights. Also watching were the gamblers, men like Boston's Sport Sullivan, who made a good living wagering—in the open—on sporting events, and they sensed too the drama of the upcoming series and the partisanship of the fans of the two cities would have people betting emotionally. The gamblers were businessmen, setting the odds on where the money—and not their hearts—went. Their favorite was the dollar, and there suddenly began a too-keen interest in the series for some newspapers, although they wrote stories and listed the odds for all to see.

On September 30, the Boston Post worried there was too much money floating around, and that this could influence the games. "There is too much at stake to risk having the series prolonged," the paper said, intimating that there was a strong potential for fixing the games. But, the paper said, "Baseball is too open to be crooked ... ask any great ballplayer if he could make an error on purpose and he would answer that he could, but that everyone would be 'on to him.'" Of course, there had long been reports about gamblers influencing the outcomes of some games, but this, after all, would be a series the whole country would watch. Ballplayers, and even owners, openly consorted with gamblers and sometimes bet on games. The pressure now, however, would be magnified.

If Dreyfuss was concerned about how the series would take with the public, he didn't have to wait long. The Pirates were to stay in the well-appointed Hotel Vendome in Boston's elegant Back Bay, right on the broad boulevard of Commonwealth Avenue. They would have a big surprise when they got there, seeing the rabid fans and gamblers. But the next day, they said to a man, they would be ready for the first pitch, and for the Americans and their fans.

The first World Series was on.

SIX

An Awful Boom in the Ninth Inning

Cy Young threw the first pitch of the first World Series and the crowd roared anew. He quickly got Beaumont to fly to Stahl in center field as the partisan crowd screamed even louder. Then Clarke popped up to Criger and Boston fans slapped each other on the back in the stands. The mighty Pirates could not stand up against Uncle Cy. Young got two strikes on the diminutive Leach and it looked like a 1–2–3 inning for him. But Leach lined a shot past Freeman in right and went all the way to third as the crowd scrambled for the ball in the outfield. Then up came Wagner and the first confrontation with Young.

The wily Wagner worked Young to throw a curve, which the Flying Dutchman lurched at and sent into left field for a single, scoring Leach for the first run. On Young's first pitch, Wagner showed no signs of favoring his badly bruised leg and took off for second, trying for a steal against the strong-armed and reliable Criger behind the plate. The throw made some people wonder if too much money hadn't been bet on the game.

Wagner, who had 46 stolen bases during the regular season, looked like a runaway freight train on the base paths. He had heard the taunts of the Boston fans in the Hotel Vendome lobby and he had started this World Series with a hit and now wanted the stolen base that had become his trademark as much as his bat. Criger delayed his throw and Wagner slid in safely, easily, and Ferris looked quizzically at Criger, wondering what had taken him so long. Criger looked, as an irked Murnane noted, "like a fur overcoat in July." Even people in the stands were looking around at each other, befuddled by Criger's reluctant throw.

Boston's battery of catcher Lou Criger (left) and pitcher Cy Young. The man in the moustache in the stands is the leader of the Royal Rooters, Nuf Ced McGreevey (courtesy Boston Public Library).

But then it was Ferris's turn to look funny. Bransfield hit a ground ball right at the sure-handed second baseman, but the ball rolled up Hobe Ferris's sleeve after he made several furtive stabs at it while Wagner went to third. On the next pitch, Bransfield took off for second and Criger threw the ball into center field, with Wagner scoring, Bransfield going to third, and the crowd shifting uneasily as their champions looked like amateurs, or suspect at least. It was already 2–0 Pittsburg, and Criger was getting uneasy looks.

Young walked Ritchey and the slow Pirate second baseman took off for second too, the visitors showing open disdain now for Criger, considered one of the game's great catchers. This time Criger bluffed his throw to second and threw to third to Collins, hoping to catch Bransfield off the bag. Bransfield hadn't moved off the base, but Criger's strategy would pay off later in the series, even if it looked suspicious at the time. Still, the Pirates had Bransfield on third and Ritchey on second and the game was in danger of turning into a rout before Boston even got up to bat. Young's control left him and he walked Ritchey. When Sebring rapped Young for a single to left, it was 4–0 Pittsburg and a gloom had spread over the crowd. This was not what they had come to see. Even the Royal Rooters had nothing to pound their drums about.

It looked, finally, like Young was out of the inning when he struck out catcher Ed Phelps, but Criger let the ball get by him for his third error in the first inning and it still wasn't over. Young struck out Phillippe but the Americans were down 4–0. The Boston team hoped the top of their line-up, the left-handed Dougherty, Collins, and lefty Stahl, could make up some of the runs against Phillippe, who had baffled big hitters with a succession of curves, slow pitches and drops, confusing their timing. But the Deacon whiffed Dougherty and Collins in quick succession, and while Stahl managed a single, Phillippe struck out the mighty Freeman. The Boston fans were trying to rattle Phillippe with screaming, singing, blowing tinhorns and using every noise-producing instrument they could muster, but he was unflappable. After the first inning, he came back to the Pirate dugout and told Clarke, "I think I have my curve working in pretty good shape. You don't need to worry about this game."

In the second inning, the Boston fans gave Phillippe applause after he struck out Parent, LaChance and Ferris in order. Phillippe had struck out five of the first six Boston batters. The players, and fans, were perplexed. Now the silence was replaced with razzing of the Boston players. Murnane saw it and heard it. "Good men were condemned because they couldn't get in touch with Phillippe's elusive curves when hits meant something, and rooters who would have given their shirts to see the home team win went quite wild and hilarious when some clever artist of the Smoky City crowd put up a good exhibition of ball," he noted. But, just as quickly — even with bets on the line — the Boston fans would applaud a good play by a Pirate, even if on the field the players found their tempers and rivalries rising.

In the top of the third, Wagner lined to Collins for the first out, but then the bushy-haired Bransfield hit a line drive to right that caught Freeman by surprise. The ball bounced in front of him and got behind him into the crowd behind the ropes for a triple. And then Sebring got another run batted in with a single past LaChance that put Pittsburg up 5–0. It got worse.

In the fourth, Beaumont grounded to Ferris, but the usually sharp second baseman muffed it for his second error. Clarke and Leach singled, scoring Beaumont and making it 6–0 as the crowd went silent. It stayed that way until the seventh inning, when Phillippe breezed along with an easy shutout. Then Jimmy Sebring, who despite a batting average of .277 was hitting eighth, entered the history books of baseball.

The 21-year-old, the youngest on either team, hit a loping pop fly that went over second baseman Ferris' head, as right fielder Freeman and centerfielder Stahl casually sauntered after it. The ball rolled almost into the ropes before it was picked up, but Sebring had circled the bases swiftly for an inside-the-park home run and Pittsburg led 7–0. The smell of a fix was ripe in the air. Freeman's insouciance puzzled everyone. And it looked like Dreyfuss, Clarke and Leach might be right; the upstart American Leaguers might be the champions of their league, but they couldn't stay on the same field with the National Leaguers. The Boston fans sat still in dense silence while the Pittsburg fans roared wildly, led by the mild-mannered Dreyfuss.

Wagner was putting on a show all game long, firing putouts with powerful grace, ripping groundballs off the dirt with his shovel-like hands, throwing pebbles along with the ball toward first base, sending a shower of ground toward the spectators. Finally, in the bottom of the seventh, Boston showed signs of life. Freeman hit the right field fence for a triple and scored when Parent banged a fly into the crowd in left for another triple, and it was 7–1. LaChance's fly ball sacrifice scored Parent and it was 7–2. The crowd started surging with excitement again, especially when a pitched ball hit Ferris and there was only one out. But then Criger and Young quickly struck out and the rally ended.

In the Pirate eighth, with two out, the tiny Leach hit another triple off Young, who carefully worked around the dangerous Wagner, who drew a walk. Wagner took off for second again, trying to steal on Criger, who fired the ball to the tiny 5' 5½", 148-pound parent, who was covering second. But second baseman Ferris saw Leach take off from third trying to steal home, intercepted the throw and fired back to Criger who tagged Leach out.

In the bottom of the ninth, the Americans used the defensive play to motivate themselves. Wagner uncharacteristically made an error, booting

Freeman's grounder. Parent singled, and then LaChance hit a hard liner to left field, which Clarke speared on the run over his head. With two men on, Ferris singled to center, scoring Freeman and making it 7–3 and the crowd felt there was still a chance. Jack O'Brien pinch hit for Criger and struck out and then the only native Bostonian on the team, Duke Farrell, pinch hit for Young, but, with the crowd worked up to a frenzy now, he meekly bounced back to the mound and was easily thrown out. The fans sat back on their hands, except for the Pittsburg contingent, which whooped it up as the sportswriters dashed for the telegrams to fire off their stories. There was a sense of deflation in the air for the Bostonians, who expected a different result with Young on the mound.

But then the majesty of the moment prevailed and the thousands of fans in the stands poured onto the field to meld with those from the outfield who wanted to rush to the players and touch them, and to gather with other fans to talk about the spectacle of what they'd seen. It was captured in surreal sense by photographers, some of whom took long distance shots from outside the grounds, from the roofs of the warehouses on Huntington Avenue past the left field fence. The brilliant Phillippe, who struck out 10, walked back to the dugout amid the joy of his team's celebration. The field had become the gathering place for talk, and while there was disappointment the home team had lost, the Boston fans reveled in the moment, even if the sportswriters were buzzing about the way the Americans had played. There continued to be much talk after the game about the ground rules which allowed Pittsburg to benefit from getting triples from what would have been easy fly outs, but little was said about why the Boston players couldn't hit them there too.

An ebullient Dreyfuss, cheering, turned to his Pittsburg entourage and smiled. "Why not three straight?" he said, thinking the team on which he had bet his financial life could sweep the Americans at their home field and go home to Pittsburg and win it all. That feeling would be buttressed that night when he would receive telegrams from the Pittsburg fans. One sardonic wire congratulated him and the Pirates but then sneered, "Why did you allow them to make those 3 runs?" Pittsburg had won and the Boston fans were not happy, especially with the curious first inning and so much money having been bet on the game. The long-awaited game was played swiftly, taking only two hours. The great Young had given up 12 hits, including three to Sebring and four, including two triples, to the diminutive third-sacker Leach, while the Americans could manage only three off Philippe's benders.

On Friday, October 2, in the *Pittsburg Post*, there was an I-told-you-so-tone to the story of sportswriter Gruber, who was confident the Pirates would win the series in a walk. "There is gloom in old Boston town to-night, and the gloom is intensified by the knowledge that Pittsburg has a faster team in every respect," he wrote. "The work put up by the National League champions simply made the Boston men look like counterfeit money," he added. "Local fans cannot see how their team is going to win a game, let alone a series," he said, rubbing it in.

Even Clarke was uncharacteristically excited. "Much of the credit belongs to Phillippe," he said. "The steady man had a delivery that was most difficult to solve. Deacon was never in better condition. The way he cut loose with his benders was a caution," Clarke said of the pitcher's befuddling slow curve.

One Pittsburg paper headlined "Deacon Phillippe has American League Champions at His Mercy," and Gruber proclaimed that Phillippe was "The Whole Cheese."

The *Pittsburg Gazette* said Young, the former National Leaguer whom Wagner had disdained, was rattled and beaten soundly. "The veteran twirler was batted freely and timely from the start. Home runs and three-baggers were accumulated by the Pirates in a way that drew dire dismay into the Boston camp," the paper reported.

The nearly 300 Pittsburg fans who came to Boston prepared for a long night out celebrating were shocked to find there was an 11 o'clock Puritan curfew, hard news for the men from a city where beer was important stuff indeed.

The *Globe*'s Murnane wrote, "Cy Young was hit hard. He fell considerably short of his best work, lacking speed, his winning ingredient. With Young off edge, the home players were carrying a big handicap." And he said Criger's work was especially suspicious and suggested the usually reliable catcher, one of the best defensively at that position, had an unusual letdown. There was talk of a fix, and bets were paid off in the open on the field as the players walked off and thousands of fans mingled. One of the big winners was a Pittsburg fan, Colonel Alec Moore, a stockholder in the team. Murnane wrote later too that Young "was looked on to win the money but was not on edge. He looked several pounds too heavy."

Murnane tried to downplay talk of money influencing the series. "Both teams played ball, but without any attempt at funny business. As the money goes mostly to the men, they can afford to keep their tempers. The Boston players have all the best of it in the way of compensation for their work, as the Pirates are under regular salary, and will not get three-quarters of the receipts, as will Boston," he wrote. The players were not happy with what would be their cuts of the games, and there was talk that they may have wanted to extend it for box office receipts that would swell the longer the games went. The money man, Smart, filled out a form that showed 2,684 grandstand admissions and a tally of 13,558 fans through the turnstiles. He turned over to the delighted Dreyfuss a first game share of $4,060.50.

After the game, Pulliam gushed, "No matter how the remaining games of the world's championship series terminate, Pittsburg's baseball team, the greatest in the country, cannot be deprived of the glory earned on the diamond here."

Still being talked about, and written about, was the frenzied crowd response to the first game of the first World Series. The *Pittsburg Gazette* reported, "The noisy demonstrations were continuous and deafening. Distant Bunker Hill Monument fairly shivered and looked down in amazement at the demonstration." Murnane was equally agog at the fans, but he was too keen a baseball man not to notice what was happening on the field and to the players. He saw that Ferris was constantly slipping while trying to field grounders and would wear toe weights in the next day's game, and saw that LaChance was trying to reach way outside the plate where Phillippe's curve balls were breaking away from batters. As for Dreyfuss, he celebrated by taking some friends to the theater, apparently unconcerned that, despite the loss, Boston was favored in the next game.

The game, of course, was the big news in Boston and Pittsburg. But even in cities with another series going on between American and National League teams, this series took precedence. In Philadelphia, the A's beat the National League Phillies 6–0; in Chicago, the Colts beat the American League's White Sox 11–0; and Cincinnati beat the American League's St. Louis Browns 7–6.

Clarke couldn't hold his newfound confidence down:

> We had a batting streak and the game was rather easy in consequence. Every member of the team did splendid service, but much of the credit belongs to Phillippe. The steady man had a delivery that was most difficult to solve, and I was not surprised that Boston's base hits were few. The spectators were loyal to their home team, but they were eminently fair, and the applause they gave us was gratifying. Boston has a first-class team and will not be so easy in the remaining games.

Collins concurred:

> I do not want to make any excuses. Pittsburg won today because it played the better ball. Phillippe pitched in masterly style and it was not strange that we did not do much batting. The game was decided in the first inning, and it was only the fortune of baseball that Pittsburg's four runs were scored after two men was out. Our boys will give a better account of themselves in the other games. I expect to see Cy Young get sweet revenge and am still confident that we will win the series.

He couldn't help but dwell on the disappointment, but he tried to show it was momentary. "We were licked and there is little to say. Pittsburg got away well and things broke good for them. I guess a few of the boys were rather nervous. Criger doesn't often throw to centerfield. The Pirates hit hard. Our playing was all right after the first inning, and we scored as many runs as the others did. We sized up the Pirates playing today and not a man is afraid of the outcome. I am slightly disappointed, but have no fear of how the remaining games will go," he said.

Young was down, though. "I am deeply disappointed. Those Pittsburg fellows can hit the ball. I had my usual speed and my curves broke as sharp as ever. The Pirates had their eyes on the ball. I want another chance at them. I think I can turn the tables," he said.

Almost as delighted as Dreyfuss was Pulliam. He knew that the series was even more critical for the established National League to win and his relief was great at the outcome. "I have claimed right along that the National League possessed the stronger team. The game today kind of proved it. Boston's team is fast, but Pittsburg is a trifle faster. Boston acted rather nervously at the start, but 12 hits will about win the ordinary game," he said.

For Boston, the hopes were now on Dinneen, who had been a local hero while playing for the National League Boston Beaneaters in 1900 and 1901. He had gone 21–21 in 1902 when he jumped leagues and joined the Americans, but had improved to 21–13 in 1903 with six shutouts and an ERA of only 2.26. The stolid Dinneen was supremely confident too and ready for Pittsburg. The Pirates would go with Leever and his sore arm and shoulder. That made Dreyfuss and Clarke wonder how long he would last, even if he had established himself as one of the best pitchers in the game for 1903. Clarke, for all his confidence, knew that his best chance in a long series was his aching pitching staff.

GAME TWO: *Done to Death by Dinneen and Dougherty*

Bostonians were a little wary when they awoke on the morning of October 2, 1903. They had been so confident their champions would prevail, and this day they would have to bet on Dinneen. He was a lanky 6' 1" and 190 pounds, with black hair parted evenly in the middle and slicked down so tight it looked like it was glued to his head, but in a game it quickly became tousled because he played with ultimate exertion and the sweat turned his hair up. He had dead-steady eyes and a stolid countenance, looking as much like a regular drinking customer at McGreevey's saloon as a ballplayer. He had iron nerve and total faith in his ability. Having faced the Pirates before, there was nothing he didn't know about Wagner or Clarke or the other players. He had won 35 games in two years with the Beaneaters in the National League and he was not in reverential awe of even the great Wagner. The Pirates were glad to have won the first one behind Phillippe, but they knew that without Doheny and with Leever, another curveballer, ailing,

Six—An Awful Boom in the Ninth Inning

they had to get up again on Boston before Young could recover. They were worried about the Dinneen factor, and whether Boston's Long Tom Hughes, another 20-game winner, would get to them.

The weather that Friday was cloudy and threatening rain. This time the crowd was limited to 10,000, still well beyond capacity, but the poor performance of the Americans in the first game and the loss of betting money had put some fans off. Some fans were upset too that scorecards were being peddled for 15 cents. One writer agreed. "It is squeezing the dear public hard," he wrote. There was plenty of competition today too for spectators, with the appearance in downtown of the Ancient and Honourable Artillery Company of England parading through Copley Square and drawing scores of thousands for an audience. A contingent of more than 50 Royal Rooters came equipped again with a band, American flags and, this time, a cheer to rattle the Pirates. It was written on souvenir cards McGreevey handed out to his followers and customers to take to the park. Sitting in the stands, still unable to play, his nerves shot and his mental condition unreliable, was Doheny. As a sportswriter noted later, "It is too bad he is not in form, for he is dangerous when right."

It didn't take long for Boston to come back. Dinneen was untouchable in the first inning after opening with three straight balls to Beaumont. He fired fastballs and broke off crisp curves, striking out Beaumont, walking Clarke, striking out Leach, and getting Clarke caught off first in a run-down as the fans breathed a sigh of relief after the previous day's first inning debacle. The sore-armed Leever would face left-hander Patsy Dougherty in the bottom of the first. On the first pitch, the curly-haired, happy-faced Dougherty, who finished third in the American League in hitting with a .331 average, and who had a constant look of wonderment about him, drove Leever's pitch into right centerfield. Sebring tried to chase it down, but Dougherty, kicking up dust like a greyhound, raced around the bases for an inside-the-park home run. There was bedlam to match. The crowd screamed insanely and the Boston bench erupted with joy. Clarke's worries about Leever came home on the first pitch and the Pirate captain was anxious. After Collins flied out to left, Stahl doubled to left and scored on Freeman's single to center, making it 2–0 Boston. LaChance walked, but Ferris's grounder forced LaChance out at second. Clarke pulled Leever for reliever Bucky Veil, who had gone 5–3 during the season but pitched only 70 innings. With Doheny out, Leever's arm hurting more now, and Brickyard Kennedy uncertain because of his eccentricities, the Pirates staff was suspect.

McGreevey, Jerry Watson and the rest of the rooters were rolling now. With music playing loudly and the fans screaming, the Rooters took up a cheer and waved their flags in asynchronous unison. Aiming their voices at the Pirates, they shouted:

> Boston, Pittsburg
> Who are we?
> We are the rooters for 19–3.
> We will win
> Go tell your Pa,
> We Beaneaters, Beaneaters,
> Rah! Rah! Rah!

They may have been confused in yelling the nickname of the rival National League team in Boston, one they had supported for years, but "Beaneaters" applied to just about every Bostonian anyway. And the Rooters weren't done. They came back at Pittsburg again:

> In the good old summer-time
> Our Boston baseball nine
> Beat the teams — east and west:
> Now they're first in line.
> The Pittsburgs they are after us
> O me, O me, O my!
> We'll do them as we do the rest,
> In the good old summer time.

In the fourth, Beaumont walked and Clarke singled to center. The crowd was screaming now, sensing a Pirates comeback. "Hold them down!" they yelled at Dinneen as Leach came up. The Pittsburg coaches were dancing up and down the sidelines and the Pirate runners were leaning off base, almost taunting Dinneen and daring Criger to catch them. Dinneen, though, was cool and almost indifferent to the noise and to Leach, although for a moment it didn't appear so. Dinneen's first pitch almost hit the plate and his second would have hit Leach in the ribs had the batter not backed away quickly. Dinneen tried a slow change-up, but Leach was ready. The tiny third baseman squared around and laid down a difficult bunt in a sacrifice attempt, but, sensing he could make an infield hit, went charging down the first base line. Beaumont and Clarke tore for third and second as the crowd screamed. A red-faced Dinneen, surprised, came charging in, grabbed the ball and fired quickly to first, just catching the streaking Leach, who kicked and screamed at the call, although he had moved the tying runs into position.

And coming up was Wagner. Dinneen eyed Beaumont and Clarke leading off base and looked toward Wagner, the leading run. Dinneen fired a fastball and Wagner swung for the fences, but hit only air with a vicious swat as the 10,000 partisans made a sound that could be heard on the other side of Boston. On the second pitch, Wagner hit a hard line drive that went foul into the first base grandstands as the crowd sighed. "Two strikes!" yelled umpire O'Day and the grandstands quivered with excitement, waiting. It didn't take long. Wagner swung at the third pitch with a hefty weight and cracked a shot toward right field that looked like it would score two runs.

As the Pirate runners screamed around the bases, and just as Beaumont crossed home plate, Ferris leaped as high as he could and stopped the red-hot liner in its course. The crowd was still screaming and trying to figure what happened when Ferris landed and headed toward second as a stunned Clarke tried to get back. It was too late and Ferris stepped on the bag for an unassisted double play that killed the Pirates' rally. It took the wind out of the chagrined Pirates' sails.

Veil continued to shut the Americans out, but almost didn't survive the fifth inning when Boston filled the bases — Freeman singled, Parent walked, and LaChance, trying to sacrifice, reached first when Veil fumbled his bunt. Ferris hit a weak grounder to third and Leach fired home, catching Freeman at the plate. When Criger went to a 3–0 count, the Pirates were a pitch away from walking in another run, or letting him hit into a big inning for Boston. But Veil pitched a strike, and, on the 3–1 count, Criger, still stinging from criticism of his play in the first game, hit a hard line drive at second baseman Ritchey, who turned quickly and threw to first, doubling off LaChance.

In the Boston sixth, Dinneen grounded out weakly and then Dougherty stepped to the plate and punched a dead-on line drive directly at the left field wall, paralleling the foul line to the 350-foot mark where the day before some fans had scurried atop to find a seat. It was a prodigious blow with a heavy bat and a dead ball. The ball hit the top of the left field fence and went over, only the second time a ball had left the field at that point. It was a shot which woke up the Boston players and the fans; a rare line-drive homer that went over the fence almost before anyone could blink or get comfortable whether in their seats or behind the roped-off outfield. It barely tipped the top of the fence before landing on Huntington Avenue. The score was 3–0.

Dougherty was the toast of the town now, along with Dinneen, who was so commanding that no Pirate hit a ball to the outfield until the seventh inning. He was cruising and put the Pirates down with 11 strikeouts and only three hits to take a shutout and tie the series, making Boston fans jubilant, but worrying Dreyfuss and Clarke. The contest had taken only one hour and 47 minutes and as the fans poured off the field, there was big talk about the next day's game. The big disappointment for Pittsburg had been Beaumont, who, after his argument at the Hotel Vendome with the Boston fans the day before the first game, had not gotten a hit. Wagner, after his first-inning hit in the first game, had not had a hit in five other tries, although he had walked twice.

Gruber wrote that one man, Dinneen, beat his Pirates. "He was the whole shooting match, for shooting he did, with a vengeance," the Pittsburg writer put it. But he stood behind his Pirates too. "Although the Pittsburgers were unable to hit Dinneen, they never lost heart. There was not a quitter among them. They fought hard to the last ditch, and the pitcher was compelled to do his best to the very end," he wrote.

The *New York Evening World* reported that Pirates and National League fans were still boldly confident about beating a team from what they called "Johnson's League," referring to American League President Ban Johnson. The paper said the Pirates had too many stars for Boston to cope with: "Is it any wonder that Pittsburgers are willing to bet their last cent that the National Leaguers will win the series from the champions of the rival organization?"

More bets were paid off again, and this time one dour-faced Pittsburg fan shelled out $1,000 for his loss. The odds had stayed slightly in favor of Boston and the Pirates had to worry about the lack of time off between games. With the Saturday game the next day, when working people would be off and the park would probably be swarmed again, they had to figure how to stem Boston's momentum. The big decision was whether to go with Phillippe on one day's rest or come in with Brickyard Kennedy, a notorious eccentric who was illiterate, but who had come over from the New York Giants and gone 9–6 for the Pirates. Now, even with the series tied, it didn't look good for the Pirates, but the Boston boys were becoming confident too. Perhaps too confident.

The bedraggled Pirates that night went to see the play *Fools of Nature* starring actress Julia Marlowe, but the disappointed Leever, a proud man who had pushed his arm and body, stayed at the Hotel Vendome and soaked his arm and shoulder in hot water. He had been criticized for having not just a sore arm but also a "weak heart," and it grated on him. He couldn't stop thinking about how he had performed during the regular season and how he wanted to do so now.

GAME THREE: *Swarm on the Field*

If Dreyfuss and Killilea had been pleased with the turnout of the first two games during the weekday, Smart was ecstatic and knew that a Saturday game, especially after a Boston victory, would bring a banner crowd. It was October 3 and extra police were brought in to handle the anticipated mob, Smart remembering how people tried to shimmy up the outfield fences to get in and avoid paying. A buzz was in the air early on that Saturday morning in 1903 as Bostonians awoke with a start and crowds started moving toward the Huntington Avenue grounds earlier than ever. At 11 A.M., four hours before game time, 1,000 people were already lined up at the ticket booths, and when the gates opened at noon, thousands more poured through into

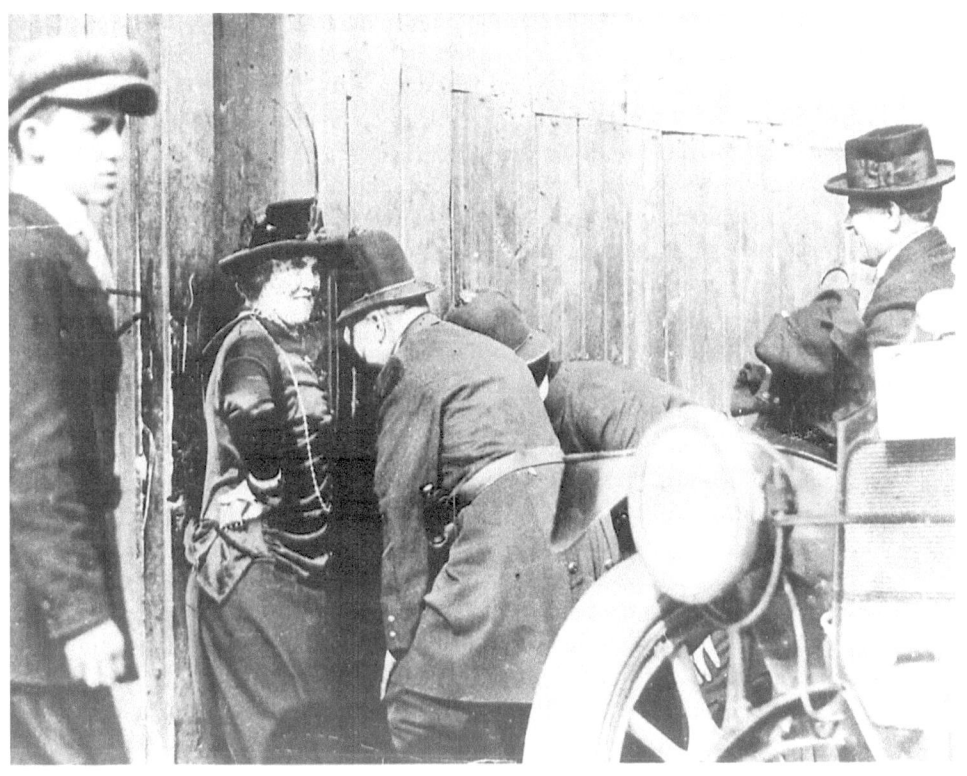

Even police wanted to get a peek at the action through knotholes in the fence, where they had to compete with others, including a well-dressed woman (courtesy Boston Public Library).

the grounds. Special railroad trains had been set up from as far as 100 miles away to meet the greatest demand ever for a baseball game.

By 1:15 P.M., all the grandstand seats were filled and a din had arisen in the lines leading to the ticket booths and spilling out onto Huntington Avenue. No one wanted to be shut out of seeing the third game with the series tied 1–1. Many boys, and some women, had spotted knotholes in the fence and were peering in. When police came, they shooed them away and took their place. Men were clambering up on each other's shoulders to reach the top of the fence and try to get in, while thousands of additional outfield standing room tickets were being sold and people were being directed to the outfield. The crush of fans trying to get into the park had become dangerous and the first day's delight had turned now into something more ominous; fans were becoming angry with each other and swarming the park and the field.

Ticket speculators were offering grandstand seats for $3 to $5 each, a large sum of money for anything, especially a baseball game. Lesser tickets were going for $1.50. The size of the crowd made it unlikely the game would start on time, troublesome for an early October game when the light might start to go if the game went too long. A 3 P.M. start was already late. Out by the centerfield fence, men had put up ropes on each side and were pulling non-paying fans up and over, many of whom fell onto the field amidst a clamor of yelling and excitement. People stood on rooftops of buildings as much as a quarter-mile away, near the New England Conservatory of Music at Massachusetts Avenue and Huntington Avenue, and a human fringe covered the outfield fences of the grounds.

By 2:15 P.M., the crowd had nearly covered the outfield in to the infield, and even 100 extra police could not handle them. When several hundred fans tried to climb into the already-full grandstands, all the police — aided by Boston and Pittsburg players in uniform — pushed them back. Smart ran into the players' dressing rooms and came out with bats he gave to the police for crowd control. Some officers wielded the bats with better results than had some of the players, whacking the most recalcitrant fans on the toes and across their shins, just hard enough to move them back. Many a courageous type wilted in the face of the wooden slugger. But even this wasn't working enough and soon even the space behind home plate was filling up and there was worry whether there would be a game. A *Boston Globe* photographer was caught in the tumult behind first base as the crowd was pushed back, and he had to be rescued by a burly officer before he fell down.

The melee had resulted in several tumbles and more than a few punches being thrown. The fresh young men who led the rush had their clothes tousled by the police and a scribe noted, "They were made to see stars which no astronomer has yet mapped." When some of the rushers reached the front row of the grandstands, like soldiers hitting the front row of an enemy's rank with bayonets, those seated started to push back to keep them out, and when that failed, resorted to throwing bunches of fives, wailing away with punches to keep their seats from the rowdies. Police behind the crowd now took to swatting some fans, with nightsticks brandished hard enough to make a number of those struck yelp with surprise and grab their behinds.

There was trouble everywhere now on the field. A few men breached the ropes in centerfield, then more followed quickly, rushing toward the third-base bleachers. A stampede overwhelmed the police and the ropes as the crowd surged for spaces in front of the third and first base bleachers. There were more than 19,000 people now on the grounds and there began yells and a tooting of horns, mingled with the cries of peanut vendors and scorecard boys seeking a bonanza. There was jostling for seats in the bleachers along the first and third base lines, but more good-natured than on the field where

Six—An Awful Boom in the Ninth Inning

the pushing and shoving had become dangerous. Every few minutes, more fans fell from the outfield fences like leaves in the autumn wind.

Then, along the first base line, there came a pair of screams that startled everyone. Two women had fallen during pushing and shoving and had screamed in their fear of being trampled. Beaumont, the boastful Pirates centerfielder, saw what was happening and, with the aid of two police, pushed through the crowd, which parted on seeing his uniform, and rescued the two fallen women who were sobbing and shaking with fright.

Chaos and confusion continued as the police, in their formal blue uniforms and high rounded hats, pushed against a sea of people, most of them men in suits and hats and shiny shoes, resisting because they wanted to be close to the game. The Huntington Avenue Grounds outfield was large and deep but fans soon consumed nearly half of it. One boy ran off with second base before being stopped by police. Clarke and Collins met with the umpires to set a new rule: fly balls that landed in the crowd would be ground-rule doubles instead of triples because there was barely 200 feet from home plate to where the crowds stood thousands deep. The teams decided to start batting and took infield practice in hopes the crowd would move farther away from the field, and, for a short time, it did. After Pittsburg's practice, though, and before Boston could come out, the outfield crowds surged again toward the diamond and soon only the infield was empty and police had to move the crowd again.

Collins pleaded with them to move because the Pirates had to take infield practice. Finally, a giant police officer weighing almost 300 pounds threw his arms in the air and ran like a mad bull into the midst of encroachers. Other police, emboldened by him, soon followed and a phalanx of them succeeded in getting the crowd back far enough for the game to begin. Pirates catcher Eddie Phelps saw four men, apparently friends, holding onto each other, wobbling from liquor, trying to stay steady in the front of the crowd. The police made them lie down on the fringe of the field, then suddenly the people behind them made a move to the front, trampling the poor fellows, who had to upright to stay alive.

A *Boston Post* sportswriter couldn't believe what he was seeing and tried to write down a description of what was happening on the field. "A surging, struggling, frantic crowd, a sea of faces, a perspiring mass of humanity that fringed the fences, packed and jammed the stands, encircled the diamond and fought both police and players ... a mighty host, whose murmur was as the roar of the sea, whose cheering volleyed and thundered, shook the roofs of the stands and rolled across the open fields beyond," he wrote.

But now there were 25,000 to 30,000 fans everywhere in the park—in the outfield, along the baselines, hanging from the fence, 20 to 30 feet deep in front of the stands, and threatening the roped-off VIP areas and where the band was settled. After a discussion, police decided to let the sideline fans stay until the game started, knowing a few hard foul balls into the crowd would be more effective in moving them back. Ironically, there was room aplenty behind the outfield crowd. No one wanted their view disturbed from being pushed back against the fence. Many along the sidelines were so close they could have tapped players running down the baselines.

At 2:40 P.M., police headquarters received news from Huntington Avenue Grounds that the force there was inadequate to keep the crowd back, so a deputy superintendent telephoned 10 stations to send more. A reserve contingent of police arrived about 2:50 P.M., 10 minutes before game time, but the crowd was too big, and the roar so loud no orders could be given or followed. But the police had a new tactic and weapon. They brought out a long, thick rubber hose to replace ropes for crowd control, stretched it across the crowd and started shoving back. Startled fans started to backpedal and there was fear of a backward crush. But the police moved systematically and the unhappy crowd started to go back in order. Boston's groundskeeper got his feet tangled in the hose and the crowd yelled even louder so he would be noticed and not knocked over.

The Boston players tried to warm up by throwing to each other and few noticed when LaChance was hit on the finger with a throw and went off looking for a doctor. The players were ready and the game would pit Phillippe against Hughes, a Chicagoan who had gone 20–7 for the Americans, with five shutouts and a 2.57 earned run average. Clarke was confident, even if Phillippe had little rest. "You stood them on their heads the last time and you can do it again," he told Phillippe.

It would be the crowd that would be the decisive factor in the day. There were so many people that the players couldn't even see their benches, much less get to them, and sometimes they had to sit on the grass near the catcher. The crowd and players were tingling together now, witnesses to a sports spectacle that had never been seen, even in the biggest of college football games of the day. The crowd was like a living entity, a single giant mass of humanity. Even as the game began people could be spotted falling over the outfield fences into the park. But once the game began, all thoughts of hectoring the police stopped and rapt attention was paid to the proceedings before the throng.

In the first inning, Collins speared a hard hit by the speedy Beaumont and threw the ball like a rifle shot to first to just nab him, drawing forth cries of approbation. "That's the boy!" some yelled and hundreds of fans in the bleachers shouted, "He eats 'em alive!"

Then Bransfield, up next, hit a foul tip that was described as "pinfeathers all horned" as it came back and smacked into umpire Connolly's mask. "Ah-r-r, he catches 'em in his teeth. Can't hurt that boy. Give him another and he'll eat it!" came a loud cry.

The crowd continued to roar when Clarke hit to third and Collins gracefully pounced on it and put him out with ease. It was the beginning of a series of great defensive plays for both teams. In the Boston first, Dougherty smashed a shot just to the shortstop side of second but the big Wagner, moving gracefully for all his size, grabbed it on the run and tossed Dougherty out to the amazement of the crowd. He may not have been hitting, but Wagner's presence in the field could win games too, as he ranged easily from side to side and threw runners out with ease. Rarely, though did he smile, his devotion to the game done with a pious intensity and no desire to embarrass his foes.

In the second, Ferris threw out Wagner and Bransfield, but Ritchey's easy pop fly to Dougherty curiously fell a few feet away from the outfielder, who let it drop for an error, allowing Ritchey to reach second base. After Sebring walked, Phelps confidently strode up to home plate, wielding a thick bat. He quickly smacked a high fly ball toward center, and Stahl, eyeing the crowd close behind him, was confounded as the ball fell again for an error, allowing Ritchey to score before Parent threw Phillippe out. Pittsburg led 1–0.

With two out in Boston's second, LaChance hit a hard line drive deep to left-center, rolling toward the 450-foot mark, which might have been an inside-the-park home run but for the ground rule which made hits into the crowd a double. LaChance stopped at second and was stranded there when Ferris grounded out.

In the stands, the newspapermen were busy trying to take their notes and record the game, and there were 18 telegraph wires running out the news to more than 50 afternoon newspapers around the country. More than 25,000 words were filed during the game, with writers rushing to the telegraphers to send running commentary to their papers. In other cities, even where the National League and American League rivals were playing their exhibitions, it was the series with Boston and Pittsburg that fans were following because it was for the championship of both leagues, and it sent fans in other cities squaring off for their favorite leagues as well as players and teams. And in those cities, people gathered everywhere — outside department stores, telegraph offices, newspapers — to see the running scores posted and talk about the games, to argue and debate the merits of baseball.

In the third, Beaumont walked, and Clarke's fly ball to the outfield, a routine out on any other day, fell into the roped-off crowd. He went to second and Beaumont stopped at third. But then the tiny Leach hit a ringing single to center, scoring Beaumont and sending Clarke to third. That was enough for Collins, who pulled Hughes and brought Young in to relieve him. Leach promptly stole second when Criger let a ball get by him, and the nervous Young plunked Wagner in the ribs with a fastball, loading the bases with none out and the Pirates leading 2–0.

The Boston fans were anxious again, the huge crowd rolling back-and-forth in trepidation. So attached were they to the goings-on that few noticed a small fire that began under the grandstand seats. Two fans saved the day, and lives. Jerry MacKay and Frank Rose arrived at the game too late to find seats, but once inside saw some fans standing on barrels and boxes, shutting short men out of view. The two went looking for something to stand on and were under the third-base seats when they saw a small fire among debris. They stomped on it before MacKay ran to a tonic stand and rushed back with buckets of water. "The American League grounds would have been a bad place for a fire on Saturday with nearly 20,000 persons on the field and in the stands," the *Boston Globe* reported.

In the stands the betting was furious, going on between innings and even when players were at bat. Freeman, the powerful slugger, was getting a lot of money his way to poke a ball into the crowd or even beyond it, and hundreds of dollars were wagered each time he came to the plate.

Young, drawing on all his experience, got Bransfield to foul out to LaChance, the runners holding. Ritchey hit a hard shot to Collins who threw home to force out Clarke and it looked like Young would put out the Pirates. But Sebring hit a hard grounder to short which Parent couldn't hold and Leach scored to put Pittsburg ahead 3–0 as the crowd groaned in great despair, especially when they saw Wagner round third and try to score on the same play. Parent recovered, though, and fired home, catching Wagner in a run-down, which ended when Criger caught the Dutchman trying to get back to third.

In the fourth, the police pushed the crowd back about another 100 feet, a tactic that, if had been carried out in the beginning of the game, would have prevented the Pirates' cheap fly balls into the crowd. Now though, it would mean that long Boston hits that would have been doubles in the crowd would be fly balls for outs. Boston tried to rally and scored when Collins singled to center, Stahl walked, Freeman moved them along on an infield out and Parent hit a sacrifice fly to Sebring, with Collins coming home. LaChance walked with two outs, but then Phillippe, who shut the door, struck out Ferris. The crowd closed ranks when Pittsburg outfielders tried to catch fly balls, and opened up in the outfield when the Boston outfielders roamed back, trying to give the home town team the advantage, but it was the Pirates who were reaching into the outfield crowd to earn doubles.

In the eighth, with one out and the crowd getting restless, Wagner got his first hit since his first time up in the first game, doubling to right when his liner hit a fan in the leg. He went on to third when Young bumbled Bransfield's easy grounder. Ritchey hit a scorching shot to third, which Collins muffed, and Wagner scored to make it 4–1. Sebring flied out to Dougherty in left, and the Boston outfielder gunned a throw to third, catching Bransfield trying to advance and completing the inning-ending double play.

The huge crowd of Boston fans, most of them standing, was uneasy. Young opened the Boston eighth with a hard ground ball to the second base side of the diamond but Wagner, moving like a cat on a hot sidewalk, scooted over and grabbed it and fired to first to catch Young. The play was so smooth and spectacular even the Boston fans applauded with zest. The fans on the fences banged the boards with their feet and swung their hats to cheer the man they tried to run out of town the first night he came into Boston. With two outs, Collins hit a fly toward right field and the fans converged to let it drop amongst them, giving him an automatic double. He scored when Stahl hit a hard line drive to left field and it was 4–2 Pittsburg. But Freeman hit into a force play and the Americans were down two runs with one inning left.

The ninth was anticlimactic although the big crowd tried to yell Boston back into the game. Phillippe, getting stronger and sensing the end, disposed of the Americans in order, ending the game with a flourish, striking out Ferris again and throwing his arms akimbo to celebrate. Young had given up only one run in seven innings of relief, but it was too late and the game belonged to his rival, Phillippe, who had given up only four hits and three walks.

Killilea told Dreyfuss, "Phillippe is certainly a warm proposition." The Pittsburg owner smiled and said, "I told you so." They both had reason to smile. The turnouts in the first three games had brought in revenues of about $25,000. Even after figuring the costs of transportation and player shares, the owners were going to make a lot of money on the series. Dreyfuss figured the 2–1 lead would ensure big turnouts in Pittsburg too and expected the fans in that city to be waiting for the team when it came back on the train the next day. An ebullient Phillippe said, "I feel just as good now as I did before the game. My superb physical condition surprises even myself. I never felt better in my life. I could pitch again tomorrow. It was easy today. I never even thought of getting tired. But I didn't do it all. Don't forget that my support was of the gilt-edge order. Without those boys behind me I could not win so easily," he told Pittsburg reporters. "If Fred [Clarke] will let me, I'll pitch two more games of the series and I should win them both. It's easy money," he said happily.

The crowd had cost Boston. Pittsburg had hit four doubles into the outfield fans. Despite the loss, the huge crowd was more orderly at the end than at the beginning and most were happy just to walk across the infield, making it a point to step on home plate as the players headed straight into their clubhouses to get away from the press. Although Wagner had gotten only one hit, a sharp double in his last time up, he had played grandly in the field. Photographs from a distance showed the field covered with people in a surrealistic scene of half-light, a silhouette frozen forever in time.

One segment that wasn't happy was the gamblers. The men who had come wading into the Hotel Vendome waving money and betting on Boston had lost and some sportswriters were openly wondering, and writing, that it seemed unlikely Boston had played its best, especially after the dismal first game showing. There was still a sour taste for some disgruntled fans and sportswriters who were wary of what had happened. "There is no use in attempting to disguise the fact that Thursday's defeat at the hands of Pittsburg was a revelation to Bostonians and that Saturday's amazing exhibition filled local baseball followers with disgust," the *Post* reported. "Wholesale charges of 'throwing the games' have been going the rounds of the city since Saturday evening. Men who took the two defeats most bitterly to heart have not hesitated in saying that at least one of these three games was 'not on the level,' that Boston 'could have won' the series had it chosen."

Most fans, though, dismissed the stories as the sour grapes of losing bettors, and backed Boston, believing in Collins and Young and the others when they said they could still come back to win the series. In Pittsburg, gamblers were finding it hard to find bettors who would go against the home team there, especially with the Pirates up 2–1. "This change is indeed significant. A week ago the odds were very strong on Boston, and Pittsburgers were holding out for still longer chances. Now it is almost impossible for them to get their money up at any odds," the *Pittsburg Press* reported.

Crowds standing in front of the offices of the *Press* shouted "Hurrah! Hurrah! Hurrah!" three loud, long cheers for the Pirates when the final score was posted on the window bulletin board. "The enthusiasm in Pittsburg yesterday afternoon and evening was greater than ever manifested, and, in the result of a baseball game. The people here are baseball crazy just at present, and what this is so is not at all unnatural," the paper reported. "The present series for the premiership of the world is interesting people who never before even listened to a baseball score," it added.

But even though Boston was down in games, something magical had happened in the city and in American society. More than 50,000 people had turned out in the three games to see baseball and it was apparent that the game was taking a hold on the American public unlike any other sport. The game was being played by men who, if not for baseball, would be among the working-class that made up most of the audience, men who could run and fight and spit and swear and walk into a saloon and hoist a few beers with the same people who had been watching and cheering them, or even castigating them for bad play or because they were on a rival team. Side by side, in the stands and on the field, ministers sat and stood next to laborers, college professors with men who carried ice or drove wagons full of coal, doctors and ladies talked with workers, businessmen mingled with servants, and all spoke the same language: baseball.

The next day, a *Boston Globe* writer would wonder what had happened. "Where is the genius who can explain the wonderful hold baseball has on the American public? It was no inhumane desire to see a bull fight or a bloody contest that drew the immense throng yesterday to the American League park, but a wholesome boyish desire to see the greatest ball teams on earth come together for supremacy."

If the players and fans were disappointed, one who hadn't lost confidence was McGreevey. The Royal Rooters had made a racket during all three games, trying to distract the Pirates players, but — despite their odd parody cheers — hadn't really rankled the visitors. McGreevey felt the Rooters had to have a signature song, something they could sing throughout the game, something annoying enough to ruin the Pirates' concentration. He hadn't found it yet, but he had rounded up scores of Rooters to take the 10:15 A.M. train on Sunday to Pittsburg and it was there he hoped to help bring Boston back.

They're Off for Enemy's Country

McGreevey's men were ready. Calling themselves The Invaders now, they got on the train at South Station in Boston bedecked in suits, ties and hats and quickly took over several cars. They were a ragged bunch of professional gamblers, rogues, and ne'er-do-wells, including the moustachioed, passionate Jerry Watson, who liked to stand on the dugout and wave the American flag to lead the Rooters in cheers. Boston's business manager Joseph Smart was helping organize the trip and McGreevey had an able helper in Charlie Lavis, who had worked with him to organize other trips when the Rooters were supporting the National League Beaneaters. The *Boston Globe* ran a large picture across the top of one page showing the smiling and confident Rooters, who were getting almost as much coverage as were the players. The names of the Rooters were becoming as familiar too: McBreen, Handrahan, "Kid" Noonan, "Blutch" Shea, "Doc" McKenna, Baxter, MacQuade, Collins, and "Slap" Cohen. So devoted was Shea that the night before, some of his friends and family held a party for him at his brother-in-law's house in Jamaica Plain and gave him a valise and diamond ring for the trip. Then they gave him a bouquet of flowers before he got on the train. It was a tumultuous scene at the station. Sport Sullivan couldn't make the trip, but he came to see friends off and ask them to take care of his business interests in Pittsburg, where plenty of bets would be placed.

Collins, a popular figure with the players and the writers, was nonetheless under some criticism for his handling of the team in Boston. But he was getting some hometown support too. "Baseball is his business and he is chock full of business," one writer recorded in the *Boston Herald*. "He never made a grandstand play in his life. There is nothing spectacular about him. He's a plain, every-day sort of fellow that gets along with every one."

The Rooters got on three different cars, called the "Madeira," "Sioux City" and the "Clifton" while the players got on another, the "Antharis," on the same train. Only reserve player Duke Farrell and Candy LaChance were on hand, though, as Collins and the rest of his boys got on at the next stop, at Back Bay station. It would be a long ride because the train had to travel through Albany and Buffalo, but the travelers liked the time to socialize and gamble on the way. A special car had been attached to the *Washington Express* for the Pirates so they players could be more comfortable on the 23-hour ride back. The Pirates were confident when they boarded the train to Pittsburg. "We've got them on the run and should finish them in Pittsburg!" yelled Kitty Bransfield, who, with the lost Ed Doheny, was a Massachusetts resident glad to have stuck it to the Bostonians.

Even the humble Wagner felt caught up in the wins. Wagner wouldn't even crack a smile because he feared it would demean another player, although he wasn't reluctant to use his tongue and spikes on someone he felt deserved it. "No use dragging it out any longer than we have to. I don't want to go back to Boston. I've got some hunting to do," he said.

Manager Clarke was less satisfied. He overheard the remarks on the train and cautioned his players, remembering how tough Young could be and not forgetting Dinneen had shut his team out on three singles and 11 strikeouts. "Well, don't forget that second game," he said. "We still got to do our winning on the ball field."

Wagner laughed. "We'll take care of that Dinneen when we meet 'im again," he said.

The players of both teams found it hard to sleep and some mingled with fans who stayed up late, playing cards and practical jokes. As the train finally arrived, Royal Rooter Alec Smith, who had managed to sleep, was awakened with a bucket of cold water, ice and all, dumped on his astonished head.

In Pittsburg, more than 2,000 fans were waiting at Union Depot in a pouring rain to welcome the team, and they rushed the players as they got off. One who got away, though, was the one they wanted to see the most — Wagner. Shy and wanting to be near his family, Wagner ran across the platform and was pulled aboard another train by a brakeman to go home to nearby Carnegie, where he'd grown up and still lived. As Wagner waved, Clarke stood on the platform in the middle of the adoring crowd. "Hans' work was a real eye-opener to Boston," he said before cheers drowned him out. Wagner had had just a single, double and one stolen base in the first three games, but had excelled in the field and was even more popular in

Pittsburg for his play and demeanor. Hans Wagner badges had just come out in a fan club and more than 200 of them were already adorning the coats of members.

The other hero, of course, was Phillippe, winner of the two Pirate victories in Boston who shut down the vaunted Boston batting order with his slick curves and change of pace pitching. He was tired though, he said, from hurling so much and concentrating on trying to keep the Boston hitters off balance. As the crowd surrounded him, he told writers and fans to be wary.

"The Boston boys are nearly all long hitters and hard hitters, so to keep them from landing the balls into the crowd was my business. I never before pitched a game where I had to work all the time as I did on Saturday. In an ordinary game with two out a pitcher can ease up and trust to the batter sending a ball to the outfield. This momentary rest helps a great deal, but there was no rest for either Young or myself on Saturday. We had to keep pegging away. It was rather wearing," he said.

Clarke said he wasn't sure if Sam Leever could pitch again, so Phillippe would do the bulk of the throwing. "Every man will stick to the finish unless he loses a leg," Clarke said.

Sunday was a travel day and the fourth game was slated for Monday at Pittsburg's Exposition Park, on the city's north side near the Allegheny River, a field Dreyfuss and the players hated equally because it was wont to flood. On the 4th of July in 1902 the river had flooded badly, covering large parts of the outfield with a foot of water, making hits there a ground rule double, as had the outfield crowd in Boston. The park had been built in 1891 and was already showing signs of age, although its seating capacity of 16,000 was much more than the Huntington Avenue Grounds. It was symmetrical too, with the left and right field fences an even 400 feet and 450 feet to dead center. There were twin spires behind home plate on the roof of the grandstand. It was right along the river, just on the other side of Mt. Washington, where onlookers could get a glimpse of the goings-on if they had a mind to.

Behind the scenes there was a lot of work going on. Dreyfuss, caught in the crush of the crowd in game three at Boston, didn't want that happening in his park or city. He had workmen build temporary sets of seats behind home plate and in front of the grandstand to hold an additional 2,000 fans. Accommodations were made for sportswriters from 25 newspapers across the country and for telegraph lines so they could file often during the game. Around the city, special places were set up where the results would be posted for those who couldn't get into the park. Dreyfuss, who did not like to give out free tickets, sent one to the local weatherman because the report for Monday was for a cold rain and he was looking for some good luck to keep the momentum with his team. It didn't work.

Monday morning rain was pouring and the *Pittsburg Dispatch* kidded that the weatherman must be "holding out for a box" to get a better seat for the game that had become the most wanted ticket in the city. The rain helped Boston and its fans. The Boston players and McGreevey's rooters didn't arrive until 10 A.M., three and a half hours late, and only five hours before the scheduled 3 P.M. start, but by noon the field was so soaked the game had to be called off. The day off gave the writers from Boston, Pittsburg, and other cities more to write about. Murnane was the star from Boston, but Jake Morse from the *Boston Herald* and Walter Barnes of the *Boston Journal* had national reputations too, as did Gruber and McQuiston of Pittsburg. But it was J. Ed Grillo of the *Cincinnati Commercial-Tribune* who put the ongoing series in its historical perspective by what he foresaw. "The best thing that ever happened for baseball is the world's championship series between the two pennant winners, Pittsburg and Boston," he wrote.

> Nothing that has been done for the game in recent years has stirred up the interest that have these games, and the good effect of it will be felt next season, not to speak of the revenues that the two clubs are harvesting this Fall. The result of the games so far shows that the two teams are fairly well matched. That the opening game proved to be a one-sided struggle was really to have been expected, for the team which got the short end of the breaks in that game was bound to have become nervous and lose confidence.

It was believed that more than $100,000 would change hands during the series, making it a record revenue event.

The day off bought Collins more time to plan his pitching rotation and give Young some additional rest after his long relief stint for Hughes. Dinneen, the second-game winner, was going to start game four while Young would go in game five. Despite the losses, the Boston gamblers thought the Americans could come back and that Pittsburg had been lucky in Boston, especially in game three with cheap ground rule doubles into the outfield crowd behind the ropes. And for the Pirates, Otto Krueger, recovering from being hit on the head by a pitch late in the season, was in uniform, although still not fully recovered. As in Boston, the idea of a world's championship had caught Pittsburg's full attention at a time when the city was expanding to its suburbs and residents were being offered the chance to buy lots on the outskirts of the city for as little as $2 down for the chance to live near a growing industrial area.

The weather in Pittsburg continued to be ominous. The dark, cold October rain combined with the omnipresent smoke from the steel mills to cover Pittsburg in a shroud that had electric lights burning all day Monday, October 5. The field was not just wet, but muddy and slippery, and the forecast was not promising. To kill time on the off day during the rain, Murnane got into an engagement with a group of fans. Murnane said Pittsburg

Six — An Awful Boom in the Ninth Inning

was 25 percent better than any other team in the National League, including John McGraw's Giants, and that the Boston team was similarly stronger than any other team in the American League. And then he said, to their delight, "You may not coincide with my views when I say that the American League champions are 25 percent stronger than Pittsburg, but with the galaxy of pitchers on the Boston team it isn't difficult for me to compare the comparative strength of the leaders of the rival leagues.

"Pittsburg, we all know, has a grand ball team, but in my opinion Boston has a better one," Murnane added. "It makes me smile to read some of the comparisons of the two teams in which Boston is rated in a class below the Pirates."

The Boston gamblers couldn't wait to put down their money. One rooter, John Keenan, said, "We realize we are up against it. How is the betting around town?" He was told to go to Newell's, a place where bets could be made, and he found the odds were running 10 to 8, still favoring Boston. Keenan couldn't see why.

"Say, who do the people here want? They'll get nothing of that sort from us. We realize what we have. It was all right before the series started," he said of the odds, but not now, although the Boston men were trying to hedge their bets at the same time they thought the Americans could still win. "After we saw them together with the Americans, we have changed our mind," Keenan said. "There's nothing to it but Pittsburg and we know that, so don't talk 10 to 8 ... we came here to support the team and we are going to do it, but the Pittsburg people will have to let us have something in the way of a chance," he said.

Not all the Bostonians were as confident. Another rooter said he wanted to put $2,000 down on the Americans, not expecting any takers. But one of Pittsburg's top gamblers, Sam Hyams, was in Newell's, and he asked the gentleman, "Do you wish to bet $1,000 even on Boston?"

"Yes," the man replied. "And $2,000 if you want it," he smiled.

Hyams didn't blink. He reached into his hip pocket, smiled back and said, "All right," and pulled out a bundle of cash, more than $2,500. "I'll take Pittsburg and here's the $2,000," said Hyams as a crowd watched the engagement.

The Boston man gulped and said, "I'll have to see my partner," walking out before he could have a bet taken.

Stories abounded about a pool of money worth more than $100,000 being formed in which six affluent Pittsburgers were interested and that the whole amount would be placed on the Pirates to win. It was a fortune that made even seasoned gamblers weaken. The *Pittsburg Post* reported that Pittsburg gamblers were confident of winning big and had put down $30,000 to $50,000 when in Boston. "This was on the series, and though not yet pocketed, the money is considered as good as won by the local sports," the paper reported. There was so much money going around now that the gamblers were getting nervous about the outcome of the series. The rooters may have been emotional for their teams, but this was business for the moneymen and some apparently tried to make sure all their bets were covered.

Criger, who had opened the series in such an ignominious fashion with his errors in the first inning that it looked as if he was throwing the game, was approached in the lobby of the Monongahela Hotel by a man he recognized, a gambler named Anderson who had been introduced to him two years before by John McGraw. He had spent an afternoon with McGraw and Anderson at a country bowling club near Baltimore. But Criger was surprised to see him in Pittsburg and even more surprised at what he said Anderson offered him: $12,000 in cash to throw the games so a man the gambler represented, a millionaire who had bet $50,000 on the series, could win a big wad of cash.

"Why did you single me out for this crooked proposition?" said Criger, who was making $4,000 a year.

"Because you are the only one capable of turning the trick," Anderson said.

Criger refused, in terms that left no doubt how swiftly and certainly he had rebuked the idea. The gamblers wouldn't give up there. Anderson, Criger said, then threatened him and his family, but the catcher stood firm. And if the gamblers couldn't get the catcher, they would try to get the best pitcher in the game: Young. For all the talk of gambling and the circus sideshow atmosphere outside the games, many of the players were devoted to their own code of integrity and with playing hard all the time, no matter how much money was riding on the outcome.

While all the side action was going on during the rain delay, McGreevey sent his trusted aide, Lavis, out to find a band to play during the game. Lavis came back and said he had engaged the 20-member Greater Pittsburg Band to accompany the Rooters, who had reserved more than 100 grandstand seats. The band would even lead the Rooters from their hotel to the field in a parade. The Rooters were sporting badges and had rehearsed the songs they sang in Boston, but McGreevey was still looking for another song that would rouse the Americans and roust the Pirates. He sent one of his gang, Tom Burton, off to a Pittsburg store to find a suitable song. Burton was a pianist and the musician in the group. He carefully culled over music scores, looking for something rousing but sweet. He looked at "Goodbye My Bluebell" and "Rocky Road To Dublin," two of the day's most popular scores, but didn't think they were right for baseball or had the kind of harmony that could be carried by 200 men. Burton came back with a ditty called "Tessie," written by Will Anderson for a musical comedy called *The Silver Slipper*. The song was sweet and whimsical, sung by a beau wooing the saucy Tessie. McGreevey wasn't sure. The song didn't have the rousing militaristic or sports fervor the Rooters liked and was, in fact, almost sappy, although it would get in your head and not leave:

> Tessie, you make me feel so badly,
> Why don't you turn around?
> Tessie, you know I love you madly.
> Babe, my heart weighs about a pound.
> Don't blame me if I ever doubt you.
> You know I couldn't live without you.
> Tessie, you are my only, only, only.

But the tune was catchy and easy to carry and — most importantly — had an annoying quality when repeated enough, a slightly manic melody that could distract a person. It was just what McGreevey wanted for the Pirates, since that would be the only time the Rooters would be singing it. The Rooters took to Smithfield Avenue in the heart of downtown and serenaded the citizens of the city with their practice songs and cheers for the next day, making a spectacle that delighted their opposing fans.

Fans in Ohio — in Youngstown, Cleveland, and Alliance — made plans to come to Pittsburg, even though Cleveland and the Cincinnati Reds were playing a series. Coming too were fans in small towns of western Pennsylvania. The game was bringing in fans from cities and towns and places without ballparks. The players were known to fans throughout the land, for they had played in many parts of the country at the beginning of their careers, including Boston outfielder Patsy Dougherty, who had begun his career in Homestead, a few miles from Pittsburg, where fans were still talking about the games he won with his fierce drives.

Indeed, baseball was overtaking the American consciousness because the players were so accessible and had the same roots as most of the fans. Expecting a huge crowd, the police said they would bring out extra men, but promised the fans would be treated cordially. The demand for tickets was unprecedented in Pittsburg and box seats had already been sold out. There were complaints that speculators were set to offer seats for high prices just before the game.

Clarke and Collins, the two managers, met at a headquarters set up for the games in Pittsburg and immediately set out to rankle each other. Clarke thought Pittsburg would win and said so openly. "The Pittsburgs, with the exception of Sam Leever, are in as good shape as when they left home, and the boys are eager and ready to do the best playing they have ever done. The trip to Boston only sharpened our game," he said. Unsaid was what was happening to Doheny, the crafty left-hander whose mental condition was deteriorating back home in Massachusetts.

Clarke said, "We will take three games from Boston in Exposition Field. From the present outlook, Leever cannot be used in this series and, of course, this is an unexpected handicap and means that Kennedy and Veil will have to shoulder some of the work, but they can do it, so do not worry." Collins was unruffled. "We were kind in Boston but intend to get down to business here," he said, his competitive fires stoked and thoughts of good-natured appreciation suddenly set away. Collins even took off after his former colleague in Louisville, National League President Harry Pulliam, who told him, "I am glad to see you, but sorry you won Friday's game."

Collins came right back. "You should be happy over the fact we did not get more."

That night many players from both teams went to see a musical at the Duquesne Theater, where Clarke had to fend off reporters' questions about whether the extra day off would let him bring back two-game winner Phillippe. Collins said he was confident the Americans could win two of four in Pittsburg and have a chance to win the series back in Boston. Meanwhile, the series that had started in such competitive rancor in Boston was showing signs of becoming one of mutual respect. The Pittsburg players said that despite their initial greeting, the Boston fans had appreciated their play.

J. Palmer O'Neill, a former National League president, said he thought the Boston players might even be presented with bouquets. "It was a surprise to learn that our boys had received such handsome treatment in an American League stronghold, but then Boston has always stood for the best in ball," he said. Pittsburg was full of players from other cities, including some old-timers thrilled at the idea of a series to determine the champion of both leagues.

Collins didn't blink when it was reported that the managers of theaters in Pittsburg had set aside reserved seats for the players of both teams, decorated with miniature pennants representing each side. Even in the theater they would be competitors for everyone to see. Collins was reticent, but his fire to win smoldered and he told a Boston sportswriter, "The worst we will get here is an even break. That will take us back to Huntington Avenue where we will take the fourth and fifth games."

Later, Pulliam took another shot at his friend Collins. "I am in Pittsburg to see the finish of the championship series between Pittsburg and Boston. I will stay here until the matter is settled. It will take only three games to decide the world's championship. The Pirates will win three straight from their opponents. Of that I am supremely confident. I saw two of the games in Boston and certainly had a wonderful time. The boys played wonderful ball," he said. Pulliam could sense the championship had a growing hold across America and a future.

At the Duquesne Theater, Murnane walked up to Collins in the lobby. "What are your chances, Jimmy?" he asked.

"I figure that our boys will field as well as they did in Boston and bat much better, which should give us at least two of the four games here," Collins said. But Collins wanted more. He didn't want to go back to Boston down 4–3, and he knew he couldn't fall behind 3–1.

And when he woke up Tuesday morning for game four, he found out that Clarke was going to pitch the Boston-killer Phillippe again. And it was raining. And he was in Pittsburg.

GAME FOUR: *Boston Takes No Chances, Failure to Do So Proves Costly*

On Tuesday, October 6, the day started in spitting rain. By game time the skies were cloudy and the field was muddy and slippery despite a liberal dosing of sawdust. The outfield was especially treacherous and the threatening weather ruined Dreyfuss's expectations of an overflow crowd, as only about 7,600 people showed up. The Royal Rooters and their brass band, which led them in a quick double-time march to the field from the fans' hotel, stationed themselves in grandstand Section J behind the Boston bench, determined to make a racket the whole game.

The Pirates fans looked on, astonished at the raucous Bostonians, whose behavior was incongruous with their splendid attire. But when the Americans came onto the field for a short practice, the Pirates fans did not applaud, and it was only McGreevey, Watson, Lavis, Shea, Cohen and the rest of the Rooters making any noise for the American League champions. The Rooters' band struck up a tune and the Pirates fans tried to figure out who the Boston players were, although they recognized Young and applauded, and the pitcher doffed his hat in return. When he turned around, Young was surprised to see among the people milling around the grounds two men in civilian clothes who came up to him. They introduced themselves as representatives of gamblers and offered him, it was later reported, $20,000 if he would not "bear down," or do his best when his next chance to pitch came.

They miscalculated. "If you put any value at all on your money, you'd better bet it on me to win," he said. Young was puffed up with indignity, and he was going to face Phillippe. The Pirates were counting on their ace again, a reticent, modest man who never seemed ruffled. He had a tall, imperial air that was not arrogant, a sturdy, oval face with a square jaw and he liked to part his dark hair just a little left of center instead of down the middle. Phillippe, the 31-year-old Virginian, took the mound for the third time in four games while Dinneen was pitching for Boston.

In the first inning, Dougherty hit the first ball thrown in the first World Series game at Pittsburg. It was to Ritchey for a groundout. Boston went out in order as Phillippe continued his mastery of the team. When the crowd saw Phillippe, they roared. The unostentatious right-hander had become the toast of Pittsburg with his two victories. "Make 'em eat out of your hand, Deacon," one fan shouted. "We'll show those phony champions what a real championship club looks like," yelled another.

But the Rooters were having none of it. When Dinneen came out, Rooter Mike Regan yelled for everyone to hear, "Just give 'em more of what you give 'em in Boston," he shouted. The rivalry born three games ago had taken on a new intensity and the pride had swept from the ballplayers to the fans to the cities to the leagues because so much was at stake. The weather worsened and a cool drizzle started that would keep up throughout the game.

The Pirates got to Dinneen quickly. The big right-hander was confident after his shutout in Boston, but this time Beaumont led off with a single and, after Clarke forced Beaumont at second and Leach went out, Wagner and Bransfield singled, bringing in Clarke for a 1–0 Pirate lead. But Wagner made another base running error trying to go to third on the single, only to be caught 10 yards off third base by Chick Stahl's rocket throw to third. Collins chased Wagner down and tagged him out as the big Dutchman slipped in the mud trying to get back to second base. He wasn't the only one. Ferris fell down trying to field a grounder and the other players looked like they were on greased roller skates trying to navigate the soaking ground.

The returns were being fired off by wire to other cities, and fans who couldn't get to the park in Pittsburg could see the running results being posted down at Miah Murray's billiards parlor, which turned out to be a popular spot. It was the same in cities across the country. Fans stood outside hotels and barber shops and newspapers and businesses, watching the results being put up, looking at the numbers as if they were at the game, watching baseball unfold, and talking about it non-stop. Baseball had seized America.

In the fifth, the Americans tied the game after Dinneen had settled down. With one out, LaChance singled. Ferris was thrown out on a grounder to Leach, but LaChance went to second and scored on Criger's single as the Rooters began to howl and their band struck up loudly. McGreevey himself jumped onto the top of the Boston dugout, singing and screaming and waving his arms like conductor's batons, leading the Rooters in song and cheer. Even the Pittsburg fans laughed at his enthusiasm. But the tie didn't last long.

In the bottom of the fifth, Stahl misjudged the speedy Beaumont, who drove a liner to center. Stahl first came in and then ran back but couldn't get the fly that fell behind him as Beaumont went to third. Clarke fouled out to Criger and when Leach hit a grounder to LaChance at first, it looked like Beaumont would be held at third. But the Boston first baseman went face first into the mud as he fielded the ball and Beaumont came home to give the Pirates a 2–1 lead. In the last game in Boston, it had been the big crowd in the outfield and the Pirate fly balls there that befuddled Boston. This time it was the weather and the grounds and the Bostonians were getting more frustrated as the game went along. Even the Rooters were glum. Collins was worried.

The players were feeling the pressure and complaints were being made to the umpires. Ferris badgered Connolly so much the umpire threatened to toss him from the game if he didn't cease his protestations. "Any more cheap talk from you, and you go to the bench," Connolly warned him.

Then Collins, fuming over a poor play by Dougherty, got on his leftfielder hard in the dugout between innings, causing curious Pittsburg spectators to look on in bemusement. The situation showed signs of getting ugly as hot, hard words were exchanged between Collins, whose quiet nature belied his furious temper when he felt the players weren't giving it their all, and the curly-haired Dougherty, whose look may have been a touch angelic, but who could spit out profanity when the occasion required. And it did now. While Collins yelled at his player, Dougherty stood with his arms folded in defiance and put the blame on Collins for what was happening on the field. Both men, it was said, paid compliments to each other in unmistakable language until Collins disgustedly screamed at Dougherty, "If we lose this series, you will suffer for it, I tell you." Collins and the Americans were feeling the pressure now for sure and needed something to help bring them together.

In the seventh, the Pirates struck again, and this time Phillippe himself started it. The Pirate pitcher hit a single down the third base line and went to second when Dougherty, slipping and sliding in the outfield pool, couldn't get to the ball in time. Beaumont then hit a little bunt grounder down the first base line to LaChance, but Dinneen, falling asleep, didn't go to the bag to take the throw. Phillippe went to third as Beaumont raced to second. Clarke hit a shallow fly to Dougherty and Phillippe held at third. Down 2–1, Collins brought his infield in to try to cut off a run at the plate on a grounder.

But the strategy backfired when the little Leach cracked a grounder past the drawn-in LaChance at first and the ball went down the right field line, bringing in two runs as Leach went to third. When Wagner, rejuvenated by playing in front of his home town fans, singled again, Leach scored and the Pirates were rolling 5–1. But Wagner had gotten too eager. When Bransfield struck out, Criger fired to second to catch Wagner trying to steal second. After his shaky start in game one, the nifty-fielding Criger had shown why he was a favorite catcher for Young and the other Boston pitchers.

The Americans had one last chance in the ninth and they almost made the most of it. When Collins walked slowly up to the plate, he was surprised to hear a roar go up from behind the Boston bench. It was McGreevey and the Rooters, exhorting the Americans. McGreevey sensed this was the moment. He jumped up again and told the band to play "Tessie" and the Rooters promptly started singing as one, to the bewilderment of the Pittsburg crowd: "Tessie, you make me feel so badly, Why don't you turn around? Tessie, you know I love you madly. Babe, my heart weighs about a pound. Don't blame me if I ever doubt you. You know, I couldn't live without you. Tessie, you are my only, only, only...."

> The Rooters were like a 200-man barber shop group now, their harmony melding with the brass band, the song soaring in their hearts, taking over curiously, pumping them up like a new anthem. They sang it loudly and repeatedly, Collins looking around as he came to bat. He felt it too. He gripped his bat tightly and stepped into the box like a rock.

Collins responded, cracking a single to center. Then Stahl and Freeman singled too, making it 5–2, and "Tessie" was sung with a new abandonment. The Rooters were waving their hats, standing on their feet, whistling, stomping, ringing bells and creating chaos. Leading them were McGreevey, Watson, Lavis, and Regan, while the Pittsburg-hired band kept up a crescendo to match. They kept it up even as Parent's grounder forced Freeman at second, because Stahl scored to make it 5–3 and the Rooters and Americans thought they were finally getting to the unflappable Phillippe. Then LaChance singled and Parent moved to second, and Ferris hit a soft single to right so short that Parent couldn't score, but the bases were loaded. The Boston sportswriters didn't see it that way. They thought Collins should have sent Parent home.

There was one out, Phillippe was weakening, and the World Series had its first real dramatic moment when it seemed an inning could swing the momentum and perhaps the championship. Criger was due up next and Collins felt the light-hitting catcher needed someone else to hit, so he chose a Boston boy, mustachioed Duke Farrell, who could also catch. The crowd was nervous and the Rooters were frenetic in their cheers as the Pirates contemplated what would happen.

Farrell, 37, had been in the major leagues since 1888 and was heading toward the end of his career. He had gone 21 for 52, had a .404 average in 1903 and was a clutch hitter. Farrell came through, lofting a deep fly to Clarke in left that scored Parent to make it 5–4. It looked like Boston would have the rally the Rooters had waited for. With Dinneen due up, Collins pinch-hit again, sending up utility outfielder Jack O'Brien to hit for the pitcher. Dinneen had only 17 hits in 106 at-bats, while O'Brien had hit .259 during the regular season, but had three home runs and 38 runs-batted-in and Collins had confidence in him, although he also had Jake Stahl, a great star at the University of Illinois, on his bench. Stahl, 23, had joined the team in mid-season and had five hits in 12 times at bat. The Rooters were wailing "Tessie," sensing a win, standing and shouting like a boisterous music class trying to impress their teacher, and out-shouting the opposition. Phillippe was sweating, wiping his brow with his left arm and his tiny glove soaked. The Rooters were standing and screaming like maniacs now, their polite jibing gone.

Collins' move didn't work. O'Brien, with a chance to be a hero, took two called strikes and then weakly popped up to Ritchey at second base as the Pirates and their fans, back pedaling in the face of the constant caterwauling and commotion caused by the Rooters, breathed a sigh of relief.

The Pirate fans poured onto the field as Phillippe staggered off the mound, winner of three games in the World Series; he was worn out but happy that his team had what looked like an insurmountable 3–1 lead. Fans grabbed the weary pitcher and hoisted him on their shoulders and carried him to the Pirate clubhouse. Poor Phillippe couldn't get dressed for a half hour because everyone wanted to shake the hand that had beat Boston and shut up the Rooters. It had been a good game for the Pirates, even with the nerve-wracking ending. Wagner had come through with three hits and a stolen base while Beaumont had broken out with two triples, a single and a renewed confidence.

Boston had lost, but the Rooters weren't down. They ran down on the field to be with the Boston players and have their photographs taken with them as a souvenir of their trip to Pittsburg. The pack of Rooters piled onto a bus to return to the Monongahela hotel, where they were staying, carousing until 11 P.M., listening to their band, and getting ready for the next day's game.

As guests of the Avenue Theater, the players were cheered mightily as they were ushered to their private boxes, new celebrities in a sport that had now become part of the American fabric and American dream of success and stardom. The biggest cheer was for Wagner, who felt embarrassed by the attention and headed to the rear of the team box, where he sat the rest of the night.

Dreyfuss, meanwhile, wondered where the fans were and if they would turn out now that it looked like their blue-collar champions would become champions of the whole baseball world and, more importantly, of the two leagues, saving the day for the proud National League over the league they considered inferior. The Boston sportswriters felt let down, too, and roasted Collins for his decision-making, despite the rally that had just failed. They thought Boston could have tied the game in the ninth and they let the readers know it. The *Boston Globe* wrote for readers who awoke on the morning of October 7 to find out their home town team had lost:

In the ninth inning, Boston lost a chance to tie the score because of the lack of a little courage and heady coaching. With Parent on second, Ferris hit to right field. Parent was held at third, when the chances were ten-to-one that he could have scored from second. Parent would have drawn a throw to the plate, allowing Ferris to make third, from where he would have scored the tying run on Ferris' long fly to left. It was the refusal to take a reasonable chance that beat Boston, and the taking of a similar chance, which won for Pittsburg. Sending O'Brien in to bat with Jake Stahl ready, and where a hit would have turned the trick, was another illustration of a lack of judgment.

It had taken only 90 minutes, the fastest game yet.

With Pittsburg now up 3–1, and with the next three games in their hometown, the betting odds had switched to 10–7 in favor of the Pirates and a Boston sportswriter lamented, "The Boston men are not putting up the kind of ball that won the American race." Cy Young wasn't having much of that talk, telling a Pittsburg reporter that a story claiming Boston expected to lose the series was not truthful. "I haven't even talked to a local reporter and I am still hopeful of winning," he said.

Collins would hear no talk of defeatism. The feisty manager was still outwardly showing a confidence that hadn't been proved on the field, and he had been stung by the criticism of his managing, especially after a season of adoration. The weather had been bad, and his team, even with its rally, had been worse. But after the game, he laid into his players anew, still hot over the affair with Dougherty and not satisfied with the rally falling short, although he had sensed a rejuvenated spirit in the players. He didn't want it to die and during an after-game meeting at the Monongahela Hotel he openly criticized some of his players, a bristling captured by the *Pittsburg Chronicle Telegraph*.

"Collins was furious over the style of play followed by some of his men yesterday and he wants better work from his men," the paper reported. Dougherty got into it again with Collins, and was joined by some others who said he could not suspend them as they technically were not under contract after October 1, and had only agreed to play in the series on certain conditions. "The team was given a good shaking up and faster work is anticipated in the second game," the *Telegraph* said.

But the Boston manager was upset with Ferris's easy talk on the field to the umpires and called him aside. "Any more cheap talk like that, Hobe, and you won't get a cent out of the money coming our way," Collins told him. Ferris had to tend to business after that.

The series had taken a turn for which Collins wasn't prepared. He had opened with the great Young, confident of using him several times if needed, but now Boston was on the brink of defeat and he had to bring Young back

Six — An Awful Boom in the Ninth Inning

after the long relief stint in Boston in the third game. The Boston manager remained unhappy with the play of Criger. The Boston sportswriters were certainly scrutinizing the Boston catcher, under criticism from the first game with his poor play and under the cloud of talk of gambling influencing the series. Still, Criger was the best the team had at going after foul flies, although Collins was considering benching him in favor of Duke Farrell, even though Young preferred to have Criger behind the plate. If Boston lost the next game though, Criger would sit down. Collins could only hope that their last-ditch drive to catch the Pirates in game four would carry over into the next game because he knew they still had a chance in a nine-game series. This was the one he knew they could not lose if they wanted any chance of winning the championship, or even of bringing the series back to Boston. Killilea, the team president, had to worry too.

The Pirates couldn't keep their enthusiasm to themselves and got caught up in the swirl of back patting and adulation from the fans. But while Pittsburg was going wild and feeling good, McQuiston, a savvy follower of the game, wrote what a lot of people in Pittsburg didn't want to hear, including himself, since he had picked the Pirates in a walk when the series began. The championship was so close now, just two games away, that they felt it belonged to the National League champions and that the American Leaguers couldn't play with them.

McQuiston wasn't so sure. His story was picked up by the Boston papers and must have been like a wet balloon to the fans and backers of the Pirates, but McQuiston said he felt uneasy about the way the fourth game ended, the rousing Boston rally coming so close and the Americans tearing down the base paths with abandon, oblivious to their position, catching momentum like a runaway train. Pirate fans, who had felt so good after the game, later read his startling caution:

> By Frank McQuiston
> Pittsburg Dispatch
> There are a lot of people around town who think this Boston gang cannot play ball. It's a good bet to make that they don't know what they are talking about, even if one has to loan them the money to bet. On the last turn of the wheel yesterday, Boston did some grand and lofty tumbling that made people shiver.
> The gang filed out of the park pretty well satisfied that the only time when it is a cinch that Boston is beaten is when the other team is 1,000,000 runs ahead, and such people as Collins, Dougherty, Stahl, Freeman, Dinneen, Young, Criger and some others are locked up. Even then they are liable to turn in with the subs and do a whole lot of damage.
> Yesterday's score was 5 to 4. Thank goodness is has been decreed that a baseball game shall only be of nine innings duration. As the thrice cham-

pions fled under the wire with every sail set in this the fourth round of the championship of the world, those Bostonians were reaching for them at every jump. They came so near that the Pittsburgers could feel their breath as they flew. Coming? Why, they were hitting the ground so hard with their flippers that the mud was flying clear into the grand stand.

Another finish like that and there will be a wholesale canceling of life insurance polices in Pittsburg. Heart disease got an awful boom in that ninth inning.

SEVEN

They Didn't Do a Thing but Turn the City Upside Down

The gamblers knew, though. The money was going to Boston because Phillippe had already pitched three games and Collins was coming back with Young, eager to redeem himself from game one and still rolling from his stopper relief stint in game three. Young hadn't liked the boast of the Pirates that he was an old man who was through with the game, and Clarke, with Doheny out and Leever still hurting, thought he might have to pitch Veil again, a prospect that had the money shifting toward the Americans.

Instead, to the surprise of everyone, Clarke selected Bill "Brickyard" Kennedy, a loveable if eccentric and boisterous wild man, on his 36th birthday. Kennedy brought in a lot of friends from his hometown of Bellaire, Ohio, for the occasion and he was determined to give them a show. He was a man who would spit into the wind; he was bellicose and not given to giving up and Clarke liked his fighting spirit and demeanor. Kennedy might not know how to read and write, but he still knew how to pitch and Clarke thought he would come right at the Boston players. He'd have to be ready because Young couldn't wait to get at the Pirates again.

This time Dreyfuss wasn't disappointed either. Buoyed by their boys' victory, the Pittsburg fans turned out and 12,322 of them jammed Exposition Park, standing in the outfield behind ropes as the Boston fans had. The sellout had many more standing on nearby hillsides trying to get a peek at what was going on. Boston's owner, Killilea, hadn't come to Pittsburg though, and neither had American League President Ban Johnson. Their absence was noticed.

For a long stretch along Grandview Avenue outside the park, up on top

Fred Clarke, manager of the Pirates, 1900–1915. One of baseball's greatest hitters (courtesy Carnegie Library, Pittsburgh).

of Mt. Washington, hundreds of people stood to get a good look at the game without plunking down 50 cents for the privilege, although some needed field glasses to see. The Boston gamblers were putting their money on the Americans. One, Moses Handelberg, put up $150 against $500 from Peter McCool of Pittsburg that Boston would win the series. "Young will beat Kennedy or Veil and it is heavy odds against Phillippe beating Boston a fourth straight time," he said.

But now it was game time.

Clarke and Collins met with the umpires, Hank O'Day and Tom Connolly, and agreed that hits into the outfield crowd behind the ropes would be ground-rule triples, instead of doubles as they had in Boston when the crowd was even closer to the infield. While that was going on, some Pittsburg fans thought they would try to rattle the Rooters and they walked over and presented Nuf Ced McGreevey with an umbrella of many colors. They did it with a pretended solemnity, but he wasn't accepting their act.

When the people of Pittsburg awoke on Wednesday, October 7, they felt that their long-maligned steel city would finally get the attention of the rest of the country for something other than smoke. Tom Hughes of Boston, like Sam Leever of the Pirates, continued to have arm troubles so Collins, the Boston manager, had already decided to go with Young and Dinneen the rest of the way, no matter how long or short that might be. And Clarke, the Pirates manager, was hoping to somehow not lose the next two games if he had to go with Veil, Kennedy or Leever because he thought Phillippe could close out the series for him. His gamble was on Kennedy, whose age was against him, but whose ferocious determination could be counted on when emotion was riding on a game.

Leach and Wagner, meanwhile, were becoming irritated by the constant droning of "Tessie" that McGreevey and the Boston Rooters were singing endlessly. They didn't want to show it, but Leach told some friends that the song was starting to pound endlessly in the Pirates' heads. "Sort of got on your nerves after a while," said the normally unflappable Leach, whose hitting had been a surprise that spurred the Pirates. They didn't know McGreevey had a variation ready for the great Wagner, who was virtually playing on one leg because of his injury, although he refused to grouse about it.

For five innings, it looked like the Clarke gamble might pay off. The teams stood at a scoreless standstill. But when Wagner came to the plate, the Royal Rooters started singing "Tessie" again, this time changing the lyrics to rattle Wagner, who had hoped his hustle, if not his hitting, would push the Pirates to victory. He was a quietly and deeply proud man, perhaps the most respected in either league, but McGreevey, whom Leach called "that Boston character," felt the great Dutchman could get distracted by the constant razzing.

The Rooters had been singing since the start of the game. But when Wagner came to the plate in the first inning, McGreevey himself jumped up so hard it looked like he had been lifted up by the handlebars of his big mustache. The Pittsburg fans still couldn't fathom the zealotry of the Boston fans, and wondered what the enmity was when the Rooters started singing lyrics penned by McGreevy himself, with musical accompaniment from the Pittsburg band Lavis had hired. Wagner was trying not to pay attention to the damned racket that could be heard even over the roaring of the Pittsburg fans who admired his every move, and his dedication to the game and to them. So he was even more startled when he came up to bat, expecting to hear the strains of "Tessie" again, only to hear different words to the same tune. The Rooters directed the words right at him, almost spitting them out in parody, and it would reverberate through him the rest of the series, unsettling the normally unflappable Wagner.

> Honus, why do you hit so badly?
> Take a back seat and sit down.
> Honus, at bat you look so sadly,
> Hey, why don't you get out of town?

Then they would repeat the refrain. Ceaselessly. Constantly. Wagner grounded meekly to Ferris at second and was out easily as the Rooters roared. In the fourth inning, Wagner struck out and McGreevey's men went wild again.

In the first four games, Wagner had gone 1 for 3, 0 for 3, and 1 for 3 before breaking out with his 3 for 4 in the fourth game. He wasn't really hitting badly, but had made some mental mistakes, especially on the base paths, and at times he had been handled easily at the plate, especially by Dinneen. The tension in the game built as the scoreless innings went by. Young was mowing down the Pirates and Kennedy was coming right at the Americans. Collins knew the Bostonians had to get to Kennedy and win this game or risk being embarrassed as well as defeated.

Collins was angry with himself, too. In the first inning he tripled with one out. But when Stahl hit a grounder, the Boston manager tried to come home, only be thrown out at the plate on a relay by Wagner that killed a chance to take a 1–0 lead before the Pirates even came up. After Collins' out, Stahl stole second, Kennedy deliberately walked the dangerous Freeman, and Parent beat out an infield hit to load the bases. But then LaChance popped up weakly to Leach at third. Collins knew that with a lead, Young was even deadlier, mixing his fastball with sharp curves that had had the Pirates' batters leaning the wrong way several times.

In the third, Collins singled and stole second, this time colliding with Wagner's outstretched left arm on a hard slide. Wagner winced as Collins hit him, holding the arm in pain, but walked back to his position. He wouldn't say how much it hurt.

Boston threatened again in the fifth, and again had what Collins kept calling some hard luck. Criger was called out on strikes and argued vociferously with plate umpire Connolly. Young then singled and went to second when Leach, overplaying the ball, turned and fired wildly into the crowd behind first base. But then Ritchey robbed Dougherty of a hit with a grab of a hard ground ball, and Collins, trying to redeem himself from the first-inning blunder, hit a hard line drive that looked like a hit, only to have it snared at the last second by rival manager Clarke in left field.

Pittsburg almost took the lead in the bottom of the fifth when LaChance muffed a throw from Parent on a grounder by Sebring, who went to second when LaChance let the ball get behind him. Phelps' sacrifice put Sebring on third, but Kennedy popped up to Parent, who had to run into shallow left field to catch it, and he turned and fired to third, almost doubling up the dancing Sebring. And then Collins threw out the dangerous and speedy Beaumont at first.

But Kennedy, holding the Boston batters at bay almost by sheer willpower as he fatigued, couldn't handle them in the sixth. The series started to turn, almost on cue with the constant refrains of "Tessie" that were so maddening to the Pirates. The harbinger was an easy pop fly by Chick Stahl to shallow left field that Clarke came in on, Wagner running from shortstop directly toward the charging Clarke. It was a routine out for either, but impossible for both to make at the same time. They veered off as they sensed a collision and the fly fell in for a single, although at the last second Clarke made a lunge for it and the ball fell off his glove.

When slugger Buck Freeman ripped a screaming line drive to center, sending Stahl to second, the rally was on and the Rooters were up and wailing louder than ever. So was the Boston bench, sensing they were getting to Kennedy. The Pirates were so close to squeezing out a fourth victory and being one game away from a world's championship that would have made the boasts about the American League being inferior seem real to the fans across the United States. In the working-class city of Pittsburg, the Pirates were the icons for people in steel mills and coal mines, for men who walked to work and ate lunch out of a box and came home with grime and sweat on their brows, and for the city's intelligentsia too, men and women who saw them as symbols of what hard work could achieve and who idealized them for their humility, even if they sometimes had to forgive the profane manner the game and its competitiveness necessitated. Boston may have had its culture and its Brahmins, New York its growing financial center, but Pittsburg had the Pirates, the three-time pennant winners. And Pittsburg had Honus Wagner, the Dutchman who fans knew would somehow find a way to bring them a world championship.

Then came Wagner's worst moment.

Rattled by "Tessie," under inhuman pressure to perform in front of fans who thought he could do no wrong, Wagner missed a play and opened the door for Boston to have a big inning. Parent bunted to move Stahl and Freeman to third and second, expecting his sacrifice would have him thrown out at first. But third baseman Leach, charging hard, scooped the bunt and turned and fired to Wagner, who made an alert play to cover third for a force out. He didn't even have to tag Stahl, just hold onto the ball.

But he dropped the ball, to the astonishment of the Pirates fans and the unexpected delight of the Rooters. There was no stopping Boston or the Rooters now. The dejected Wagner walked back to shortstop. The bases were full, nobody was out, and Kennedy was wilting.

It was the highest drama of the World Series: Boston batters dancing on the bases, Kennedy nervously eyeing them, the fans standing, the band playing, the tension filling the air like smoke pouring out of a steel mill. LaChance worked the count to three balls and Kennedy walked him to force in the first run. The door was open and McGreevey and the Americans felt the tide they had ridden in the ninth inning of the fourth game wouldn't be stopped this time.

It got worse for Wagner and the Pirates, even if it wasn't all his fault.

With the Pirates fans yelling encouragement and McGreevey, Watson, Lavis and the Rooters yelling in derision, Ferris slapped a ground ball to the rattled Wagner, who made a clean play and fired to second, but there was no one covering the base and the ball sailed into the outfield as Parent and Freeman scored to make it 3–0. A second error was charged to Wagner.

Criger then laid down a sacrifice bunt to Bransfield, who threw to Ritchey covering first, as Ferris moved to second. Then Young showed he could hit too, driving a long fly ball into the crowd standing behind the ropes in left field, giving him an automatic triple and allowing LaChance and Ferris to score and make it 5–0. Dougherty promptly hit another triple into the crowd in left to make it 6–0 in the series' biggest inning. It looked like a rout was on, although Collins lined softly to first and Stahl, up for the second time in the inning, grounded to Wagner who threw him out easily to end it. And, for a change, the Bostons had their band strike up "There'll Be a Hot Time in the Old Town Tonight."

Inexplicably, or perhaps because he felt the game was already out of reach and wanted to save hit pitchers, Clarke let Kennedy go back on the mound in the seventh inning. The Americans turned the game into a rout as the Rooters changed the chorus of "Tessie" into a new refrain for the occasion:

Kennedy, you seem to pitch so badly,
Take a back seat and sit down.

Kennedy, you are a dead one
And you ought to leave the town.
Pittsburg needs a few good pitchers
Such as Boston's pennant lifters
Phillippe, you are the only, only, only one

And then, the song ringing in his ears, Kennedy came apart. Freeman beat out a hit to second and Parent singled. Then Ritchey made a brilliant save of a hard grounder by LaChance and forced Parent at second as Freeman went to third. Ferris' single to center scored Freeman and when Criger walked, the bases were loaded. The Rooters started singing and screaming so loud that one Boston sportswriter noted that "by this time, Boston's loyal rooters acted more like escaped patients from an insane asylum." The Pirates fans fumed and raged.

Young made another bid for a hit with a hard grounder to Ritchey, but the Pirate second baseman threw him out for another run and an 8–0 score as the Pirate fans sagged in despair. Then Dougherty hit another fly ball into the crowd in left field for a ground rule triple, scoring Ferris and Criger to make it 10–0. The decision to make the fly balls into the crowd a triple had cost the Pirates in the same way the ground rule doubles had hurt Boston at their home field. Collins grounded out, but the game was already out of reach. And the ground rule triple would hurt Pittsburg again.

In the eighth, with Thompson pitching in relief of the battered Kennedy, Stahl opened with a line drive into the crowd in right for a triple and scored on Freeman's ground out to first to make it 11–0. It was the last inning Kennedy would ever pitch in the big leagues.

Young was cruising, but lost his shutout as the Pirates tried to stage a frantic last-gasp rally in the eighth. With two out, Beaumont hit a grounder to Ferris and appeared to be out easily, but umpire O'Day called him safe over the loud Boston protests. Then Parent fumbled Clarke's grounder and two were on. When Leach tripled, it was 11–2, but the sore-armed Wagner was thrown out on a grounder to Parent.

That was all Pittsburg would get. Boston won 11–2 and was down 3–2 in games but back in the series. A Boston loss would have finished his team and Collins knew it. Young had given up only six hits and should have had a shutout. It took only two hours — and "Tessie" — to do it. And Collins was more confident than ever, because he could come back with Dinneen while the Pirates would have to bring back the sore-armed Leever; Phillippe couldn't go on one day's rest again after having pitched so much already. What was unsaid, but felt, for Pittsburg, was the loss of the crafty left-hander, Ed Doheny.

Wagner left the field dejected and feeling the loss was his fault, and the writers tried to be kind to him without ignoring what had happened. "It was

Wagner who must bear the brunt of the defeat," one writer noted. "But as Hans does not do tricks of that kind often the cranks can afford to forgive him." His two errors had opened the door for Boston and he had gone hitless in the face of what was called Young's "hypnotic benders" and the relentless craziness of the Royal Rooters and "Tessie." They had shouted themselves hoarse and were blue in the face with exhaustion and joy. Wagner had promised to run Young out of the game, but it was the old man pitcher who had beaten his old friend into the ground instead.

Now it was the Pirate fans' turn to howl about whether their team was trying to win. The *Pittsburg Post* reported, "Some wild-eyed fans estimated that the Premiers did not try to win the game. This is ridiculous. When men throw base ball games, they will not do it by making errors. They will duck the hits, etc. It was unjust to the Premiers to even insinuate that they did not try to win. The men worked hard for the game. Bungles are part of the pastime and will ever be made." But some fans were so upset that a rumor swept the city that Dreyfuss had released Wagner, which quickly proved untrue, but a measure of the passion that had become part of the epic.

Charley Lavis Refuses to Be Held Up by Band

It was a wild night for celebrating for the Boston fans and the maniacal Rooters, whose antics at first had amused the Pirates fans but was now was growing more irritating by the moment, especially with the Boston win and the sense that McGreevey's boys were feeling part of it. At 11 P.M. the night of the Boston win, as they were stepping out of the Grand Opera House where they had gone with both teams, McGreevey and his right-hand man, Charley Lavis, who had hired the band in Pittsburg, were served with papers by the authorities and charged with breach of contract by the Greater Pittsburg band. They were ordered to appear before Alderman John Groetzinger at 10 a.m. Saturday, the day after tomorrow, to answer.

The band leaders said they had been promised $80 per day for performing and were hired for four days, but had been paid only $80 and let go when Lavis hired another band instead, charges which Lavis denied emphatically. He was fighting mad, as was McGreevey, because they did not want the music or the singing stopped. The Rooters with them started shouting and, amid the hubbub, said they would start a pool to raise the money to fight the action and spare McGreevey and Lavis the expense. They had some unexpected support.

Some of Pittsburg's wealthiest patrons said they were outraged by the action against the Boston visitors and said they would put up the money to fight the charges, while several lawyers coming out of the theater, attracted by the noise, came over and offered their services without charge. Lavis was upset:

> I am sorry that this has come up but I will stick and fight it out. I will not be held up, and this seems a clear attempt to do this. When we came to Pittsburg we thought best to have a band and the manager of the Greater Pittsburg band came to us and wanted to make a deal. I told him that the chances were that I would be compelled to pay most of the money out of my own pocket and that I could deal with him but for one day.
>
> I told him that if the money came in right that we would likely want the band for the four days that we would be here, and perhaps a little at night too. I meant by that that if we won the first game that we would have a whole lot of money, and that we would go through with the program, which we hoped to carry out.
>
> This seemed perfectly satisfactory and so I closed with the Greater Pittsburg band on a basis of $80 per day. Well, it is known that we lost the first game, and our boys fell heavily in a financial way, so we decided to dispense with the high-priced band and I paid it off. Today we got another band, as we had a perfect right to do, and we will continue to hire whatever band we see fit. We did not come to Pittsburg to be bulldozed, nor will we.

He said the gambling losses had set the team back and that he had not deceived the band. "I did not hire the Greater Pittsburg band for four days. I hired it by the day. We had it one day, for which I paid. They must show me before I pay for the other three days' service, which we did not want, nor did we bargain for, nor will we have," he said.

In a flourish, he finished, "I desire to thank the good people of Pittsburg for their generous offers of assistance. We are surely not without friends, even in an enemy's country."

Collins was glad to have them and said, "I do not know what I would have done without them. Their aid in encouraging us to victory has meant lots and lots to us in these games. They share in the victory with us." Collins couldn't be caught up in what was going on off the field, even if the Rooters had become nearly indispensable as cheerleaders and had lifted his boys' morale when they had been down and seemingly out. He was going to bring Dinneen back, while Clarke had to counter with the lame-armed Leever, hoping the "Goshen Schoolmaster" could bring himself up to a performance as extraordinary as had Kennedy in the first five innings of the fifth game.

The attendance was listed as 11,556 and the grandstands were filled early; strings of people lined the ropes in the outfield again, and the ground rule triple rule was invoked again. Thursday, October 8, 1903, was now almost as important for Pittsburg as for Boston. The weather had gotten very cold, and it was difficult for the players, especially the infielders, to handle the ball. Young batted infield practice for Boston. "I'll give 'em enough to do," he said, whacking hot grounders to Ferris and LaChance, whom he called his "rabbits" for the way they chased the ball.

The Pirates fans, anxious to outdo the maniacal Rooters, had something ready for big Dinneen when the Boston pitcher came onto the field to warm up. They threw baskets of confetti in the air trying to distract him. A local firm, though, had donated multi-colored parasols to the Boston rooters, who started to twirl them, creating a crazy kaleidoscopic effect from the stands that, with their singing coming from behind them, made their section seem like a mad house. They ran up and down the aisles, swinging and twirling the parasols and ringing tin cans and making a loud nuisance.

The 31-year-old Leever, his arm pounding with fatigue and hurt, was a gamer and he shut Boston down in the first two innings, which finished scoreless. But with two out in the third, Dinneen, the pitcher, who had only 17 hits in 106 plate appearances during the regular season for a .160 average, lined a single past Wagner. Then Dougherty walked, Dinneen went to second and there were two on with two out. The Rooters could smell a rally. Boston was down 3–2 in games now and a victory here would even the series and send it back to Boston for sure. Collins, on whom there had been so much pressure, came through with a single to center, scoring Dinneen to make it 1–0 as Leever rubbed his arm in hurt.

Then Stahl singled too and Dougherty came home to make it 2–0, and Collins went to third, as the Rooters wailed like roosters. Then came "Tessie" again and it was all the Pirates could do to keep from putting their hands over their ears. When the band tried to strike up another tune, the Rooters jumped to the feet in protest. "No, no, nothing but Tessie!" the terrified Pittsburg band was told. And so the strains repeated themselves, over and over and over and over and the lilting little melody was filling the air of Exposition Park with maddening insistence. And worse, for the Pirate fans, it was working for Boston.

Tessie, you make me feel so badly, why don't you turn around?
Tessie, you love I love you madly....

Stahl then promptly stole second base. When third-baseman Leach fumbled Freeman's slow roller, Collins came home to make it 3–0 as Freeman took first, but Parent grounded out to end the inning, and Boston had the first blood.

The players were feeling the tension now too. As the Pirates took the field, some of them barked at the umpires about calls they felt were missed. Boston's LaChance, protesting that O'Day had called a ball fair that went into the crowd, got it right back from the umpire. "Perhaps you think I am going to hand you the game on a plate?" he said, looking at the big first base-

Seven—*They Didn't Do a Thing but Turn the City Upside Down*   113

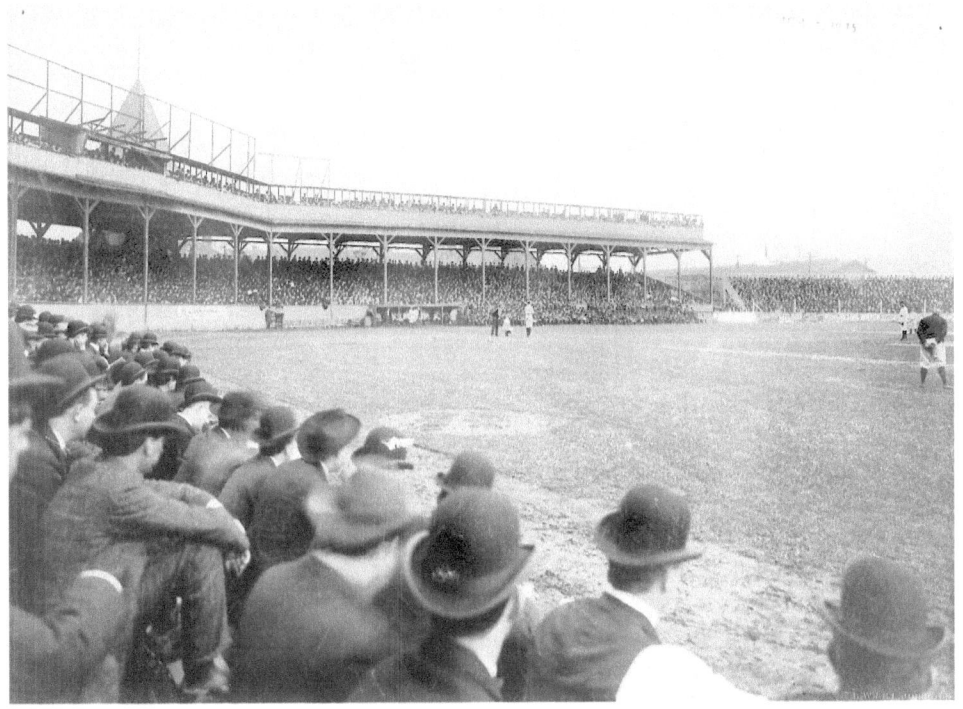

The Royal Rooters' vantage point for the games in Pittsburg was far down the first base line, but it didn't keep them from singing "Tessie" incessantly, to the annoyance of the Pittsburg fans and players (courtesy Boston Public Library).

man. "You are mistaken, my boy. You will get just what belongs to you and no more," O'Day said.

In the fifth, Stahl opened the inning with a tremendous blast, the longest hit of the series, but it landed deep in the back of the crowd, giving him a ground rule triple. Freeman hit a sacrifice fly to center and Stahl scored to make it 4–0. Leever, reeling and hurting, hit Parent with a pitch as the crowd winced too. After LaChance flew out, Collins put the hit-and-run on, sending Parent with the pitch while Ferris singled and the hard-running Parent tried for home, hoping to beat a relay from the deadly Wagner, who had gone to the outfield to take the throw and cut off yet another Boston run. The strategy worked. Wagner, rushing his throw, made a wild toss and didn't get Parent at the plate. Boston scored to make it 5–0 and the game seemed to be slipping away from the Pirates, their confidence fading as fast as the sun behind the smoke of Pittsburg.

It didn't stop there. In the seventh, after Freeman struck out, the little Parent tripled into the crowd and LaChance doubled down the right field line, scoring his best friend and putting Boston ahead 6–0. Dinneen, meanwhile, was having little trouble with the Pirates and it looked as if he might throw another shutout at them, as he had in the second game in Boston that saved the Americans from being swept there.

Dreyfuss was uneasy now too, sitting in the stands in his home city, his fans around him, expecting an easy Pirates victory over the American League collection of league-jumpers and old men. They rallied against Dinneen in the bottom of the seventh.

Sebring opened with a single to right and went to second on Phelps' single. Leever grounded out, advancing both runners. Beaumont singled to center, scoring Sebring as Phelps went to third. Pirates manager Clarke doubled hard down the left field line to make it 6–3 and Dinneen was rattled for the first time after cruising through the first six innings. Leach flied out to Freeman in short right field, bringing up Wagner as the crowd screamed for their hero to save the series. It was all on the sore shoulders of the game's best player and Wagner walked up stoically, his huge, bow-legged frame bent with determination.

Dinneen, concentrating on Wagner, didn't see Clarke take off for third and the Pirates manager stole the base, sliding in with dust flying and cleats high. The Pirates fans were on their feet, sensing the comeback. The wily Wagner, knowing Dinneen would be expecting him to be overeager, worked the cagey hurler for a walk instead and now there were two on. The tying run was at the plate. Then Dinneen walked Bransfield intentionally to fill the bases and set up a force out at any base, but the Boston pitcher was wearying and it was the Rooters' turn to worry. A ground-rule triple into the crowd here could tie the game and give the Pirates a chance to put Boston away.

Now it was up to Claude Cassius "Little All Right" Ritchey — all 5' 6", 167 pounds of him. The second baseman had been steady during the series in the field but had gone only 3-for-17 at the plate, and Dinneen had handled him with ease in the series. The Boston players felt Ritchey had been one of the best Pirates players during the series. Collins' managing had been criticized by some of the Boston media but he felt Dinneen could get the light-hitting Pirate second baseman to hit a grounder. He was right. Ritchey topped an easy roller to Parent, who fired to Ferris at second to force out the hard-charging Wagner and end the Pirates' rally.

Before the rally ended, Pittsburg sportswriter Gruber saw what was happening too, and he was as excited as the fans, thinking the Pirates were going to make the unlikeliest of rallies. "Men who could write their checks in six figures stood on chairs alongside of the day laborer and yelled until black in the face. It was not one short, sharp outburst, it was a prolonged siege of yelling and rooting, under which they hoped the Pittsburgs would come to the front," he reported.

Seven—They Didn't Do a Thing but Turn the City Upside Down 115

The Pirates hadn't won three consecutive pennants by quitting and they didn't in this game either. After the fatigued Leever managed to put Boston out in order in the eighth and ninth innings, the Pirates came up for their last chance in the bottom of the ninth. The Rooters were screaming again and the Pirate fans were trying to match them with constant shouts of "Hooray!" but the real work was to be done on the field, where Dinneen was on the slab and the Pirates were pounding their bats in the dirt, eager to take him on. The big Boston right-hander had done them to death and they didn't want him getting out of town without doing more damage.

Beaumont, playing brilliantly, got his fourth hit of the game with a single over second base. Beaumont was the Pirates' fastest man and he was leaning off first base, looking for his third steal of the game or a big jump on a hard shot that would give him a chance, as had Sebring, to come all the way home or at least get to third and give the Pirates a last-gasp chance to win. Pirates manager Clarke came up and scorched a low line drive that looked like it might get past Parent into left field as Beaumont broke. But the little Boston shortshop, whose fielding had bedeviled the Pirates much of the series, shot out his fielding glove and caught the liner just above the ground and, in one motion, wheeled and fired back to LaChance at first base to catch Beaumont for a double play. The Pirate crowd, up in anticipation at the crack of the bat, sagged back into the seats.

But the drama wasn't done.

LaChance didn't see that Parent had caught the ball because the line drive was so close to the ground, so the Boston first baseman fired to Ferris on second base, who blocked the bag as the Pirate headed straight for him, determined to make it, even if he had to knock down the 5' 8", 162-pound Ferris. And Ferris, concentrating on the oncoming Beaumont, dropped LaChance's throw, but Parent grabbed the ball and put the tag on Beaumont, who still thought he had a chance to make the bag safely. By the time the drama was done, so were the Pirates. Beaumont had been out two ways and then Leach, the last man to face Dinneen's music, popped foul behind the plate and Criger caught it in stride near the grandstands to give Boston the victory, 6–3, and tie the series at three games apiece. After the game, Watson and McGreevey danced on top of the Boston dugout and a weary, grimy Dinneen, his hat off, stood in front of the Boston bench debating the merits of the game with Pittsburg police officers who stood guard, as Ferris looked on. Young had come into the series as the game's biggest name on the mound, but Dinneen had notched his second victory and it was he was confounding the Pirates.

The gamblers who'd bet on Boston to come back were raking it in, but Dreyfuss was doing all right financially too. The turnout of 32,000 fans in three games had been a windfall for him, but the Pirates owner wasn't thinking

Following a big win in Pittsburg, Boston pitcher Bill Dinneen (bottom center, no hat) and second baseman Hobe Ferris (bottom left, cap askew) struggled to get back into the dugout during the celebration of some Boston fans (courtesy Boston Public Library).

about money when Leach's popup ended the game. He saw the sad-eyed Pirates head slowly back to their clubhouse and headed after them.

The players were surprised to see their owner in their midst and stood fast when he came in, not knowing what to expect. He was one of the hardest losers in the game and the Boston writers said Dreyfuss wanted to win the series badly, so the players might have been expecting a roasting. That's not what they got. Dreyfuss, standing elegantly still, said, fighting his German accent:

> Boys, I'm proud of you. You have made a fight the likes of which no other team ever made. You'll win yet. None but you and myself know the handicap under which we went into this series. We had but one good man in the box, Phil," he said, looking at Phillippe and talking about the injuries that had clipped his club.

"Yet, knowing this, you took up the task and you've fought like demons. They have hard, strong club boys, but they cannot beat us, crippled as we are. We will win tomorrow, and then we will then go to Boston and give them the final blow in sight of their own people, Monday. If they beat us tomorrow, we will beat them two games at home."

He continued, to a Pirate clubhouse of silent players, "I have faith in my boys and I'm prouder of you right now than if you had won the championship in five straight games. You don't know how to quit. If you should lose — but you can't — I'll love you in the same old way. Cheer up," he said, and walked out, leaving behind a proud team more determined than ever. After all, the series was still tied and Dreyfuss still believed in Wagner and Clarke. And he thought he had a strategy to help them, something that depended on the next day's weather.

Pat Egan, the clever and colorful baseball scribe for the *Pittsburg Times*, let the Smoketown fans know there was a reason to worry, though.

> Boston's infield worked like a clock yesterday, and everybody on it took part in one or more hair-raising stops or plays. Collins demonstrated that he is as fast as ever, when he jumped with the agility of a cat for a short bunt down along the third-base line and threw out the runner by a block at first. The clever manner in which he executed his plays served notice on the Pirates that they would have to take desperate chances if they bunted the ball in the neighborhood of the Boston captain. LaChance showed to much better advantage, while Parent made it clear enough to the crowd that Wagner has nothing to speak of on him. No infield ever worked better, and several of the chances were extremely difficult to handle.

The *Post*'s Gruber wrote about the new feeling in Pittsburg, fright that was bordering on panic. "It is an unusual thing to see Pittsburg divide honors with a rival in baseball that the local rooters looked scared, but only for a moment." Dreyfuss knew now that the Pirates' only real hope lay on the tiring shoulders of Phillippe. The ghost of Doheny's absence, the sore arm of Leever, the idiosyncrasies of Kennedy, the uncertainty of Veil, had turned the Pirates' staff into something which neither he nor Clarke could count on.

The *Boston Globe* noted the growing pessimism in Pittsburg, especially with National League President Harry Pulliam, and his old mentor, Dreyfuss. "They acknowledge the American League has a grand champion team in the Boston club and can see that Pittsburg must do some great ball playing in order to take the series, or two out of the next three games played," the paper reported as soon as the sixth game ended.

Collins, who had gotten over his tirade against Dougherty after game four, said he felt a lot better now that the series was tied. "I will confess that I was a bit nervous and anxious when things were breaking so badly, but I am not now, and am positive that we will win the series. I felt sure from the start that we had the best team in the country, but defeat will come to the best of clubs. We have done just what Pittsburg did—taken two games out of three in the opposing camp, and we will take the rubber game Friday. Phillippe will go up against us just once too often," he said.

Jake Morse in the *Boston Herald* was told by a joyous Boston player after the game, "Say, it was worth a journey of 700 miles to see, don't you think?"

Morse obviously agreed and couldn't resist rubbing it in a little when he wrote, "Hushed is the hilarity of the National Leaguer rooter tonight, while the American Leaguer is crowing." Morse said Pittsburg fans had told him Boston was "not in our class" after the first four games. "But it is now a different story and it is agreed that the Boston American League team is the only one in the land today that has a right to dispute with Pittsburg the matter of baseball supremacy," Morse wrote. Baseball has imprinted its mark on the nation's consciousness, taking the game into another realm, past the days of monopolies and pure rowdyism into a sphere of competition that had captured the attention of old fans and made new ones. It was, for sure now, the national game, as thousands of fans across the country continued to stand in front of department stores and other places where the inning-by-inning scores were being announced.

There was another element—again—in the Boston victory, and one that was grating on the Pirates and their fans—the Royal Rooters. Boston's maniac fans had endeared themselves to Pittsburg with their wacky manner and unfettered celebratory methods when they first arrived in the city, but now it seemed they were having an effect on what happened on the field.

At game's end, the Rooters and their band marched across the field, out the gate and through the streets of the city, rooting and tooting and blowing horns and celebrating with gaiety, all the way to their hotel.

People in Pittsburg, meanwhile, had been mesmerized by the series, even if they felt their confidence slipping in their hometown boys. Baseball was all most people were talking about, especially as the players for both teams made grand night tours of the city, going to restaurants and theaters and being cheered as celebrities. Even the Boston players were treated royally by most people and had become as recognizable as the city's most well-known businessmen and leaders. The players reveled in the attention and restaurant and theater owners hoped to lure them with free tickets so they could attract patrons who would come to see the players. Young, of course, was the grand old man of the game and treated as such, but even players like Candy LaChance, with his big 1890s style moustache, and the little Parent, whose dazzling fielding had vexed the Pirates, were getting some quiet hurrahs too, as Parent was playing Wagner to a standstill in the field.

Even one Pirate official chimed in with plaudits for the little Boston shortstop. "Talk about Wagner. I cannot see where the big fellow has anything on that little Boston wonder. Why, he seems to be everywhere and makes no fuss about it," he said.

The people of Pittsburg were becoming used to the sight of the rabid Rooter fans, wearing their red badges and Boston symbols, carousing at night and partying up a storm in a city of working people. Lavis retained the band for the night celebration of the series being tied and the group played loudly at the Monongahela Hotel, where the Boston fans had taken over. As they laughed and joked and sang, the Rooters seemed supremely confident, hoisting their drinks with aplomb and razzing the Pirates. But then they got an announcement, just at midnight, as it was raining hard outside.

One Pittsburg fan, who had heard enough of "Tessie" and the Royal Rooters, had engaged a 40-piece band for the locals to engage in a battle of the bands with Boston's hired group. Worse, it was the band that the Rooters had discharged and which was suing them.

The music stopped.

The drinking stopped.

The Boston fans, still in their suits and ties, even if looking a bit ragged and sounding a bit hoarse from singing and shouting and carrying their lady "Tessie" everywhere, were indignant.

They sputtered and fumed and put down their drinks.

"And what's that for?" one said.

"They aim to drown out 'Tessie.' They think it is a hoodoo," the Rooters were told.

"No! No!" the shouts came. The Rooters were rooting as much now for "Tessie" as for the players, and were willing to put their money up. One party of Rooters put up $560 for Boston against $700 offered by a Pittsburg gambler, Buck Cornelius, but turned down lesser odds, so confident were they. And other peculiar bets were made. One Pittsburg gambler bet $200 against $600 that Pittsburg would win game seven, Boston would win game eight, and that the Pirates would win game nine. But he refused to bet at even money that the Pirates would win the series in any other fashion other than what he had presented.

The Pirate band had been instructed to play "Hail, Hail the Gang's All Here," when they heard "Tessie," and a medley of other songs, including "The Smoke Goes Up the Chimney Just the Same."

"The band has received orders, and the first and foremost one is to put a crimp in that 'Tessie' business," the Pittsburg papers reported. It would take more than that to stop Boston now.

Sparring for Wind

The seventh game was scheduled for the next day, on Friday, October 9, but the weather was worsening and Dreyfuss was trying to find a way to buy time to bring back the Deacon. He felt the first World Series slipping away from his proud champions. As soon as the sixth game ended, Collins was asked about the idea of postponing the seventh game until Saturday, when a huge crowd could be assured, although the Royal Rooters had reserved train seats for late Friday night to get them back to Boston. It was an arduous trip which required planning.

Even with the inter-league play going on in other cities at the same time, more attention had turned to the Boston-Pittsburg series the longer it had gone on. The stands in Pittsburg and Boston were filled with sportswriters from around the country and there was a sense there was something grander going on than just another series of baseball games. The idea, the games, had seized the country just when a sense of optimism had infused itself into the American psyche. The waves of immigrants coming to the United States, many to Boston and Pittsburg, had hoped for better lives and opportunity. For many, the game provided not just a pastime or entertainment, but a common language avenue toward better times.

Everyone shared the joy of a hometown hit or the sorrow of a loss; everyone delighted in the unbridled joy of the players who were being paid to play a little boy's game. And for the working classes especially, the games were their circuses, a giant saloon where thousands of them could gather to talk and drink and swear and bet and let loose from the grinding labor of the new industrial revolution. For others, it was a place to take family members for an introduction to the American way of life.

And if Dreyfuss was worried about the outcome of the series, he didn't have to worry about the financial or popular success of the series or the games in Pittsburg. All anyone wanted to talk about, it seemed, was baseball, even if the fans were becoming begrudgingly respectful of the Americans. Pittsburg had become used to the Pirates winning championship after championship and even to their team becoming so dominant the thought of them losing a critical series to anybody was not considered. Dreyfuss had hoped to lay over the series to Saturday for other reasons too. The Westinghouse Company had ordered 1,000 seats and the Pirates were sure of another big house for a weekend game, unlike Friday games, when many people could not come because they had to work. For them, the news would come by word of mouth or from people who had stood in front of store windows watching scores being posted.

Boston's two victories though were unsettling to some, including McGraw, who had confidently predicted the Pirates would easily defeat Boston. "They realize that Pittsburg must return to Boston for the toughest proposition of a lifetime," a Boston writer noted. Boston was confident now, even if they didn't win the next game, that they could finish it in Boston.

Parent, normally not given to boasting, said he could feel the surge and

Seven—They Didn't Do a Thing but Turn the City Upside Down

took a few verbal swipes at the Pirates. "Boston will win. These fellows stop once you get a lead on them, and they have nothing on us at any time," he said. The Rooters, and the gamblers accompanying them, figured Phillippe couldn't put the hoodoo on the Americans a fourth time, and that Young was ripe for business.

But then Dreyfuss got what he wanted. It started to rain hard late on Thursday night and the prospect of a Friday afternoon game was dubious. By midmorning Friday, the temperature was 57, but a stiff wind was blowing and it seemed a lot colder. It was an unpleasant day under any circumstances, especially to play or watch a baseball game. "It was too cold for football, not to speak of baseball," the *Globe* reported.

Phillippe walked in to see Dreyfuss. "It's awful cold today and my wing feels stiff and sore. I am not fond of working under such conditions," he said, swinging his right arm like the pendulum on a clock.

"You don't like cold weather?" Dreyfuss said, his face falling in fear. "Well, we'll see about that. Send for Fred Clarke," he said.

The Pirates' manager was called into the office and surprised to see Phillippe there waiting. "We're going to call the game off," Dreyfuss told Clarke, who didn't want to disagree. Dreyfuss, citing cold weather and windy conditions, said the seventh game, which would be like the first in its tension and importance, would be postponed a day to Saturday. It didn't sit well with the Boston players or management.

Collins wasn't informed until 11:30 A.M. and angrily went to the Pittsburg club headquarters and confronted Dreyfuss and Clarke.

"What is the game called off for?" Collins demanded. "What is the matter with you people?"

Clarke looked at him starkly. "The weather is too cold and tomorrow being an open day, we called the game off." And then he stopped talking. Collins didn't like what was happening because he felt part of the reason for the delay was to rest Phillippe.

"We're willing to take a chance. What's the use of waiting a day? It is likely to be just as bad then and we want to finish these games here and get away. I think it's a shame. What guarantee do you have the weather will be better tomorrow?" Collins snapped.

"Why," Clarke said slowly, "the weather reports are for fine weather tomorrow."

Collins wasn't buying it. "We are leaving for Boston tonight," he said, the threat of taking his team away with the series tied and no resolution without the final games sufficient, he thought, to change Dreyfuss and Clarke's mind and play.

Then he turned to Dreyfuss, the gentlemanly owner and spat his words in anger. "What does this mean? You have no right to do this. We are ready to play and you are simply sparring for wind. You think I can't see into this thing, but I can. What are you going to do when you get to Boston?"

Dreyfuss pulled out some papers and said to Collins, "You had better read this first." The Pirates' owner produced the agreement he had with Killilea that said Pittsburg had the right to call the game either for wet or cold weather. All Collins could do was read the words and simmer.

There, in paragraph two, were the words typed out:

> Providing however, in the event of the weather being such as to prevent a game being played on either of said days, such game shall be postponed until the next succeeding day when the weather will permit such game to be played at the city where scheduled. And in that event there shall be a moving back of the aforesaid schedule for the day or days lost on account of said inclement weather.

The Boston captain measured his words carefully and made one last plea. "We are ready to take our chances and play ball when possible and a little wind should not interfere with these games. Let us get through the business at once," he said, waiting for the reply. The air was thick now, as Clarke knew he had been called, but he was steadfast.

"It is impossible to play good ball under the conditions and unfair to ask the public to sit outdoors in such weather," Clarke said.

Collins could do nothing else, but he said, "We will go to the grounds early tomorrow and take all the time we want in warming up. We didn't have enough practice in the first game, as the grounds were too wet and slippery to stand on." When he heard the news, Killilea, who was still in Milwaukee, sent a telegram to Collins, stating, "Your great work is an honor to the American League and all are proud of your great team." But he still hadn't shown for the Pittsburg games.

Later, reporters asked a still-angry Collins what he thought about the delay. "I think we will get on to Phillippe tomorrow and win out, and then we should have no trouble to win our game in Boston, as Dinneen can beat Pittsburg any time he is right."

Clarke, having enough of Collins' ripostes, came back at him. "We have Boston beaten with Phillippe in good shape tomorrow, and can certainly win one out of two games in Boston," he snapped. And, despite his weather report, the weather for Saturday was expected to be cloudy and cool again.

Young, relatively quiet during the series, was emerging as the best in the game again and said he was ready. "I feel in first class shape and it will be the aim of my life to win this game, and I feel confident, with a fair field and good umpiring, we will come out ahead," he said.

Some Pirates officials were still confident though, or at least put on the front. "We would have won today anyway," one said. "Putting it off a day makes it all the easier for Phil," Deacon Phillippe, in whom the players and management believed fervently.

The layover meant the Royal Rooters would either have to change their plans now to get another train, since their reservations were for Friday night, or leave. McGreevey, Lavis, Watson and the rest of the rooters would not have it that way, though. They were determined to stay and believed that their encouragement, along with the timely appearance of a lady named "Tessie," had put the Pirates adrift in their own ship.

When they heard of Dreyfuss' decision, and Collins' failure to change the Pirate owner's mind, they gathered at the Monongahela hotel to talk about it. There was much bickering and anger, until one rooter, Charley Waldron, stood and yelled for attention, which he got in a room full of sputtering men. He looked them over calmly and started to speak slowly. "We should stay here until the last game is played … I propose to remain, even if I am the only one, and take the band to the Grounds and give the Boston boys some encouragement," he said, to loud cheers and a steadfast unified front. The Rooters would not leave on the Friday night train.

Lavis, who had hired the band, was indignant. "Why, Barney Dreyfuss intended from the start to hold the Bostons here for a Saturday game. It is a case of showing the white feather and Boston should never stand for it," he said, spouting rage. They asked Dreyfuss to change the starting time of the Saturday game to 2:30 P.M. so they could catch a 6 p.m. train back, but the Pirate owner refused. The Rooters were irate, but the day off gave them a chance to appear before Alderman John Groetzinger, who was hearing the suit brought by the first band the Boston men had hired.

At 11 A.M., they stood before Groetzinger to make their case while Prof. W. William Guenther, head of the band hired by the Rooters, brought his lawyer, Charles A. Robb, to make his case. Guenther said he had been hired for three or four days, the length of the expected stay in Boston for the series, and was due $285. The band was to march and play from the Monongahela Hotel to the park, at the park, back to the hotel and then gives an evening concert at 9:30 P.M. Guenther said the band was to be paid $96 for 18 members, or $105 for 20 members.

But when the time came for the Rooters to leave the hotel for the first game, and as they lined up outside to march behind the band, they were told Guenther would not march with only 18 men and that the band wanted to ride to the ballpark. An infuriated Lavis said he had to quickly find a conveyance for the band, from which they played.

"And I was applauded all the way down Fifth Avenue," Guenther testified, before a Rooter chimed in, "But that hasn't anything to do with the case." Groetzinger tried to keep order and prevent bedlam as the Rooters and musicians squared off before him, the two groups ready to bark at each other in his presence.

Guenther said the next day, Wednesday, he came with his band to the hotel again, only to be surprised to hear "another band making noise in the hotel." He said he put his men outside while he and three of his group's members went to investigate inside, where the Rooters confronted him.

"Your services are no longer needed," a shocked Guenther said he was told. He recovered and replied, "Then I intend to serve notice that I will expect compensation for the four days for which I was engaged," he said, storming away.

Lavis testified that he felt Guenther was merely jealous that another band had taken his place. "It is most unlikely the band would be hired for four days when there was the possibility we would be going home at the conclusion of the third," Lavis said, and McGreevey gave the same testimony as to his orders to Lavis, who said, "I am a dead stranger in the city and what I done, I done honestly," claiming Guenther was motivated by jealousy.

Another rooter, William Pink, said, "The Rooters had come to Pittsburg with the intention of walking behind a band, and not to follow a band in carriages." Robb asked what business Pink had trying to be an expert on band business. "I have been in the minstrel business 18 years," Pink said, and Robb withdrew his objection. But then the Rooters and the musicians began arguing with each other loudly, as a patient Groetzinger listened before he stopped them.

"Gentlemen, gentlemen!" he said. "I have heard the testimony from both sides and I shall give my decision at 5 o'clock this afternoon." The alderman left to let the debate continue.

It was indicative of the passion the games had created that the contest between the Rooters and the band was getting significant coverage from the many Boston newspapermen who had accompanied the team. Back home in Boston, the series was front page news every day, with many adjoining stories about the characters and events surrounding the games.

And with newspaper competition for coverage of the series becoming as fierce as the games, and with so much money at stake now, the *Boston Globe* jumped into the event too. On the morning of October 9, with the game postponed, *Globe* editor Charles H. Taylor sent a telegram to Collins:

> The Boston Globe, believing that victory is within the grasp of you and your comrades, offers to present to each player of the Boston team of the American League, if it brings to Boston the world's championship, a valuable gold medal, which can be worn as a watch charm, and be treasured as a reminder of the most notable achievement upon the diamond.

The tiny medals could be worn as a watch chain. Each had a globe on top and the front showed a pair of crossed bats behind a catcher's mask and the words "Boston American League Team, World's Champions, 1903" engraved on it. Taylor had a good reason. In a front-page story, the paper explained the hold baseball had taken on the American public because of the series. "Never before have the leaders of two great leagues battled for supremacy in the national sport. The public interest in the final result is therefore unusual," the paper reported.

Collins was delighted, even though ballplayers generally were superstitious about gifts. "It is pleasing to get such recognition, and such loyal and liberal support," he said. "The boys will do everything in their power to win the honor for Boston, which has given us the best treatment, even when we were not having the best of luck," he added. Reserve catcher Duke Farrell, a Boston native, remembered that eight years earlier the *Globe* had put up a pot of $1,000 for a pennant winning game if the Boston Beaneaters had won, and which the paper had paid although Boston lost.

Even the Pirates' captain, Fred Clarke, thought the idea of the medals was helpful to the game, even if it offered extra motivation to the Americans. "It looks well to see the press recognize the game and the players in this way," he said. "The Boston boys are to congratulated upon having such a supporter, but Pittsburg intends to take the series and prevent any handing over of the Globe's gold medals," he cautioned.

The *Globe* knew the games were good for readership too, and said so on its front page. "Wherever in Boston men gathered last evening, whether in hotels, in theatres, clubs, bowling alleys, billiard rooms or street corners, the general topic of conversation was baseball — the championship series between the Boston Americans and the Pittsburg Nationals ... the excitement is more widely spread and more intense over this contest between the champions of both the great leagues than ever was known in the history of baseball in this city."

Back in Boston, a city assessor named Daly said the games had overtaken the city. "The national game is the greatest ever invented. There is no pastime like it. Its patrons are found in every town and city of our great country. Its' votaries are to be found on every lot big enough to toss a ball or swing a bat on. It is essentially American — vigorous, powerful, strong," he said, defining what others had been unable to, explaining how baseball had become part or the fiber of a new America.

The talk of gambling influencing the outcomes had died down somewhat in the excitement of the subsequent games, but hadn't been forgotten. One account noted, "Every fan in Boston apparently believes that Boston will win, although there are those who do not overlook the fact that the Pittsburgs are a mighty strong team and stand a good show. Here and there one hears talk about the games not being 'on the level' but the majority believe that these games are on the square and are being played for 'blood.'"

The players had many friends attending the games, and even people who knew little about baseball had been captivated by the series. "There are men who care nothing about baseball, but they hear so much about Honus Wagner, Cy Young, Lou Criger, Kitty Bransfield and Pat Dougherty that they go out to see them work," the paper said. There was more than gold at stake, though. The six games had brought in more than $50,000 in revenues, at a time when false teeth cost $5 a set, ladies' suits were $12.50, cigars were 10 cents each, boys' top coats were $2.98, men's underwear was 19 cents, and men's ties 59 cents.

Even after paying expenses, there was already a pool of about $46,000 to divide. The Boston players were going to receive 75 percent of their team's share, to be split among 16 players and Smart, the business manager, and the owner. The estimate for the whole series was that the players would be getting about $1,300 each for about 10 days' work, a handsome sum indeed for the times. And through the first six games, only three members of Boston's team, Jake Stahl, Gibson, and Winter, had not played.

Then came some news that embarrassed Killilea and raised talk among the players. Dreyfuss had already decided in September that if the Pirates won, he would take only enough to pay his team's expenses and let the players divide the profits. He went to Clarke and told him about it and the Pirate manager told the owner to keep it under his hat so the players would be thinking only about pride, and not about money. But the word leaked out among some and the stakes had been raised even higher for the Pirate players, and Killilea had some thinking to do about his team's shares.

Dreyfuss had said if the Pirates lost the players would still "be taken care of," but that was taken to mean that the owner would keep money for his team's expenses and his lost wagers before the pool was established. But then a bet was put down in Pittsburg that even if the Pirates lost, they still would get more money from Dreyfuss than the Americans would get from Killilea. Dreyfuss said, "If the Pittsburg team beats Boston in the championship series now on they will receive every cent of money coming to Pittsburg less expenses incurred." It was a powerful incentive because the sum was up to about as much as one-third to one-half a season's salary for some players. And that didn't include pride, of which Pittsburg had plenty.

With the series assured of returning to Boston for a Monday game, the demand for tickets in Boston had been as high as for the first three there. Orders had also come in from Pittsburg, New York, Philadelphia and other cities as the series intensified its hold on a fascinated American public. More than 300 pavilion seats at $1 a head had already been reserved for the Huntington Avenue Grounds, including about 200 for Pittsburg fans. The Royal Rooters had already reserved another 200 seats in the grandstands, in their favorite spot by the Boston bench. Although some tickets were available at

Barney Dreyfuss (upper left), one of baseball's greatest owners (courtesy Carnegie Library, Pittsburgh).

agents, Boston team officials said remaining seats would be sold only on game day, at 50 cents each, although speculators were sure to be jacking up the price.

There were few tickets to be had in Boston, and it had made some people looking to get into the game as angry as a kicked dog. One man who went all over town to ticket agencies looking for ducats stormed into the office of the *Globe* and slammed his fist down on an editor's desk. Complainants said tickets by the hundreds were in the hands of speculators, who were openly hawking them in front of the stores where people were supposed to be able to buy them.

But Boston Americans officials denied there was any known reselling and Assistant Manager H.A. Breen said he opened the box office early Friday morning and promptly closed it when he felt speculators were trying to buy up big blocks of tickets. He found young boys who couldn't properly have a dollar holding money and lining up to buy tickets. Breen felt the boys would be returned to waiting speculators nearby, at a limit of two per customer.

Breen said he would sell more than two tickets to people he knew were not going to try to peddle them elsewhere. When he closed down the sale, orders started to arrive by telegraph. And Pirates officials and fans said they wanted enough set aside for their delegation for the scheduled Monday game. "As the yellers from that part of the country got left on seats the last time, common decency urged they be taken care of on Monday," the paper reported. The tickets, it seemed, "melted away like the morning mist when the sun comes up as hot as were the kickers this morning."

Despite the confidence of Boston's players and officials, the game had to be settled on the field, in front of an expected huge, hostile crowd on Saturday, and against the American-killer, Phillippe, who had become almost as revered as Wagner in Pittsburg. And, like Wagner, he had a dignified and reserved manner, but was fiercely competitive and was confident he could again handle Boston.

Dreyfuss got what he wanted on Saturday, at least by game time. As in Boston, the masses of fans started to come to the ballpark early because it was a Saturday and many did not have to work. The park was full by 1 p.m. and fans had to squeeze themselves into the outfield spots. Hundreds more onlookers sat atop nearby Monument Hill, even if they could only see part of the field from there, and many more tried to get a vantage point from the top of Mt. Washington, overlooking that part of the city, even though it was quite a distance. Groups had come from Cincinnati, Louisville, Columbus, Ohio; Scranton, Detroit, Buffalo, and many small towns around Pittsburg and West Virginia, from Wheeling, Steubenville, Ohio; Uniontown, Connellsville, Blairsville, Indiana, Charleroi, Beaver Falls and Monongahela. A special train from Youngstown and Mahoning Valley brought in 1,700 people.

Lavis took to more than rooting this morning, now that the series was tied and he was in a feisty mood from his dealings with the Pittsburg bandleader who had sued him. He said in a Pittsburg newspaper that optimism was rising quickly amongst the rooters and players from Boston:

> Boston seems to hold her own with the Premiers in every department of the game, and in the box is much superior. Young and Dinneen are both in rare form while Pittsburg evidently has but one pitcher, Phillippe, and his arm, even with frequent rests, cannot hold out forever. When the Collins boys once land on him he will take to the tall timbers as have the rest of the bunch.... The Pittsburg infield, which has been touted as so much superior to Boston's and which I once thought led ours, has not shown up so wonderfully well, at least as far as averages go. Bransfield has shown slightly superior to LaChance, and Ritchey has been decidedly better than Ferris, but Parent and Collins have outclassed Wagner and Leach.

The Pirates fans had their own band now, realizing how critical the contest was, and because this was the last game of the year in their city, they organized a pep rally parade for their boys. There was a horse-and-carriage caravan across the Allegheny River from downtown with many of the city's most prominent businessmen in front in their carriages leading the charge. The crowd, nearly 1,000 persons, wore the team colors of navy, red and yellow and wore badges that said, "Champion Rooters, Pittsburg, 1903."

At the park, Collins kept his word and got his team out for practice at 2 P.M., an hour before the game, and found 13,000 people already there and another 5,000 outside, including the marching band of Pittsburg fans.

As they marched down the streets of Pittsburg, they whooped it up, trying to outdo the Bostonians in their zest, and chanted, "Phil, Phil, Phillippe, Phil; He Can Win and You Bet He Will."

It was 2:15 P.M. now and the Second Brigade Band hired by Pirates fans walked around the diamond, to the astonishment of the players, and then the Boston band — the second one Lavis had hired — broke into "Auld Lang Syne" as the Rooters sang, and the melody was picked up by everyone and sung. And then as the Pirates came out for practice, both bands joined in playing "My Country 'Tis of Thee" as the game's opening anthem, and then "The Star Spangled Banner," the words rising like the American flag as both sides saluted. The truce was warm and genuine, but didn't last.

The Pirate fans took again to chanting their "Phillippe" cheer. It was their "Tessie" and they kept singing it as they entered the park and headed for the outfield to take their positions behind the ropes that were, as in the other games in Pittsburg, the spot for ground-rule triples that couldn't be played by the outfielders. They elbowed their way into position among thousands that stood there.

The bands took up their battle again, the Boston-hired group striking up a curious medley of "Yankee Doodle Dandy" and "Away Down South in Dixie," and then finishing with "My Maryland," a relief from the constant strains of "Tessie" for the hometown crowd. The sound of the music reverberated through the park, and fans took up the songs from one end to the other, the revelry a celebration of the joy the games had brought.

Exposition Park was again overflowing, this time with a crowd announced as 17,038, nearly 6,000 more than the previous game and the greatest crowd ever for a ball game there. It seemed the city's residents had simply moved into the park and the din they were making was for the Pirates, trying to rally them back and shut up the Royal Rooters at the same time. "I didn't know there were so many people in the world," said a stunned spectator from the little town of Punxsutawney who had made his way to the big city.

It was a gray, cold October day, but the fans hoped their shouting would warm their team. "I paid $1.50 to get in and I can't get a seat," an exasperated fan said when he came in and saw the seats all taken and people standing in the outfield. "I don't care though, it's going to snow anyhow," he laughed.

He motioned to a man standing next to him, not knowing he was from Boston. The Pittsburg man looked out at the Americans and said, "That's about the swiftest bunch I ever stacked up against."

The bespectacled Bostonian next to him stood stiffly and replied, "Referring to the aggregation of professional players of the Nation's greatest game, the athletes representing the city of culture undoubtedly are superior to any similar number of opponents whom it has been my pleasure to observe."

But then there was more bad luck for the Pirates, during the warm-ups when both teams were tense. Bransfield let a bat slip out of his hands accidentally and it struck Clarke hard on the leg, knocking the surprised Pirate left fielder–manager to the ground as the crowd gasped. Not now, not again to the injury-dinged Pirates. Clarke got up grimacing, rubbing his leg and limping, trying to shake it off, but he couldn't. He was bruised and hurt but had no option other than to play, even if he couldn't go full speed.

The papers had bannered the contest as an epic, Phillippe matched again against the already-mythical Cy Young, whose stature had not been too diminished by his first game loss to the Deacon in Boston. Since then, Young had won the crucial fifth game with ease, putting down the Pirates like so many dolls at a carnival sideshow. But the Boston team was worried that the Pirates' fans again would take to throwing confetti into the wind to distract the Boston players, even though it hadn't helped before.

It was a trick that had brought calls of unsportsmanlike conduct from the Boston fans and reporters, but which had added another moment of colorful chaos to a series that had become as eccentric as its players, matching character-for-character in the two cities with those on the field.

Back to Boston

As Phillippe went to the mound to open the game—with three days' rest—the Pirates' rooters gave a loud cheer, but McGreevey's boys were ready and they struck up the dreaded "Tessie" again, although the Pirates' band and fans tried to counter. There was in the air an excitement that had been unmatched in any athletic contest in Pittsburg or Boston or anywhere else because so much was at stake: the pride of two leagues, of the players, of the fans in both cities, and the interest of Americans everywhere, it seemed.

And, of course, the stakes included the new riches the players and owners

Seven—They Didn't Do a Thing but Turn the City Upside Down

would enjoy, and the publicity they couldn't buy, across the country. It was baseball everywhere, thanks to this newfangled idea of a real World Series between the league champions. The grounds were hard and the winds blew harder as the summer game was swallowed by the gray chill of October now, made grittier by the background of smoke and industrial buildings which surrounded the park in Pittsburg. The eerie start was captured perfectly by Murnane in the *Boston Globe*. "The scene was a weird one. Clouds of black smoke from the large steel works came sailing down the two rivers that meet here from the Ohio, while a bright sun shot needles through the whirling sheets of light and heavy smoke, and every face was focussed on the home plate as Boston's curly haired boy and his favorite club stood ready for business," he wrote as Pat Dougherty stepped to the plate.

Phillippe bore down as Dougherty came up and the crowd kept up its loud, reverberating cheer, though through it he could hear the haunting, maddening tinkle of that damned "Tessie" again, and he looked into the crowd and could see the thousands of fans, most depending on him to win for the home team, mostly men in suits and their formal wear expecting a celebration today.

There arose a din that carried across the field like an elongating cumulus cloud of noise. That gave Clarke time to talk to umpire Connolly, but a fretful Collins came over to complain and Clarke walked back to left field for the game to start up again. The noise didn't let up, even when Dougherty bounced to second for an out. But it did cease when Collins lined a shot to left and it fell into the crowd for a triple, which had been a Boston trademark throughout the Pittsburg games. As the crowd had done to Boston in Boston, the Pittsburg crowd had bedeviled their hometown team by being so plentiful. Worse, it seemed Phillippe's pitches had lost their zest or sting and the Boston players were sitting on them, just waiting. No confetti would interfere with their concentration today, although the field was muddy and the players slipping as they tried to field the ball.

As the Rooters roared through their megaphones, a frustrated Pirate fan yelled back at them. "He's not home yet," he said, pointing to Collins at third.

Then, the curse of the triple struck again like a lightning bolt on a man holding a metal umbrella in a storm. Stahl hit a rising liner that rose over the speedy Beaumont's head in center and landed in the crowd for another triple and Boston had a 1–0 lead before the crowd had even recovered from the opening moments, the echoes of the bands still ringing in its ears.

Freeman hit a hard ground ball to Ritchey at second and he fired home to catch Stahl at home plate in a close call. The Pirates fans sighed instantly in relief, thinking a run had been saved, but catcher Phelps, holding the ball momentarily, dropped it on Stahl's hard slide and it was 2–0 Boston. A quick wave of panic came over the crowd faster than had the steel mill smoke. Phelps redeemed himself briefly when he threw out Freeman trying to steal second, and when Parent grounded out to Wagner, the Pirates were still in the game as they came to bat.

But Young was in form and all business. In the bottom of the first, Beaumont bunted down the third base line, surprising Collins, and making first on his raw speed. Then LaChance bobbled Clarke's roller to first, putting two Pirates on with no outs. But with the Pirates fans howling, the usually reliable Leach, a clutch hitter throughout the series, bounced into an untimely double play and then the great Wagner struck out on three fast Young pitches, and the crowd fell into its seats.

Young shut the Pirates down easily for three innings and Phillippe recovered from his shaky start to shut Boston out for the next two innings as well. The Pirates were still down only 2–0 going into the third, when Phillippe came to the plate and, suddenly, the game stopped. As the Pirate hurler looked around in amazement, a group of Pirate fans came strolling out to the plate where he stood. Still holding his bat, he was handed a gift. It was a diamond stickpin, paid for by the fans. A proud Phillippe stood stock still, his Pirate hat with the bright yellow "P" looking like the top of a scarecrow stick, his heavy wool uniform hanging from him, while it was presented. A spokesman said, at the top of his voice to the cheering crowd, "We hope this pin brings you good luck today, Deacon, and in your remaining games of the series, if you again are called upon to pitch." And then players from both teams gathered around him at the plate, their rivalry forgotten for the moment, as the whole crowd — including the Boston Rooters — cheered the Pirate hurler.

Phillippe was genuinely appreciative, despite ballplayers' superstitions about receiving gifts; many thought a hex would be put upon them if they accepted a gift before a game or a series is won. But he responded, hitting a rifle shot single while his fans roared more than ever. Beaumont was thrown out on a grounder to Ferris and Clarke hit to Collins at third and the ball was thrown low to first. It was getting very chilly in Pittsburg now and the players moved constantly, trying to keep warm, batting their feet into the ground, pounding their fists into their gloves. The fans, though, buoyed by Phillippe's hit, kept screaming for more, but Young was equal to the task and he struck out Leach.

But in the Boston fourth, the hard-hitting Freeman rifled a drive over Beaumont's head again, and the centerfielder had to give up on it because of the crowd, into which it landed for an automatic three-bagger. The ground rules caused by the crowd had crowded the outfielders from both teams and cost them chances to make outs. Parent hit a grounder to Wagner too soft for the Pirate shortstop to make a play to the plate as Freeman scored to make

Seven—They Didn't Do a Thing but Turn the City Upside Down   133

it 3–0. After LaChance went out, the light-hitting Ferris added to the triple parade with a line drive into the crowd in left center and then scored to make it 4–0 on Criger's single.

With the crowd behind them in desperate exhortation, the Pirates tried to come back in the bottom of the fourth against the speedballs Young was throwing. Wagner, pressing now, tried to bunt his way on but was thrown out. Bransfield finally got a Pirate crowd-triple and then scored on Ritchey's infield out to stop Young's bid for a shutout and close the gap to three runs. The crowd picked up its vocal support again, but a determined Young stopped the rally right there with a couple of quick outs. In the fifth, Pirates fans took to ringing cowbells in an inning-long chorus, but that didn't work either, as Beaumont was picked off first by Young and caught in a rundown until he was finally, as a writer noted, "shut off like a steam valve." And with it went the steam out of the fans and the Pirates too. The game had turned into a disaster, errors combining with the bad weather and sloppy field to make decent baseball a precarious business.

In the top of the sixth, Parent opened by beating out a slow roller to first. LaChance put down a sacrifice bunt which Phillippe fumbled for an error, putting two men on with no outs. Ferris sacrificed on a bunt to Bransfield, who threw to first to Ritchey who came over from second to cover. Then Criger, who had had a rough series defensively, came through with a single to right, scoring Parent and LaChance to make it 6–1. The Pirate fans felt the game slipping away as Phillippe was wearying, although he got Young to hit into a double play. The Pirates fans were serenaded, again, with "Tessie," as McGreevey and the Rooters were jumping with delight and making a racket the likes of which hadn't been seen at a baseball game.

The Pirates were game, though, and they weren't going to give up. Since the fourth game, when he'd gone 3-for-4, Wagner had been hitless in nine trips to the plate. Bransfield had not hit in games five and six and Ritchey was struggling at the plate too. Clarke tried to get his team back into the game when he opened the sixth with a triple. After Leach struck out, Wagner was coming up. It was the game's best pitcher against the game's best hitter and the Pirates fans were so desperate you could almost hear the growl in their throats.

Young stared down the big Dutchman, but they had had this confrontation many times before and Young's heaters did not intimidate Wagner. He surprised Young when he hit a hot grounder right back to the pitcher. Young looked Clarke back to third before throwing to first to get an out on Wagner. But at that moment, Clarke, knowing how desperate Pittsburg's plight was, made a mad dash for the plate as a startled LaChance threw to Criger, hoping to cut off the Pirate manager.

Clarke slid in spikes high, off the plate, as Criger put the tag on him, but Connolly called him safe over the mad protests of Criger. "He didn't touch the plate!" the Boston catcher screamed in vain. Connolly wouldn't yield and the Pirates were back in it at 6–2 and plenty of time left to catch Boston. If only they could hit Young. They couldn't, and he got out of the inning with just one run given up.

The tension in Pittsburg was palpable now, but a grim-faced Young went back to the mound and simply shut down the Pirate bats. In the eighth, Boston got another run when Parent hit another Boston triple — the team's twelfth in Pittsburg — and scored when a worn-out Phillippe threw wild with LaChance at the plate. Parent danced easily across home plate as the pitch flew past a bewildered Phelps, and, with it, it seemed, the Pirates' chances to stop the Boston roller coaster that had begun, maddeningly, with "Tessie" back in the first game in Pittsburg. They kept it up, serenading Young when he came up to bat in the ninth; confident the big man had done it again. When he heard his fans sing in uneven unison, "Tessie, Tessie, you're my darling," Young gave a bashful smile, stepped out of the batter's box and tipped his cap to McGreevey's men.

The Pirates weren't quite done yet. They had lost the last two games and were on the verge of losing their third straight at home, an account which hadn't been foreseen by Dreyfuss or Clarke or any of the fans who thought the Pirates could at least go back to Boston up 4–3. In the bottom of the ninth, Young had only to put out the bottom of the Pittsburg lineup, but Sebring beat out a roller to short that Parent couldn't get to in time. Then Phelps singled to center and the hearts started beating faster in the Pirates' players and fans, even though Phillippe was coming to the plate. The noise almost raised the roof off the grandstand behind home plate and even the Rooters couldn't be heard. The Deacon gave himself one more hope when he singled, making it 7–3, and there was some belief that perhaps the Pirates could mount the same kind of rally Boston had in the first game in Pittsburg, the crucial ninth inning that had turned around the whole series, it seemed now. Two were on, nobody was out and the crowd reached back for one last raucous yell of support.

Criger flashed signals and made eye contact with Young, holding up the glove in which he used to put steak to soften the blows from Young's fastball, giving the veteran time to settle himself and ignore the crowd. Young pulled up his big frame and bent over and stared down at home plate as Beaumont came up. He got the fast man to pop up. Then Clarke came up, amidst a new flock of flying confetti paper, and hit a harmless fly to left and it was Leach's turn. He had been a bedrock at third in the series and had hit well early, but Young had already struck him out three times with fastballs that had the third baseman tied in knots trying to reach. Leach hit a hard grounder just to the right of Ferris at the second, but the Boston player dove to the

Seven—They Didn't Do a Thing but Turn the City Upside Down 135

ground and knocked the ball still, and, in one motion, threw it to Parent at second for a force-out to end the game.

On deck was Wagner.

It was over in 1:45. The Pirates walked away, heads down, while Criger ran out to congratulate Young, happy with himself too because no Pirate had stolen a base on him in this game.

Boston now led the series 4–3. Wagner wasn't going to be doing any hunting. And he was going back to Boston.

The crowd rushed the field, and instead of anger or hurt or grief, there was an incongruous celebration, the Pirates fans lining up to shake the hand of Cy Young, who couldn't get off the field for the crowd that wanted to be around him, to touch him, just to be near. When it came time to leave, the Boston players, in a coach, found themselves being escorted by a procession of Royal Rooters down the main street of Pittsburg. Behind it was the band, and the players came out on top of the coach to watch the sweet madness. Several more coaches full of Rooters followed.

On the way, they passed Newell's hotel, where bets had been placed, and Charley Waldron, who had given the impassioned plea for the Rooters to stay for the Saturday game, had something to pick up and told the coach driver to stop. "Please stop until I collect my winnings," he laughed. He came back out in a few seconds with a big roll of bills to back his belief in the team and was cheered by the crowd as he stood up in his carriage and sang out, "Easy money boys, I thank you for the contribution." He had pocketed $30,000, more than 15 times what the players would make.

As the coach reached the Monongahela Hotel, the streets were jammed with people on a late Saturday afternoon, the sun going fast now, the cool of autumn covering everyone with a reminder that the summer game was almost gone for good, extended only by the extraordinary event that had enveloped American life.

The beaming Boston players filed into the hotel as waves of cheers and constant hurrahs swept over them, and once inside they saw a Rooter jump atop a chair and ask the crowd for more, as hats were doffed and thrown to the ceiling. They even cheered for the players who had played little or not at all—Jake Stahl, Winters, Gibson, Farrell and O'Brien, because they were part of the team.

Wagner had now gone hitless in three games and his slump was affecting the whole team, especially with its pitching problems. He had made five errors too in the seven games, although no one wanted to talk about nerves to a man who seemed impervious to pressure before these games. And the Pirates had stranded nine men on base against Young, squandering opportunities to get to him and get back in the game. The regrets and recriminations started too, one Pittsburg paper saying, "It is too bad that the Pittsburg

Club should be sorely handicapped in the pitching department. With Leever and Doheny in shape, there is no doubt they could have made a better showing than has been the case. President Dreyfuss was advised not to play the series with the team in a crippled condition, but he insisted upon doing so."

Wagner was taking the most criticism of his illustrious career, although many sportswriters and papers were trying to be kind to him. The *Pittsburg Post* said, "Stars of the Wagner magnitude did not twinkle as much as was desired," and the *Pittsburg Chronicle Telegraph* was even more lenient in explaining the loss: "Wagner was the main offender, but the Carnegie giant has few lapses and the crowd forgave him."

In the Boston clubhouse, the players were supremely happy and confident, if worn out. Collins, who had been getting scores of telegrams from friends, fans and admirers, hurrahs and admonitions alike, said, "It has surprised me to see the amount of interest that is being taken in this series. I never thought it would arouse so much enthusiasm. I am glad Pittsburg won the National League pennant, for this series with the Pirates has been the most exciting of any in which I ever participated. It will certainly be a high honor if we can succeed in winning the world's championship from such a sterling bunch of ballplayers as Fred Clarke has here." Pressed about the pitching choices and dilemmas, Collins said, "I felt confident Cy would do the trick and that we would bat Phillippe enough to win. Cy pitched grandly."

In the Pittsburg clubhouse, where Dreyfuss had given his speech after the last game, Clarke was more downhearted but trying not to show it. "I am much disappointed. I felt all confidence we would win today and that meant in my opinion, the series. I have not give up yet. Look for us on Monday," he said, but some of the spirit seemed to have gone out of the fighting Pirates. Indeed, after the first game, the only thing Boston had lost in Pittsburg was the suit brought against the Royal Rooters by the Greater Pittsburg band, the alderman ruling that the Boston men had to produce three extra days' pay for their contract, a decision the group said they would contest — even as they got out of town. They may have lost the suit, but the Rooters begrudgingly won the respect of the Pittsburgers.

"That loyal little bunch of rooters in Section J during the past four games did more to win for Boston than did the pitching of Cy Young or Dinneen," the *Pittsburg Post* reported. "They put heart in the boys. They dug into their socks and hired bands. They danced, screamed, shouted and sang by turns, always with eyes of love turned on their own...

"And when Pittsburg gave Boston the heel on the opening day here, making the score 3 to 1 against Boston did her rooters quit? No, not Boston. They rooted and cheered until bedtime and then sat round until daylight, waiting to get a good chance to begin rooting the next day," the paper added, giving them a "Bravo!"

Seven—They Didn't Do a Thing but Turn the City Upside Down   137

The players and the Rooters, meanwhile, had to hustle to the train station to get out so they could be back in Boston by Sunday afternoon and get ready for the big game on Monday. Clarke thought he would have to come back with the bedraggled Phillippe, whose arm had been through four complete games and 36 innings in 10 days—too much, Clarke worried, even for the grand Deacon.

The glum Pirates would have to share a train with the Americans and—even worse—with those Royal Rooters who would be sure to keep up the racket all the way to Boston. Only five days before, the Pirates had won the fourth game and were up 3–1 in games and poised, it seemed, to be the champions of both leagues and the world. But now there was deep worry in Pittsburg, and the one Pittsburg writer who had warned of being overly optimistic reminded the fans.

By Frank McQuiston
Pittsburg Dispatch

The Pittsburg club did not win the championship of the National League with one pitcher, nor had they the right to attempt to defend it with but one. They were not as strong with Phillippi alone as when they won the championship with Leever, Doheny and Phillippi, and nothing would have been lost by them saying so plainly.

It would not have been an act of cowardice for the owners of the Pittsburg club to announce plainly that, owing to the falling of Doheny and the bad cold in the shoulder of Sammy Leever, they did not feel able to fight against the American League club.

No, I think it would have been better for them to have made this statement frankly and let it go at that. Should the Pittsburgs win this series, which they will play in Boston this coming week, they will still be losers. The public will not be so well pleased.

Should the American League team be the loser the people will be sore indeed, and have a reason to be, because they will have been beaten by a one-man team.

Phillippi will, if he wins, be the most famous player in the history of baseball. He will be famous even if he loses out now, for he alone has been the man.

It should not have been so. No, there was something coming to these people of Pittsburg which they have not got in this past season's fight. There is something coming to every adherent of the National League in the other cities which the Pittsburg club has not given.

It is satisfaction.

There was plenty of that in Boston.

But there was none for Doheny, whose mental condition was worsening. The Pirates, hoping to make him feel better, had sent him his uniform. But Doheny, thinking he could still pitch, became disoriented and even more confused with the gesture. Since his initial departure from the Pirates in the summer — and even after a rest period at his house allowed him to rejoin the team in September, only to leave again just before the end of the season — Doheny had been acting confused and disoriented. He acted strangely at times, but his friends knew his propensity to worry about his ability to pitch and his deep desire to win, and thought he was just worn out and tired and gave little attention to his eccentricities and delusions.

On Saturday, the day of Boston's victory to take a 4–3 lead in the series, Doheny's doctor, E.C. Conroy, came to his house at 112 Main Street in Andover to call on him. It was a Greek revival style house in the country where the Dohenys were boarders.

"I do not need your attentions anymore," a confused Doheny said. "You do not need to come anymore."

The doctor did not believe him. "If you keep up your treatment, Edward, you will soon be well," Conroy said.

Doheny struck him in the face, and the surprised Conroy staggered back and was pushed out the door by a more agitated Doheny, who told him forcefully, "Do not return. You are not wanted here!"

Conroy went to the police station to notify them, but it was decided that Doheny simply did not want the doctor's services and he was left alone, for he had been kind all along to his wife and young son and it was thought he was not a threat to anyone.

Conroy, however, decided to send a nurse who was a well-known faith healer, Oberlin Howarth, as well to try to assuage Doheny's demons and care for him. It was Sunday, the day after the Americans' wrenching win at Pittsburg that gave them the 4–3 series lead, and when Doheny read of his team's defeat, he became all the more uneasy, blaming himself, his anxiety rising.

Howarth succeeded temporarily in calming him and getting him into bed. But when the nurse turned his head, Doheny became berserk, reached under the bed for the leg of a cast-iron stove foot rest he had hidden, and beat Howarth behind the head with it. The nurse fell suddenly to the floor, unconscious, even as he was hit again, murderously.

His wife, holding their four-year-old son, came running into the room as Doheny was beating the nearly unconscious nurse and begged him to stop. "Eddie! Eddie! Don't do that!" she screamed. The sight of his wife and child calmed him momentarily.

But the noise startled another boarder in the house, a young woman who ran outside to seek help. Two young men who were neighbors across the street, followed by another man who was walking outside, rushed into the house and found Doheny, holding a poker in his hand now, standing ominously over the fallen Howarth, looking ready to strike another blow.

Howarth was bleeding and still prostrate. Doheny pointed at him and smiled insanely. "See what I have done?" he said.

One of the men looked him dead in the eye. "Give me the poker," he said steadily, while the other two waited to see if Doheny would try to strike again, or take a swing at them.

Instead, Doheny meekly handed over the poker and the man said, "Get into bed," and he complied, the fight gone out of him, the madness with it, if only for the moment. And as he watched, the men turned their attention to the fallen Howarth, who had a severe wound on the back of his head, and disfiguring bruises to his face. He moaned and tried to tell them what happened, but they took him into the adjoining apartment so Doheny could not see or hear him.

Another doctor named Abbott was called to tend to Howarth and dress his wounds, while the men who had helped him stood guard outside Doheny's door in case he should go berserk again, as there were women boarders in the house as well. They were waiting for the police, and, during the delay, Doheny got out of bed, armed himself with another leg from the footrest, went to the window, and then to the door where the men were and ordered them to leave. Apprehensively, they waited and a moment later the police arrived and apprehended Doheny, who offered no resistance.

His wife, holding their child, told them to be gentle, as he had been under undue stress. "He needs help," she said somberly.

The local newspaper, the *Andover Townsman*, reporting on the affair several days later, said the stories that Doheny had kept police at bay for an hour and been a madman, apart from the beating he inflicted on the poor nurse, were unfounded, "notwithstanding he was a dangerous man to deal with if one was off guard."

Doheny, waltzing in and out of lucidity, was taken to the police station where Dr. Conroy, accompanied by another physician, Dr. R.M. Birmingham, examined him, declared him insane, and ordered him sent to the nearby Danvers State Mental Hospital for care and treatment, with the consent of a local judge, Andrew C. Stone of adjoining Lawrence. Doheny was taken away calmly and offered no resistance. He said nothing and did nothing, except to stare directly ahead, his eyes fixed on something only he could see.

The Pirates, en route to Boston, didn't know what had happened to their teammate. His wife explained it later, sometimes sobbing:

> The ball games between Boston and Pittsburg made Eddy go wrong.... He could not stand the strain, and when he read that his old team was losing and he not there, he just couldn't stand it. He used to moan when he would read about Leever's arm being bad, and he wanted to rush away to the club. He was confident he could beat the Bostons and when the Bostons began beating Pittsburg it was awful the way he felt. The news yesterday morning that Boston had again beaten Pittsburg and made it four victories to three was entirely too much for Eddie. It seemed to

numb and daze him. I sent for the doctor and the sight of him seemed to make my husband mad. You see, he always blamed the doctor for keeping him away from Boston when the Pittsburgs first came over. He thought he was well enough to go into the game, but he was not. So when the doctor came there was trouble and Eddie struck him....

"He had never given up the chance he could help Pittsburg beat Boston, but when he got his suit back he was heartbroken, thinking all was over. I hope my husband will be well soon," she said softly.

EIGHT

"Tessie"

It was a long train ride back to Boston for the Pirates and their fans, while the Rooters whooped it up, counting their winnings and believing fervently that their passion, and "Tessie," had been the difference. Since they started singing it in the ninth inning of the first game loss in Pittsburg, Boston had won three straight and outscored the Pirates 28–8. Even better, the caterwauling had seemed to unravel the normally unflappable Wagner, who hadn't been able to buy a hit in his hometown. The champion hitter of the National League was hitting .217 against Boston. There was great anticipation in Boston for the return of the series, with one anxious Bostonian pleading in a letter to the editor for better crowd control. "With an ample force of police, a crowd of 20,000 can be kept in bounds and a good game of ball be seen. We are entitled to this, and it is up to the management to see that we have it," wrote W.H. Preston.

The first seven games had been seen by more than 92,000 fans, 44,000 for three in Boston and 48,000 for four in Pittsburg, so the totals for the whole series would now easily top the 100,000 mark. That meant, after expenses, the players already could count on at least $1,100 a man for their two weeks' work. The ride for the Pirates was made longer when their train had to stop in Albany to allow the Boston special to catch up. But there was no mockery of the players by the lighthearted Boston fans who had enjoyed the Americans' comeback, but who also delighted in the spectacle of the series and admired the men playing it. The players and fans from both sides mingled the rest of way, although the Pirates were still hurting, and surprised to see LaChance and Parent, the French-speaking buddies, along with pitcher Tom Hughes, come into their car to talk with them.

The train pulled into South Station in Boston at 4 P.M. on Sunday,

October 11, before only a small crowd. The Pirate rooters who had come north with them were a smaller group than had showed up 12 days before. Missing too were Kitty Bransfield, the Pirates' first baseman and Hobe Ferris, Boston's second baseman, both of whom got off in Worcester, Massachusetts, their hometown, the night before to stay with their families. The fans were surprised to see the Rooters get off and give them three cheers.

Still, Sunday was one of the worst days ever for the Pirates. There was none of the lighthearted and even sarcastic banter of the first time the Pirates had come to town 10 days before. They were physically hurting and missing left-hander Doheny, the 16-game winner, more than ever. They hadn't talked about him much, but some officials and players and fans couldn't help but wonder what would have happened if he had been able to pitch even one game. One thing the Pirates couldn't escape was the Royal Rooters. By 3:15 P.M., about 600 fans were in the terminal, although the train wasn't due for an hour, and there was a joyous air of expectation in the hubbub; the series was the talk of the town. The fans screamed in delight when the train pulled in. They rammed through the gates when they saw the players alight, and Young was mobbed most of all, suddenly surrounded by scores of people as he had been in leaving the field in Pittsburg. Collins was besieged too, and the normally quiet manager was happy too as he took uncountable greetings and backslaps.

McGreevey and Lavis were pressed by the regulars at the Third Base Saloon and spent a lot of time laughing and explaining their legal troubles with the band in Pittsburg. The sound of so many people speaking at once filled the terminal. Royal Rooter Charley Waldron was celebrated too. "Well, we did not have to walk home after all," he laughed, remembering his winnings and the Boston victories he thought he and the Rooters had helped spur.

Lavis said the hearing before the alderman had been comical. "Why, some of the rooters would put Boston's best lawyers to shame when it comes to pleading," Waldron said. "You should have heard them pleading for the $285," he laughed as the crowd roared.

"Young and Dinneen pitched great ball and they deserve no end of commendation," Lavis said. "Phillippe is a great pitcher but I predicted the day I left town that Boston would take his measure and they did that to perfection on Saturday. The treatment accorded the Rooters by the Pittsburg people was most generous and when we get a chance, we will return the compliment," he added.

And then one of the Rooters chimed in: "'Tessie' did the trick. Ever since we began to sing that song the boys have played winning ball," he said. The fans waiting and the Rooters who had arrived picked up where they left off in Pittsburg, parading out onto the street and making a loud racket for all to hear.

Eight—"Tessie"

The Pirates had gotten off at the Huntington Station right near the baseball park to avoid the scene and the possibility of heckling; they hustled themselves away anonymously, looking at the pouring rain. The Pirates, crippled and down, went back to the Hotel Vendome on stately Commonwealth Avenue. It was raining and ominously dark, and waiting for Phillippe and Wagner, left by a prankster, were copies of a magazine. It was *American Undertaker*.

There wasn't even grim humor now. Clarke's leg was still sore and he was limping visibly. Leever's shoulder rendered him ineffective and out. Ritchey had an irksome infection in his hand from scratching a sore. Wagner told a Pittsburg sportswriter that his arms were "gone" and he couldn't throw hard anymore. He was almost in despair and told the writer he might even retire from the game because he was hurting so much, physically and spiritually. "His stale note raised a smile of incredulity all around and when reminded that he would rather go hungry than quit baseball," the writer said as Wagner backed off his retirement idea a bit.

Gruber remained irrepressible and wrote that the Pirates were confident yet and that Clarke would probably start Bucky Veil, or maybe even the sore-armed Leever. But even he noted how sore physically the Pirates really were. Phillippe was proudly sporting the pin he had received from the fans in Pittsburg and saying he was ready to pitch in the last game. He said that after the series, he was going to rest for a while and then go on a hunting trip with a party that included Wagner, who was deeply introspective now about his failures in the series.

When he got to the hotel, Clarke got even worse news. It was about Doheny and it numbed the normally stoic Pirates manager, and he talked to some of the Pittsburg sportswriters about what happened. "That's pretty bad news. Of course, we sometime ago gave up all expectation of Doheny's helping us in the present series, but I hoped he would be all right for next season."

Clarke remembered the September visit, after Doheny had gone home for the second time during the season, when the manager wanted to see if his pitcher could return. Then, he said, "Quite a while ago I got word from his physician that it was all off, and that Ed couldn't be depended upon for these games. I was still hopeful that his mental condition would improve and that he would be all right next Spring," Clarke said, but now he wondered about that too.

"He was a mighty good fellow, and the players always got along nicely with him. It is needless to say we never had any detectives following Doheny. The men he told me were watching him were two commercial travelers who never saw him before or since. That was simply his form of mental derangement. You may say for me and the whole Pittsburg team that we are very sorry for his wife and family and very sorry to lose so good a friend and companion," Clarke said, and he was done with it. He couldn't talk about it any more.

While Doheny's condition had cast another pall over the Pittsburg team, nothing had dulled the public's optimism about the series. J. Ed Grillo, the sportswriter for the *Cincinnati Commercial-Tribune* who had written so eloquently about the games, saw the future in it too:

> The championship series between Pittsburg and Boston has proved one of the best attractions baseball has had in many years. Nothing that the game has furnished has created as much interest as the games between the winners of the rival leagues. This has been shown by the number of persons who watch the scoreboards about town. Every one who is interested in baseball and many who have never seen a game have taken an interest in the outcome of the championship series. The game has, therefore, benefited, for new enthusiasts have been made and without enthusiasts or fans there would not be a possibility of having the game holds its popularity.

But there was some grumbling in Pittsburg now that the Pirates, and not Boston, were on the verge of possibly losing the series after a victory had seemed so sure only a short time before. The *Pittsburg Post-Gazette*, under the ominous headline "*World Series May Be Stopped,*" said Pirates fans were deeply dispirited and that talk about gambling and money influencing the series might mean its demise.

The *Post-Gazette* said the fans had thought Boston and the American League was no match: "This was largely due to ignorance on their part because they had never seen the Boston team play, and all the information they possessed as to the playing or strength of that organization was that which they had read in the newspapers. Of course, they had seen the Pirates play, and they knew that Clarke's team was the strongest in the National League, that was all they really cared to know."

But after the Pirates lost two games in a row at home, some ugly rumors were being heard throughout the city, even in the midst of the celebratory air and good times so many people were having. The paper continued, "The people who started these stories had never for a moment stopped to figure the situation out. They could not see that the team, although crippled, was against a foeman worthy of the best it could produce, and that they only had one pitcher on whom they could depend. Little things like that did not concern them in the least, and then came reports about games being 'fixed' and that the contests were being manipulated in favor of gate receipts, and the funniest part of it was that there were many who stood ready to believe these reports."

The *Post-Gazette* had a theory, though. And it was about Doheny and the midsummer problems that came back to haunt the team:

The remarkable reversal of form shown by certain players is one of the queer things in the present series. Who would ever have thought that it would be such strong and usually reliable players such as Clarke, Wagner, and Leach who would go up into the air and make mistakes that cost their teams such important games? The only possible explanation is that these players were laboring under such a strain that an explosion had to come some time, but it was unfortunate it came when there was in the box a pitcher included to be a bit flighty himself and who needed the best efforts of the other players behind him.

Cy Young was outraged over the "fix" stories. "The story is malicious. Pittsburg may win when we meet but if they do it will be because they have the ablest team and the luck as well, for the Boston team is going out to play ball to win. I am not fake sport, nor are the other fellows. We are all on the level," he said, his voice rising with anger. Young, the winningest pitcher in the game, still knew that no matter how good you were, the competition was so intense that even the best could lose, or fall into a losing streak in a short series. He was burning still about the gambling talk and the way he had been approached.

Clarke had a lot to think about for the moment. His team was hurting and he was hurting, but his mind was with Doheny. Wagner had not hit for three consecutive games and the failure was wearing on him. And he was being driven berserk by the incessant strains of "Tessie." It was hard for his teammates to see how Wagner was getting down and how much pressure he was putting on himself. He had been the star on every stage in baseball, but the World Series had put him center stage, where he didn't like the limelight, and his retiring nature was working against him. The Rooters knew they were getting to him with "Tessie," and they fired the lyrics at him every time he came to the plate.

The series seemed to be going on too long for some, too, including the players, fans and writers who had to shuffle between cities and wait out rain delays, cold weather, and the discomfort of long train rides in such a short period of time. It was continuing to rain miserably on Sunday night and prospects were slim of a game for the next day, Columbus Day, when the Americans went to the Palace Theater to see a production of *The Baby Trust*. Waldron made 100 Royal Rooters his guests and the theater was packed with people as anxious to look at them and the ballplayers as to see the play. The stage was decorated with red, white and blue bunting and shields were along the boxes where the players and Rooters sat. And there was a big sign, "Welcome, American League Champions And Boston Rooters."

Rooter Tom Wilson was asked to go on stage and sing, and he did a parody of the Americans, particularly Young, Collins and Dinneen, that brought the house down.

Then Waldron brought the Letter Carriers band on stage and they struck up a tune that made the joint jump with noise to the heart of downtown: "Tessie, you make me feel so badly, why don't you turn around...."

Lavis led the Rooters in a round of cheers and when Young and Dinneen took their seats, they were swamped with fans wanting to be near them and touch them and pat their backs. There was a feeling that the end was near for the Pirates.

By midnight the rain held and it seemed unlikely there would be a game on Monday, a break which Clarke thought may have helped the Pirates get some rest. On Monday morning, Collins awakened and looked out his hotel window and smiled as he saw the wetness. "Guess it's all off," he said to himself. He came downstairs and called to the field by telephone and was told the grounds were more suitable for a yacht race than a baseball game. He went to the field to see for himself and called Murnane at the *Globe*. "The grounds are in awful shape. We may be able to play tomorrow and we may not. A good warm sun would help out, but just now things look pretty dubious," he said.

"The boys have had a hard trip and the day's lay-off after practically 24 hours on the train will do them good and make our chances all the better for getting into the game with our best goods. Bill Dinneen never was in better shape, and with him in the box it will take just one game for us to clinch this series and win those Globe medals," Collins said.

Over at the Vendome, National League President Harry Pulliam woke up and saw the same dismal sight and came down to the lobby to talk with players and reporters. "It does not look as though the game could be played for at least two days," he said. "But the game will be played and we think two will be played, even if we have to remain in Boston until November 1. A short rest will do Pittsburg good," he said.

"We had some great games in Pittsburg and I tell you Boston played great ball. They had luck, too, but they surely put up a grand article of baseball," he said.

Pulliam, who had been crowing for the first four games, said when the game was put off on Monday he would head back to New York to conduct what he said was league business, promising to return to Boston if there was a ninth game. But before he left, a less jovial Pulliam said, "The Pittsburgs are a game lot and will fight to the last ditch. Not that the Boston boys are a bit slow. They have played splendid ball, but I still think that they would not finish ahead of Pittsburg in a season's race." And even in the bad weather, the Pirates were ready to go to the park on Monday and waited for word whether the game would be called, even as a dark, cold rain fell.

They were not notified until later in the day, which irked some of the players, especially after a report that the Americans had been told earlier in the day. Word around the city was conjecture that the late notice was a retaliation for the off-day called in Pittsburg the previous Friday by Dreyfuss. Clarke had a lot to do on the off day. At the hotel, he called the players into a corner of the lobby and told them he had met with Dreyfuss to talk about Doheny. "Boys, I'm going down to see Mrs. Doheny and her little baby. Will you all stand by me in what I do?"

There was only a slight pause before they said stolidly, but dejectedly, "Yes."

Clarke took a train ride to Andover to visit Doheny's wife and then to the state mental hospital where his pitcher had been committed. It was an awful time for the Pirates manager, who struggled to keep his composure before the ghastly looking young man who had been his star left-handed pitcher only a few weeks before. They talked softly before Doheny, surprising his manager, gave Clarke an envelope, which the Pirates manager put in his pocket after nodding in acquiescence to something Doheny said to him. It was a sad, short train ride back to Boston; Clarke sat alone on the train, watching the rain, feeling the envelope in his suit.

When he returned, Clarke was downhearted. "I had heard good reports and was hoping he would pull through all right, but from what the doctors tell me, I fear he will not play ball for some time. It is too bad. We all liked him and he was a rattling good pitcher. Still, with cares such as I know I will have, I hope he will be around for next season."

Before he had left, trying to keep his players up, Clarke had said, "We are going right out for the games and expect to land Tuesday's game. That will put us on equal terms with the Bostons. It's going to be a battle. They are due to have a change of luck. I hope that will come Tuesday. Look at the batting average of Ritchey. You cannot tell me that he has been playing his game in the batting line. He has hit the ball, but right at someone. Better breaks are sure to come to us. We had miserable breaks in the final game at Pittsburg. Boston men got the best of us in every phase."

Indeed, Ritchey had been hitting poorly for the first seven games, and things got worse for him after the seventh game when he discovered a pimple on the back of his right hand and tore at it with his fingernail, gaining an infection for his trouble and worrying whether his fielding would be affected.

Dreyfuss was more concerned now about Doheny than about the outcome. He had made sure Doheny had received his full salary for the year, even though the pitcher missed so many games and was unable to appear in the series. The Pirates had been in good health as a team for only 17 games all year and now, in the most crucial series they had ever played, they had their worst health problems. Dreyfuss tried to explain why he thought the Pirates would have prevailed with a full club without making it sound like sour grapes, but he kept coming back to Doheny, the intense competitor whose smiles were twisted with desire to win.

"There is no doubt in the world that had Doheny not been taken sick he would have won the games in which he pitched," Dreyfuss said. "Leever was really out of the game and should not have pitched at all. He contracted a cold almost a month ago. I just wish our team had its pitchers in as good a shape as the Boston men. There is no use in crying about spilt milk. All I hope is to get another crack at Collins' men next Fall and I'll promise you it will be our turn to crow," he said, almost signaling the white flag, although the Pirates still had two chances to take the series.

And, he added sadly, "It is too bad that we could not have played four games in this city at the start, then four games in Pittsburg and the odd game settled by lot. This could have been done as well as not. I cannot tell who will pitch today. The matter of selecting the pitchers lies entirely with Mr. Clarke and I never interfere with him in any manner," he said.

Dreyfuss said he would rather have lost $100,000 than lose the seventh game, and talk of a fixed series or betting having too much of an influence had faded with the intensity of the play and the passion of the players. Morse, in the *Herald*, wrote, "Every lover of the game can be assured that the conduct of the games has been beyond criticism and that each one was played strictly on its merits. Pittsburg wanted to take the series in the quickest possible time."

While much of the country was watching the outcome of the games closely, the series being a daily topic of conversation virtually everywhere, other baseball news showed how seriously the game was taken. In St. Louis, there was a report that the Cardinals were upset with their manager for calling them "malingerers," fighting words indeed for ballplayers. The *Globe-Democrat* reported:

> A number of baseball fans who will buy drinks all night if honored by the presence of a player and who revere the hand that shook the hand of a man who can hobble grounders, muff flies and strike out before the admiring gaze of thousands have been trying to work up a stream of public sympathy for the men charged by [manager] Donovan with shirking and practically throwing games all season. They are that, although it was perfectly proper for the players to shirk, it was a heinous offense for Donovan to say so. It is said that the players were justified in shirking because they had grievances. It is pointed out that the ballplayers were absolutely at the disposal and under the thumb of the club and that he had no other recourse of getting even when treated badly.

But then the paper said, in a swipe at the players:

> If he is more downtrodden and oppressed, he gets more for it than the average lawyer, doctor or minister of the gospel earns. He gets a big salary, has easy work and short hours. If it were not for baseball, the average

player would be knocking down fares or hustling vigorously for $1.30 per diem. By throwing games, for that is what shirking really means, the ball player guilty of such an offense is practically obtaining money under false pretenses for he is drawing salary for giving honest service and that is just what he is not doing. If it is justifiable to shirk because of fancied, or even real grievances, it would be also justifiable for the player to break into the office safe and take the club's money.

During the rain day, Murnane had time to contemplate the meaning of the series in the game he loved. While the Boston staff was busy lining up 100 extra police officers and getting ropes ready for the outfield crowd, he was back in the *Globe* office writing his story for the game and said he was proud that the games had attracted more than 94,000 spectators in the first seven contests. And while there was fierce competition, there had been sportsmanship and few examples of ill tempers, and even a curious kind of camaraderie had developed in the new rivalry between Boston and Pittsburg and the National and American Leagues. And, he added, the games had brought Americans together and transformed American society, creating a culture of baseball he thought would endure as a new common denominator for Americans.

"This shows that baseball is the greatest outdoor sport that has ever been known and it is thoroughly American, combining everything in the way of athletic skill, nerve, grit and honesty and all that is best in our national character," he said. Pittsburg sportswriter Pat Egan said the games had shown too that the future of both leagues was secure because of the closeness of the contests and how captivated the public was. "Ever since the American League first breached out into eastern territory it has been branded as a minor league organization in certain quarters hereabouts. These people now have a chance to see the leading team of this season in the American League perform with the champions of the National League and up to the present the Americans have the best of it," he said.

And S. Goodfriend, an old baseball writer, said: "It is the greatest series of games that has ever been played for the world's championship. Never before has there been such universal interest in a series of baseball games. No two teams were ever more evenly matched, though Boston has a present advantage in the matter of pitchers, and it is still a tossup as to which team will win out."

Toward the end of the day, Clarke was feeling a bit better and told the Boston sportswriters, "We are going to beat your chaps in the two games. There will be two games and our boys will certainly win or I am no prophet. Not only does this bad weather give us a rest, but it also affords Bostonians an opportunity to brace themselves for two days disaster. Get ready!"

By Tuesday morning, the rain had ended, but brisk winds and cool

Shortly before the start of the last game, in Boston, both teams posed for a group photograph. There were relatively few spectators in the stands because it had rained that morning and many people did not get word the game would go on (courtesy Boston Public Library).

temperatures made it a hard day for baseball. The layoff, the lengthy series, the fuss over tickets and scalping of the ducats, had worn a lot of people out, although the newspapers in both cities were still bannering their pages with stories. The *Herald* and other Boston newspapers were besieged with calls from fans wanting to know if there would be a game, but it was hard to tell early and many did not get the news until too late. One fan was so upset about the lack of ticket availability he wrote the *Globe* to complain. "I was told at all of the downtown offices that the management of the Boston-Pittsburg series had sent them no tickets and to go to the Huntington Avenue grounds." He said when he came out of the offices he saw a bunch of speculators offering tickets at $2 to $3 each, five to six times the cost.

He then went to the ballpark to try to buy tickets at 9 A.M. but said he was told the ticket seller, McBreen, had not arrived. A crowd grew to about 400 and when the McBreen arrived, he surveyed the group and promptly turned around and walked away, infuriating those waiting, who chased him out onto Huntington Avenue.

"Where are the tickets?" he was asked in hard fashion by some men, who grabbed his suit.

McBreen turned around and gulped at the anger. "Why, all the tickets have been put on sale downtown," then pulled himself away and ran off before he could be stopped.

Miller said, "Speculators were around there with their pockets full of tickets. It looks like a game of bunco as I could find no tickets by sale except speculators."

Despite the crowd at the gate and the lack of tickets — or perhaps because of it — there wasn't the rush there had been for the first three games, and much of that had to do with the lack of communication about whether the game would be played Tuesday at all. Most people in Boston felt the grounds would be too wet to play, even though the rain had stopped, and there was no way to let them know in time. If the game had been laid over a day, the crowd undoubtedly would have matched the third game swarm.

A lot of the talk about the eighth game had to do with betting. With more than $50,000 put down after the first two games, the odds hadn't changed much, nor had the amounts put down, despite some Boston windfalls in Pittsburg. American League President Ban Johnson was gambling a lot more than money. He had bet the future of his league on Collins, Young, Dinneen and the Boston bunch.

Pirates Doomed from Start

It was a wary bunch of Pirates players who made their way to the Huntington Avenue Grounds on Tuesday, October 13, 1903, showing little of the pepper they possessed 13 days earlier when they first walked onto the same field. Clarke knew his players were physically and spiritually hurting and he was worried about Doheny. He walked into the dugout and over to Phillippe, who was sitting down. Clarke had to call on the worn-out Phillippe yet again, hoping against hope his stalwart could manage one more strong game from his tired arm, but it didn't look good for the Pirates. He told Phillippe he was going with him again.

"Deacon, you're our only hope. But if you pitch as well as you have done, I'm sure the boys will start hitting behind you." And then Clarke said, "You're the only pitcher I have. You can beat those Pilgrims."

Phillippe, proud but tired, said softly, "I'll give it everything I've got."

Clarke was thinking of playing second base himself, which would put pitcher Kennedy in left field. Wagner was bone-weary and sore-armed and in poor spirits, confused over his poor play.

Collins was more robust and eager. He saw how dank the field was, and didn't know how many people would be at the game because the news had not spread throughout the city that the contest was on. "I don't care if there's 10 people at the grounds. We have as good a chance as Pittsburg and the sooner the series is over, the better for us," he said.

The stands were full again, but not as overflowing on the field as they had been during the first three games in Boston. It was a bone-chilling day for baseball, the kind of downcast October New England day that sucks the joy out of the atmosphere and was ill-suited to the summer game. You could almost hear winter whistling in the wind through your ears, but the weather hadn't dispirited McGreevey and his Rooters, who were back with the Letter Carriers Band by the Boston bench, ready to roar at what they felt confident would be victory and the world's championship.

The Pirates picked up the pace when they went out for their infield practice, putting some zip into their throws and chatting lively, trying to perk each other up, Leach and Wagner especially firing the ball hard.

When the Americans came onto the field, the band played "Mr. Dooley," but quickly broke into "Tessie" again, the song ringing in the Pirates' heads like a bad dream, a hangover that wouldn't end. When Cy Young came out to hit grounders to the infielders, the rooters began yelling, "Hobble, gobble, hobble, gobble, sis, boom, bah. Boston. Boston. Rah! Rah! Higgledy, piggledy, ain't we nice? The Pittsburg bunch will cut no ice!"

Then McGreevey jumped out and, as the band played "In The Good Old Summertime," to try to instill some warmth into the air, began twirling the parasol he got in Pittsburg and he led the crowd in singing. About a dozen of the Rooters ran onto the field near the first base line and began a joyous cakewalk, one of them carrying the McGillicuddy calling card, "Are Ye There?" on a sign.

There were far fewer people in the outfield for this game, nothing like the swarm on the field for game three, but the stands were still jammed when umpires O'Day and Connolly gathered the managers at home plate at 3 P.M. It was time for baseball again. Dinneen would have to face the two left-handed hitters, Beaumont and Clarke, at the top of the order. Boston's big pitcher was working with the skin of the index finger of his pitching hand having peeled off from so much work and each throw triggered a new burst of pain, but he had put that aside.

Beaumont dug in for the first pitch and the crowd quieted. Dinneen fired a fastball for a strike as the crowd roared again. This is what they had come to see and they wanted more. But Dinneen threw two pitches for balls as Beaumont stepped out to assay the scene. Boston's big right-hander reared back and threw two fastballs past the startled Beaumont, who walked slowly back to the bench. Boston was in good form, it seemed already. "Dinneen must be right to dispose of that boy so easily," an unhappy Pirates fan sitting near Murnane said.

The pressure was intense on all, as the players knew one false move could end their hopes. It was the unkindest kind of stress to put on a man because, unlike the opening games when there was always a chance for redemption or a comeback, a miscue today could prove a finality. The players were tense and pressing. Manager Clarke stepped in eagerly and whacked two fastballs foul. On Dinneen's next pitch, Clarke screamed a line drive that seemed to fly over the head of Parent at shortstop, but the little fielder leapt as high as he could and snared it in his tiny glove, not much bigger than his hand, and a sure hit was taken away. Leach flied out to Stahl and it was a 1–2–3 inning.

In Boston's first, Dougherty hit the second ball from Phillippe deep to center, but the speedy Beaumont sprinted more than 100 feet to take it on the deep run, rivaling Parent's play. Collins singled but Sebring stopped the ball before it could roll into the crowd in right and, after Stahl hit deeply to center for an out, Freeman flied out to Clarke. The Pirates were heartened and the Americans were no threat in that inning. Nor through the next two, as both teams failed to score.

Then came the fateful fourth.

Dinneen had retired the first nine men he faced with ease, in perfect form. In the top of the fourth, Beaumont hit weakly to Ferris and was thrown out. Clarke hit a fly ball that landed just foul as he thought he was heading for a hit, but was called back to the plate, his face twisted in disgust. With two strikes on the Pirate manager, Dinneen whistled one by him to strike him out. It was too much for Clarke. He threw his bat viciously and swore, a phrase that Murnane described as, "something not taught at Sunday school."

But then Leach walked. And then Wagner singled to left for the Pirates' first hit and Leach went to third. The great Wagner, weary and worried, knew he had to make a big play here. He would find a way to beat Boston the same way he had with everyone else. With his feet. With Dinneen worried now about Bransfield at the plate, Wagner suddenly broke for second on a delayed steal, disparaging catcher Criger's ability to catch him with a throw, hoping to draw a toss so Leach could go home on a double-steal and score.

Then Criger, almost run out of town after his first game series of errors, saved the inning. He bluffed a throw to catch Wagner at second with a wicked swing of his arm that seemed to signal a rifle throw, but he stopped, wheeled to his left, and fired to Collins at third to pick off a surprised Leach, who was caught flatfooted and tried to make a break for home. But Collins fired to Criger who caught Leach dead to rights.

The play almost brought tears to Clarke's eyes as he saw the championship slip away on a play by the man who had made three errors in the first inning of the first game and who had been pilloried by the Boston press and

Tommy Leach: third baseman and outfielder, 1900–1912 (courtesy Carnegie Library, Pittsburgh).

fans. McGreevey was waving his megaphone over his head as the band played and the crowd screamed from one end of the field to the other. It was a disheartened group of Pirates who left the field in the fourth. And it would get worse for them in the bottom of the inning. Clarke was counting on the gallant Phillippe to again hold off Boston until the Pirates could somehow get to Dinneen, who had mystified them all series.

By now, the crowd in the outfield was getting restless and had moved closer to the infield, pushing the ropes with them. It was their closeness in the previous games in Boston that had cost the Americans when some Pirate fly balls that would have been easy outs landed in the crowd for ground-rule triples. Now that would come back to hurt the Pirates.

The hard-hitting Freeman, who had started the first two games on a tear but had settled down to bat .266 so far, opened the inning with a long fly ball to centerfield, which landed in the crowd to give him a triple. Now the Boston fans were on their feet and the Royal Rooters were singing along with the Letter Carriers Band. The skies remained cloudy, the air windy, and the sense of rain remained. October was fading fast, and, with it, baseball, but everyone present would savor this last gasp at the Huntington Avenue Grounds. They couldn't know that October would become a month for baseball fortunes as important as the summer itself.

The little Parent, who had been an irritant to the Pirates the whole series, hit a little dribbler in front of the plate and made a mad dash down the first base line as catcher Phelps, hurling off his mask, leaped in front of the plate to grab the ball. His hands cold and fumbling, he muffed the ball and Parent reached first, although Freeman had to hold at third.

LaChance, sensing destiny now, hit a hard grounder to Bransfield at first and the tableau was frozen on the field for a moment, Parent taking off from first, Freeman edging down the third base line, catcher Phelps blocking the plate, Phillippe watching, the second baseman Ritchey running toward first to cover the bag, the fans in the stands on their feet intent on the action.

Bransfield grabbed the ball and whirled toward third as if to try to catch Freeman off the bag, knowing that was the lead run in a cold dead ball game in which the Pirates could not afford to fall behind. Then the Pirate first baseman whirled again and threw to Ritchey at first to catch LaChance just in time. There was no out and no score yet. Phillippe could breathe easier and bear down now. The lanky right-hander who had been the Pirates' stalwart stepped back onto the mound, this time to a crescendo of noise from the Boston fans and the maniacal McGreevey, and the ever present "Tessie."

But now there were men on second and third and the light-hitting Ferris was at the plate. He had managed a respectable .266 against Phillippe in the four games he had faced the Pirate hurler, but was the seventh man in the line-up because he was respected more for his glove than his bat. He stepped in and dug in and eyed Phillippe warily. Phillippe reared back and fired a fastball. Ferris hit a clean line drive to center field, Freeman and Parent dashed home with the lead runs and the Americans were up 2–0. The Pirates were pounding their gloves in fury and frustration. How could this happen? Wasn't it only 13 days ago on the same field they had laid claim to superiority; perhaps being the greatest of all baseball teams ever?

The noise of the crowd and the singing of the Rooters pounding in his head, Phillippe got Criger to ground out as Ferris made second. Now there were two out and the pitcher, Dinneen, was coming up. But he surprised Phillippe, hitting a hard line drive single to right as Ferris, breathing hard, rounded third and roared home, trying to build the lead and end the Pirate dreams in one inning. The Pirates had something left, though. The swift Sebring, a hero throughout the series, came charging hard and scooped the ball and threw it home on the fly. Ferris slid home on the hard, cold surface and Phelps caught the throw and moved down in the same motion, putting the tag on to catch Ferris a yard before he touched home plate. The Pirates were still in it.

But they couldn't touch Dinneen, who had shut them out in the second game and was still overpowering them with his fastball, and catching them off guard with an unpredictable darting curve that had them lunging. The afternoon was waning fast now, the air was colder, and the October light was fading to a surreal gray, blending with the crowd of men in their monochromatic gray and black suits and hats; it was hard to find a dot of color anywhere. With two out in the top of the fifth, Sebring drove a fierce liner to left. Dougherty misjudged the ball and the rabbit-like Sebring scooted to third. If only the Pirates could score now, they could put the dent in Dinneen. But the big Boston pitcher fanned Phelps.

The Pirates tried again in the sixth. They were playing on pride now: Phillippe hurt, Clarke still ailing, Ritchey's hand hurting. Phillippe tried to help his own cause by opening with a sharp single to left. The top of the order was coming up. Beaumont feigned a bunt with Collins closing in on him at the plate like a cat preying on an unsuspecting mouse. With two strikes on him, Beaumont didn't dare bunt and whiffed on a slow drop that caught him unawares. And, as he had in the fourth when he picked off Leach, Criger suddenly stood with the third strike and rifled a throw to first, LaChance grabbing it and tagging out Phillippe, blocking the bag as the Pirate pitcher, who had been leaning toward second, tried futilely to return.

It was a signal to celebrate, and the Rooters wouldn't miss a beat. The Pirates had been vexed at every turn today and they would have to again endure "Tessie" as the entire crowd joined in the jubilee, not stopping their singing even when Clarke singled, only to see Leach fly out to Dougherty and end the inning.

In the bottom of the sixth inning, with two out, LaChance hit a long fly ball to right field that landed in the crowd for an automatic triple. Phillippe had pitched well, remarkably so in his fifth game in less than two weeks. The Americans were not scorching him, but their hits were timely and their luck better today. It was LaChance's first triple of the series, but it made him the seventh Boston player — excluding only Criger — to have a three-bagger, aided, of course, by the ground rules and the surging crowd that refused to back up.

And back up came Ferris, the hero of the day and a real hoodoo for Phillippe. He promptly singled to right to score LaChance and give Boston a 3–0 lead, a cushion that seemed safe the way the Pirates were playing against Dinneen. But the Americans were taking nothing for granted, even as the pressure built in the game's last innings. As he trotted out to third for the top of the seventh, Collins pounded his glove and yelled out to his players: "Hold 'em boys!" Dinneen had been firing so hard that the crack of the ball in Criger's mitt could be heard in the outfield, and he worked quickly.

Collins had decided to have Young warm up with Farrell, and the two men had to go out past the crowd, through an alley, to the back of the grandstand, where they could find some room to throw. But it meant they couldn't watch the game and had to rely on the crowd noise and Farrell running out between innings to take a peek at what was happening.

Dinneen got the first two outs before Ritchey worked a walk. But Sebring hit the ball right back at the Boston pitcher for an easy out and Clarke again saw the beginning of a potential rally die. Phillippe got Boston out in the bottom of the seventh and Dinneen continued his mastery in the top of the eighth. The game was moving swiftly now and, after Boston went out in the bottom of the eighth, the Pirates were down to their last three outs. Dreyfuss was trying to hide his anxiety and the newspapermen in the stands were running back to the telegraph operators, sensing the end. The idea that had burgeoned in the heat of the summer and had come to fruition in the fall with the champions of the two major leagues meeting was pulsing toward its finish.

Clarke was the first man up for the Pirates' last chance in the last inning. Farrell walked out from behind the grandstand and came back to get Young to watch the drama unfold. Farrell told him, "Bill will stay all right. Now watch him burn them over." The entire crowd was standing now but the Pirate manager had proved a hard out and he was desperate now, even though Dinneen was throwing so hard the ball seemed like a pill. Dinneen threw a real stinger, but Clarke whacked it even harder, lining the ball viciously to left field toward Dougherty, who scampered hard for it and pulled it in like corralling a ball at the end of a rope.

The Pirates were fidgeting in their dugout, the VIPs behind the ropes

In Boston, there was a roped off area for celebrities, politicians, and Royal Rooters (courtesy Boston Public Library).

along the first and third-base lines were leaning forward in anticipation now, the Rooters were standing in unison and singing and waving their megaphones and parasols, the noise reaching above the grounds like a cloud shot aloft. Some of the Pirates fans in the left field bleachers broke out in shouts of "Pittsburg!"

Leach stepped in. Dinneen threw. A fly ball was lofted to Freeman in right, who took it in stride. The Pirates were down to their final out as a solitary figure stepped to the plate, his stance and manner a familiar sight to all in the crowd.

It was Honus Wagner.

And as he stepped in, a final act of grace was paid, even as he had suffered the ignominy of failure in his greatest test. Still regarded as the perhaps greatest player in the game, he was treated with respect, all the more so because his rivals had known what it was like to face him in a battle on the ball field.

Because it was Wagner, the crowd noise stopped. The band stopped. It was the greatest moment in baseball and everyone, it seemed, sensed it and seized the destiny. Wagner was getting to bat in near silence, made all the more momentous because the noise that preceded was deafening. His last battle with Dinneen, unless he could start a rally, would be almost in solitude, the two men facing each other alone in the midst of 8,000 people holding their breaths, and hundreds of thousands more across the country standing outside hotels and barber shops and newspapers, watching the telegraphed results posted for all to see, each strike causing a skip in their heartbeats. They looked at the scores being posted, at the out-by-out recounting of a part of history, mesmerized by the digits, caught up in the spectacle of the event that had been the table talk in homes, offices, coffee shops and wherever people gathered.

From one end of the United States to the other, in baseball cities in both leagues, in little coal towns outside Pittsburg, places like those where Wagner grew up, in neighborhoods where the ballplayers had taken their first swings, in dense inner-city streets, in the open fields outside St. Louis where little boys mimicked Wagner's bow-legged stance or threw stones at barn walls pretending to be Cy Young, where they ran along rutted dirt paths in stony fields threw together sacks for bases, men and women and young boys and girls stood as silent as those at the Huntington Avenue Baseball Grounds waited for the climax to the greatest sporting event the country had ever known.

Wagner dug in with his spikes. His gentle countenance, which sometimes made him seem sad or reserved, was replaced now with a grim determination. It was again all on his shoulders, as it had been since he came to the Pirates and made their name synonymous with the best baseball had to offer. Staring back at him, his hair slick with sweat even in the disappearing light and onrushing chill, was Dinneen. The talk before the series had been all about Young, and during the series it was about Phillippe, but Dinneen had come on to be the pitcher who knew how to seize a high ground of drama and who reveled in it.

At stake now in their personal duel was the championship of the world, bragging rights for cities and leagues and men for whom competition was more important than the big reward of money they would be getting, their thoughts of dollars replaced now with the same sense of excitement and joy they'd felt as boys playing on makeshift fields, as young men barnstorming through small towns. This was baseball at its purest and the legions of fans at the game and waiting across the country were caught up in it now too.

Dinneen looked hard at Wagner, who looked back with equal grit. The Boston pitcher fired, and Wagner took a grand swing that missed. Now the crowd was back in it, roaring for Dinneen, while Pittsburg's boys moaned.

"Strike him out!" came a roar from the stands.

Dinneen worked Wagner carefully, but the count went to 3-and-2, to what could be the last pitch of the last inning of the first World Series, and the entire crowd was standing, the outfield crowd moving toward the infield, sensing the end. Wagner dug in harder, Dinneen wiped his brow and looked toward home plate.

A new serenade started now in the stands. "Strike him out!" the Boston fans screamed.

In the stands, Murnane was watching and writing furiously, angry at all those who thought betting and talks of the games being rigged had tainted them ever so little; this being spread by people who, unlike him and those on the field, had never had the opportunity to play at the major league level. "The players had heard the wildcat stories of how the series had been fixed. It was the same obscenity started by thoughtless people and cold-blooded enemies of the national sport. It was an insult to the sport, and as far from the truth as Deer Island [in Boston Harbor] is from the North Pole," he wrote.

But all Dinneen and Wagner could think about now was the next pitch.

Murnane described it. "Dinneen got a firm foothold and then started a short easy preliminary swing to the music of 8,000 heartbeats. The Boston boy increased the speed of his swing as his long arm cut a circle for the second time and then with all the force at his command, he shot the ball across the plate, past Wagner's chest and into Criger's hands."

But Wagner was ready too, and he took a mighty swing, the force of which could be felt from Boston to Pittsburg, a blow for baseball that was being watched across America, his strong shoulders tearing around, the bow-legs straightening, the power rippling through him as if it would be the last time he swung a bat, the ball seeming like a will-o'-the-wisp, it was coming so fast.

Years later, those who were there would remember the moment. The mighty Wagner had struck out, the ball cracking into Criger's mitt with a resounding finale to the draining, wearying series and the efforts of men who had put their being into playing and winning. It was 4:40 P.M. on Tuesday, October 13, 1903; the dusk was rushing toward the field faster than a Dinneen fastball, the cold of autumn right behind it.

Criger threw the ball high into the air and pandemonium erupted, the crowds pouring out of the stands at once, the outfield crowds rushing the players, Wagner the lone Pirate left on the playing field as he tried to turn and shrink away. The roar sounded, Murnane said, "as if a thousand lions were doing their prettiest." It could be heard across Boston, and then across the land as the sportswriters rushed for the telegraph wires, the invisible clicking and clacking of sound waves being translated into the result for the millions in other cities and towns to see.

Dinneen had won his third game of the series and his second shutout and had come through with his best. He had given up only four hits, walked only two and struck out seven, his fastball besting the Pirates all afternoon.

Jerry Watson, one of the leaders of the Royal Rooters, took to a dugout top to wave the flag and scream in joy after Boston won another game. He was among the most rabid of the fans (courtesy Boston Public Library).

The Boston fans poured out onto the field—jubilant, singing, shrieking, dancing and fighting for the chance to touch their heroes. They picked up every player, put them on their shoulders of fans, and carried them around the field.

The Rooters' Watson danced on the dugout roof with an American flag while the band picked up its pieces and stormed the field as well, surrounding the fans holding the players aloft. "Everyone in the crowd seemed anxious to secure one of the victorious players as a human souvenir," Murnane wrote.

Wagner got a single in the game; his only hit in his last 14 times up, to finish at .214 for the eight games, and he had six errors. The gallant Phillippe had pitched five complete games but lost the last two. Still, he came out of the dugout and looked for Collins, and offered his hand in congratulation. It was taken, before Collins was hoisted up too.

People were tearing at Collins now, trying to grab and touch. His cap fell off and his uniform was torn and he was surprised to look down to see he was astride the shoulders of one of the city's leading politicians, smiling back up at him. As Collins bobbed and weaved on the shoulders, he could look across a sea of people and see his teammates being held similarly high, trying to keep their balance as they were carried across the infield toward the dressing room, their hats gone too, waving their arms high in victory, the band sounding louder than ever now, "Tessie" being played again, as if to follow the Pirates out of the park, back to their hotel, onto the train, all the way to Pittsburg, and for the rest of their lives.

One player was missing though, and he was making a mad dash through the crowd trying to escape when he was spotted and someone yelled, "Get him! Get him! My gosh! Get him! It's Ferris!" Hobe Ferris was hoping to be overlooked in the chaos, but a fat man with a megaphone had seen him and alerted the crowd, which swirled toward him like hyenas on a wounded animal. Ferris was quickly picked up by a group of people and paraded around like the rest of the Americans.

Ferris and Dinneen were the heroes of the day and the fans wanted them to know it. Ferris had hit .290 and had five runs-batted-in, but the last three were the most important. He was ridden back and forth until his wife, in the grandstand, almost became hysterical, fearing he would be hurt, and she screamed for him, but it couldn't be heard in the din and the dusk.

Parent was getting favorably rough treatment too, the mob in approbation that his first inning leap to take away a hit had set the tone for the rest of the game. Criger was being carried around too, but Murnane thought the little catcher, who started the series so badly, who labored under rumors of taking a fix, had resurrected himself in the final game with his pickoffs of Leach at third and Phillippe at first. He showed why he was Cy Young's only choice as catcher.

Not seen were the Pirates, a sad, silent bunch, pride shattered, gray uniforms dirty with defeat, the sweat cooling to chills with the twilight autumn air. They limped away across the field, hoping not to be seen, although Dreyfuss stood in the stands and watched them, his heart heavy too. Wagner's whole body was in pain, Clarke was limping, Phillippe was sore-armed. Clarke was crying openly.

Murnane felt for them. He thought they were probably done when Killilea and Dreyfuss agreed to the series when the Pirates' pitching staff was being decimated by injuries and he knew, as a former player, the despair settling in on them. "These boys had not flinched from the issue when two of their pitchers fell by the wayside, leaving only Phil. Beaten not disgraced was Pittsburg, and her tears were manly," he would write.

The Pirates, still in uniform, made their way back to the Hotel Vendome, coming into a now quiet lobby, heads down. There was no longer a taunting crowd. The jovialities and niceties were dispensed with and they wanted only to be together and then to be alone. But there was one more matter to be conducted. Clarke had left behind the mysterious envelope given him by Doheny and he told Ritchey to go to the lobby desk to get it. The other Pirates, heads down, didn't see him, as they waited for their room keys.

The letter was addressed to him in a neat, feminine hand — Mrs. Doheny's. Ritchey, bedraggled and down, opened it carefully. As he did, two $1 bills fluttered to the floor, landing softly amidst the gray uniforms and cleats.

Inside was a note. "Eddie said he owed you $2 and asked me to pay you. Here it is," she had written.

Ritchey stifled a sob and handed the note to Clarke, who looked at it as the rest of the Pirates watched.

"Poor Eddie," he said, returning the note sadly. "I hope they don't tell him where he is that we've lost the championship," Clarke said.

Ritchey headed for the elevator, but stopped and said, "I hope they'll tell him, anyway, that he or his family can have anything I have."

He hadn't read aloud the letter because there was more. It told of how Doheny had gone mad and attacked his nurse and how, as he was being taken away to the mental hospital, had turned to his wife and said "I owe only $2, that to Claude Ritchey. Won't you pay him?"

Phil Sorry He Lost Two

Dreyfuss, stung, was gracious nonetheless. "Boston won on her merits as the teams stood. I wish we had had our full string of pitchers. I say this, not to detract, but in simple justice to my own. I am as proud of them as if they had won every game of the series." And, he added, "The Boston club has won the World's Championship squarely, playing the cleanest kind of baseball ... my confidence in my team remains unshaken, for no one knows better than I what a game fight my players put up under most distressing conditions ... next year I hope it will be our good fortune to engage in a similar series with a different result."

That night, both teams went to the Colonial Theater and received a rousing ovation from the audience. Dreyfuss put on an informal banquet for his team and the Pittsburg sportswriters at the Vendome, and made his announcement about giving the players all the money. Almost forgotten now was the yeoman performance of Phillippe, who had almost single-handedly defeated the American League champions with his three victories and five complete games in less than two weeks, under trying conditions and in bad weather too. Phillippe, though, still thought he had let down the Pirates fans.

"I have nothing to regret, save that I lost two of my five games," he said in a statement to the fans. "The players of the Pittsburg team fought bitterly and under fearful odds. I am glad it is over and sorry we lost. My arm is numb and I am tired. A dull pain has been in my right arm since this bad weather set in. It did not hurt me when in the box, but on the bench it bothered me like a toothache. I believe I have caught a bad cold in my arm," he said.

Ban Johnson could barely contain his delight. Collins had kept his promise to win against the team regarded as the best in baseball and brought the championship to the American League, insuring its prosperity and acceptance, but even Johnson was amazed at the unbridled popularity of the series and how it had ingrained itself into the fabric of life. There could be no going back now.

He used the opportunity to crow about the style of ball played in his league, proclaiming it cleaner than the roughhousing of the National League, although during the series both teams had gone at each other ferociously on the field, but were sportsmen afterward.

"Clean ball is the main plank of the American League," Johnson said. "There must be no profanity on the ball field. The umpires are agents of the league and must be treated with respect." He ordered his owners to make sure their stadiums were patrolled to keep down rowdiness, an act that would bring in new audiences and spread the game to a growing population attracted by the sensational reception of the series.

The speech didn't get unanimous acceptance in baseball, and would come back a year later to cause problems for Johnson. One sportswriter declared that Johnson was guilty of self-aggrandizement and said, "Ban Johnson never missed an opportunity to make a speech. It was always the same speech: all about how he, single-handed and alone, had made baseball a gentleman's sport, and it must be kept forever clean because sportsmanship spoke from the heart of America and he would lay down his life to save our beloved nation, at which he would begin to cry."

And Johnson's old foe, McGraw, who had jumped to the American League only to jump back after confrontations with Johnson, pooh-poohed the American League president. McGraw had been fined several times for baiting umpires and encouraging his players to start brawls, which he would join as one of the game's best scrappers. After McGraw was ejected from his last American League game, Johnson took a shot at him and said, "I am glad [the umpire ejected] and humiliated McGraw. Rowydism will not be tolerated ... and the men who disregard the organization rules must suffer the consequences."

Sportswriter Francis Richter said, "The public is bound to hail both teams as the very best exemplars of the one great, clean and honest national sport. In all respects has the great World Series been a credit to and good thing for the game of baseball."

A Pittsburg paper reported that:

> the games between the two clubs meant something more even than the supremacy of the Boston American league club over the National, for it was claimed by many that Pittsburg had the better team and that the American teams as a whole were inferior to those of the National League. Consequently, almost every National League rooter rooted for Pittsburg and every American league rooter for Boston. It is the first championship that has been contested for between a National League club and an American league club, and it has been the greatest thing for baseball known in years.

The criticism was swift and predictable and hurtful for the three-time pennant winners from Pittsburg, even though Clarke had a decimated pitching staff that was far from the group that had thrown 56 consecutive scoreless innings that summer. Some writers and fans felt Clarke should have used Leever more, and there was antagonism against Chesbro and Tannehill for jumping the club after the 1902 season.

Pittsburg sportswriter Ralph Davis wrote that he still didn't think Boston was a better team. "It is a pity that the Pittsburg pitchers were not right for the Series, for, under the present circumstance, there will always be a doubt in the minds of the fans whether Collins' team could have triumphed had the local twirlers been at their best. For myself, I do not think they could."

And, both sides agreed that the loss of Doheny was perhaps the most critical factor in swaying how the series concluded. Both sides praised the work of Dinneen and Phillippe, who had overshadowed virtually everyone else. The other stars were Sebring, who hit the first home run in the first game and finished with an average of .367, and Chick Stahl at .303. Wagner, who had led the National League in extra-base hits, managed only one in eight games in the series and committed six errors, leading to several key unearned Boston runs that helped turn the series. It was a performance he would have to live with for the rest of his career, and one that would grate on him all the rest of his years in a Pirates uniform.

Dinneen had two shutouts and four complete games, while Young had two victories. Phillippe, even in defeat, had thrown 44 innings in two weeks, had thrown five complete games, and had walked only three batters for World Series records that would stand for a century.

For the Americans, the heroes were Dinneen, with his three victories, and Young, who garnered the other two. Ferris, besides his hits to win the final game, had finished at .290 with six runs batted in. Freeman and Parent had both hit .281. Young had an earned run average of 1.59, while Dinneen, with his two shutouts, posted a 2.06 ERA and, more importantly, had been untouchable in the last game.

The Pirates had fared miserably in hitting, having only a .237 team batting average that, coupled with their sore-armed and star-crossed pitching staff, had been their undoing. Leach had hit .273, and Beaumont and Clarke .265 each. But, besides Wagner's .222, Bransfield hit only .207 and Ritchey was the worst, with only three hits in 27 at-bats for a .111 average, worse even than the pitchers. The Pirates had been outscored 39–24, including 28–8 since the appearance of "Tessie" in the fourth game, and Phillippe had been the only pitcher to win any games for them.

It didn't help the Pirates' demeanor the next morning, October 14, when they awoke to prepare for the trip home and saw the Boston newspapers. The *Herald* banner was "Boston Americans Champions of World," proclaiming almost exactly what the *Globe* and other papers did.

Murnane wrote, "Never were ball players more bent on winning a game, and the spectators will have a story to tell about the most important game ever played and won since the sport was introduced at the Elysian fields of Hoboken in 1845."

At 10:40 A.M. on Wednesday, the Pittsburg Pirates and officials and rooters entered a special railroad car for the return trip. Before they left, Dreyfuss gathered them for something to eat and told them he had an announcement. "I told you I would give you all the net receipts of the series if we won. It was not your fault that we did not win, and now I want to tell you that I am going to give you exactly what you would have received had you won, and you will get your checks as soon as possible after you arrive in Pittsburg," Dreyfuss said as the players applauded.

The series, after all, had been a huge financial success too, with more than 100,400 paid admissions, bringing in $55,500 in revenue. Each Pirate would get a check for $1,316.25 while the Americans got $1,182.18. Killilea kept his share of $6,699.65.

"The boys deserved it," Dreyfuss told Clarke. "They've won three pennants for me and they stuck by me during the American League raids. I'm glad to do it."

There was unanimity about one other thing. No one was going to sing "Tessie" on the long train ride back to Pittsburg.

The Pirates arrived back in Pittsburg on Thursday morning, October 15. This time there was no fanfare and that afternoon they gathered at the club offices to get their share of the revenues Dreyfuss had promised. It was a handsome take for all, and Krueger and team secretary W.H. Locke were voted full shares, but Locke refused his. Partial shares went to trainer Ed LaForce, groundskeeper John Murphy and newcomers Thompson and Carisch, and to Doheny. Each married player's check was made out to his wife, which caused some grousing among the men.

Dreyfuss told them, "Your wife's stockings are longer than yours." He added later, "I'm tired of this business of the boys getting money and spending it. There are a lot of married boys who don't know how to save money, but their wives do. I'm for that hearthstone, and if any of the boys want to get sore because I made out checks to their wives [they] can influence their wives to return the checks to me. I'll take the money back. There are some of these thrice-champion Pittsburg team who have no more sense of the value of money than a rabbit. They've got to learn."

Dreyfuss then walked over to his safe and pulled out some papers and carried them over to Phillippe. "I have something else for you, Phil," he said.

"Here are 10 shares of railroad stock which I want to give to the player who would have pitched all the games for us if we would have let him, and would have won them all if he could," he said, producing a torrent of applause from the players and glad feelings all around, almost erasing the bitter tea of defeat they had been forced to drink.

Locke stepped up to Dreyfuss and told him the players had something for him. Locke gave Dreyfuss a split-second watch engraved with each of their names on the back, and he gulped, almost overcome with the gesture. He stared at it as the Pirates looked at him and Locke said,

> Deeply as we regret the defeat suffered at the hands of the Boston team in the struggle for the world's championship, we cannot but admire the spirit of true sportsmanship shown at the finish by yourself, and we are all convinced that the sporting world has at last produced something which hitherto did not exist — a good loser. Your kind offer at the close of the season, made in spite of the fact that your team had been beaten is appreciated by the players to an extent that cannot be expressed in words, and as a token I have the pleasure of presenting to you on their behalf this handsome timepiece. Its value is nothing compared with the well wishes that go with it.

Dreyfuss was dumbstruck. He stood still, holding the watch, looking at it, trying unsuccessfully to hold back a tear as the Pirates looked at him, sheepish with emotion themselves. Dreyfuss finally looked up and looked from one player to the other, plainly surprised at the gift.

"I had not the least suspicion of any such scheme on your part, boys. What I did was no more than right, for I know you fought to the last ditch under a handicap that few teams have ever experienced. No one not on the inside can realize the conditions under which the series was played, for in addition to the fact that we had only one pitcher in shape for work, there was hardly a sound man on the team. I shall prize this handsome gift as long as I live and cannot express my thanks in words," he said.

Then Dreyfuss turned and walked toward a window so the players would not see him cry, made all the harder when they burst into singing "For He's A Jolly Good Fellow."

Dreyfuss went back to looking at his watch and fooling with it, trying for a while to get it running because it had a complicated split-second watch hand. Finally, exasperated, he yelled, "Fred!" calling for Clarke.

The manager came over. "What is it, Barney?"

"How the hell do you get this watch going?" he said forcefully. Clarke laughed.

They also gave Clarke a watch and charm, and the Pirate manager repeated the tearful scene of Dreyfuss, worn out, worn down, hurt and sad and now glad. It was an emotional meeting because the players knew it would be the last time they would see each other until the next season. Dreyfuss had made sure that the missing Pirates were taken care of too. A check was sent to Mrs. Doheny and another to Otto Krueger, who had been badly hurt when beaned by a pitched ball late in the season. Brickyard Kennedy insisted not on a check, but cash, including a $1,000 bill. "This is more money that I ever had in all my life," he said.

The emotional gathering had other ramifications. Clarke had been on the outs with Dreyfuss during the latter part of the season because the manager's contract was up and he wanted more than the owner was willing to pay for the 1904 season. But the hurt ended when Dreyfuss rewarded Clarke with a new three-year contract worth $7,500 per year, 50 percent more than the $5,000 deals Wagner would earn each of the next four years under his contract. It made Clarke one of the best-paid players in history at that time.

It didn't hurt Dreyfuss to be generous. The Pirates drew 326,000 fans in 1903, up more than 80,000 from the year before, and giving him a profit of $60,000, second only to the Giants' $100,000 in the National League. Dreyfuss, besides giving up his World Series share, also lost an estimated $7,000 in wagers on the games, a large sum indeed, but a lot less than one Pirate gambler, Shad Gwilliam, who reportedly dropped more than $29,000.

Locke said later, "Clarke and Dreyfuss have been working together for 11 years and they never had a serious disagreement. In all that time Clarke was never released, which is a record unparalleled in baseball history." He said the players were disappointed to lose, but not disconsolate. "We are not complaining. Boston won and their team certainly played baseball."

Clarke, delighted with his watch and charm — and new contract — left that night for his farm in Winfield, Kansas. Before he did, he said, "I have signed again with Pittsburg; this time for life, that is, my baseball life."

He also said he thought the Pirates would do very well the next year and that their future was good:

> I think it is very bright. We will have just as good a bunch as we had this year and I believe that means that we will win the pennant again, but I do not believe we will have any more trouble winning the pennant again for the fourth time than we had cinching it this year. Our infield and outfield will be the same as they were this year. I know of no changes in them. The only new faces will be in the pitching and catching departments. We may have a new catcher and we will have several new pitchers. We have some good, young twirlers signed and one or two of them should certainly show class. They, in addition to Phillippe and Leever, should be able to pull us through. It is difficult to tell much about a youngster in advance. It requires several weeks of championship work to show what is in them. But I am sure we have some comers.

Beaumont left for Wisconsin, Leach to Cleveland, Phelps to Albany, New York; Sebring and Veil to Williamsport, Pennsylvania; and Brickyard Kennedy to Ohio, his career over. Wagner had only to go a few miles to Carnegie, but the games went with him. For Wagner, the games didn't end in his mind or in those of the fans and media of Pittsburg, where he was an icon and sports hero. His teammates would be states away, but he had to read the Pittsburg papers every day about his failure.

The Sporting News crucified him with a story entitled "Hans Wagners' Showing in World Series a Blot on the Great Player's Record." The paper's correspondent, a Boston writer, declared that "while Wagner is a fast, gingery player he is not a wonder as regards courage." It was perhaps the most stinging rebuke of all, especially when it continued, "I am half inclined to think he has some yellow in him." The Pittsburg press was kinder to the man they still revered, but McQuiston wrote, "What would have happened if Wagner had batted at his usual clip in these games? We would have beaten them even though we had but one pitcher. But Wagner didn't."

Wagner wanted nothing but to go back to Carnegie and forget what had happened, but he told sportswriter Hugh S. Fullerton he was more upset about what his failure had meant to his teammates. "I wouldn't mind it for myself— but the boys deserved to win." He felt personally responsible for the defeat of the Pirates and the hurt still stung in Pittsburg. He would get his chance to redeem himself in a few years.

The *Post*'s Gruber took the loss harder than did many of the Pirates. He wrote on the way home, "The Pittsburg champions are hastening toward the Smoky City, but not like a team that has been beaten for the world's championship, but like winners." Gruber characterized the Pirates as gallant losers who were jolly in defeat and the Americans as avaricious mercenaries who wanted the money more than the pride or the glory. "The Boston men beat their way to the box office to ascertain the size of the crowd and the amount of the receipts. The Bostons fairly lived in the box office and wanted to know the amount of the receipts to the last penny. It has even been hinted that they were hand-in-glove with the speculators who fleeced the public vigorously and charged 10 and 15 cents for a poorly printed score card."

The Boston players got their money on Thursday, October 15, about 2:30 P.M., each handed a check. Collins got a call from state Senator Michael Sullivan, who said a grand banquet had been planned for the team at Faneuil Hall, the great place where planning for the American Revolution had been done, but Collins said the players were all ready to leave for home. They were worn out and did not want to attend, although he said they appreciated the gesture.

Criger had something as valuable as the check. It was the ball Dinneen threw for the last out and the last strike to Wagner, the Pirate great. It was bloodstained, as Dinneen's finger was bleeding at the time. The ball would travel with him to his home in Elkhart, Indiana.

Some doubts lingered about whether all the games had been on the up-and-up, although Boston's victory seemed to erode any validity that Criger or even Young had been reached by the gamblers. The criticism of Criger's play in the first game didn't jibe with his claim that he had been approached by the gamblers only after the first few games in Boston, and Young had been a workhorse on the mound. Collins snapped at a *Boston Post* sportswriter after the victory. "We won ... the games have been cleanly played, and no one can say otherwise.... Our victory should make those 'knockers' ashamed of themselves. It is impossible for baseball to be played dishonestly," he said.

For all the pandemonium during the series and right after the last game, though, there was no citywide celebration that matched the mood of the event while it was going on. *The Sporting News* criticized McGreevey, who had fired up his rooters during the games, as being just another businessman trying to get customers for his drinking saloon. "Some of the head people worked it for all it was worth and one cheap guy who runs a cheap barroom near the ball grounds schemed it out for a big ad and a big drinkfest at his saloon. He had the band and some of the Rooters headed over toward his gin mill before the rooters were wise," the paper said. The Boston and Pittsburg papers had a bonanza, though, with the intense interest the games had brought.

Many of the players had lost weight during the grueling series; Criger dropped six pounds and Cy Young eight pounds. But now they had all winter to get fat and get ready to play in 1904. Buck Freeman headed home to Wilkes-Barre, Pennsylvania, and Tom Hughes went to Chicago. Collins was going to Buffalo and Chick Stahl to Fort Wayne, Indiana. LaChance had already settled in at his home in Waterbury, Connecticut, while Patsy Dougherty headed for Troy, New York, where O'Brien also lived. Ferris, the last game hero, only had to go to Providence, while Parent headed north to Sanford, Maine, and said he would spend a few weeks bird shooting.

The series was barely over, but still pounding in the players' heads and they needed to get away now. It had been a grand idea for them to play, but people who didn't have to battle on the field or face the stress of competition and the pressure to succeed had put the proposal forth. The players could use the time to heal, to think, to be with their families, to get ready for the next season. The baseball writers were done with their work, although there would be expectations for the continuation of the World Series in 1904, and speculation whether Boston and Pittsburg could repeat and do it all again.

Collins told *Sporting Life* that the success of the games was not just what happened on the field, but what had happened to American life and public expectations. "I should not be surprised to see postseason games each fall as long as there are two big leagues. There is no reason, when the games are played out on their merits, as they were in this case, why they should not be successful. They give the public a high article of baseball and enable the championship teams to pick up a bit of prize money for the cold winter."

Johnson could gloat with the victory of his American Leaguers and think the future of the American League secure. Dreyfuss, gentlemanly even in defeat, could accept the loss with grace because he still believed a healthy Pirates team, with pitchers intact and players not injured, would have defeated Boston. He could think about next October, imagining an even grander series.

The afterglow of the success of the first World Series was warm indeed, with fans and sportswriters buzzing for weeks about how great the games were and how much they looked forward to 1904. Would there be a Boston-Pittsburg rematch? Would the Philadelphia A's challenge the Americans? Would the Pirates be able to capture four pennants in a row and hold off McGraw's New York Giants?

On November 1, 1903, Murnane wrote in the *Globe,* "The local situation is very satisfactory. Jimmie Collins will handle the world's champions and all of last season's players are either signed or on the reserved list." A week later he talked about how the competition of two leagues and the win by the

Americans had forced National League owners to reassess the teams they had been fielding. The Americans had such a large advantage in attendance over the National League Boston Beaneaters — better than 450,000 — that the National League entry was scrambling to sign better players. They had lost McGreevey and his rooters when they raised prices a few years before and now they were in danger of losing the fans altogether. As Murnane noted of them, "There is no chance, however, for the present aggregation to make a one, two or three finish, and this is always needed in this city to fill up the bill for the local fans. The local National League boys will have a big contract on hand next season to shine in the same class with the world's champions — no winter dope champions, but a team that defeated the great Pittsburg club in a walk and could repeat without extending itself."

Murnane took a slap at some of the Pittsburg sportswriters he thought had made excuses where the Pirates themselves had made none, even knowing how hurt they were and limited in manpower. "I would like to bring to the notice of the writers who claimed Boston won in a fluke the fact that the members of the Boston club carried off the prize without any cheap talk about their antagonists. The Boston men had the nerve and knew how to play ball. Dinneen out pitched Phillippe, although the Pittsburg man was given all kinds of praise for his effort."

Indeed, while Phillippe was justifiably lauded for his five game, three-win performance, Dinneen still somehow remained overshadowed not just by him, but by Young, although it was Dinneen who had really carried most of the pitching load for the Americans when it counted. Murnane said in comparison to Phillippe, Dinneen had really been better. "His work in every particular was far superior, and when it came to a showdown for condensed nerve, the Boston man had everything his own way," Murnane wrote in his Sunday column.

Americans owner Henry Killilea found the victory faded for him too, as the Boston scribes belittled him as an absentee landlord and greedy for not giving the players the same share Dreyfuss had for the Pirates, and for letting scalpers get tickets. He responded by trading 20-game winner Tom Hughes to New York for Jesse Tannehill, the former Pirate.

The winter would be toughest on two people. Wagner would not get over the loss and it would fester with him, the injuries no excuse, and it would be many years before he would reveal his true unhappiness and his performance. He did have his family to support him; his brothers knew what athletic disappointments were too.

And 20 miles from Boston, in a mental hospital far from the fields where he was on the verge of becoming one of the game's best left-handed pitchers, Ed Doheny sat staring out a window, his thoughts known only to himself, no one else knowing whether he was thinking about pitching or

Eight—"Tessie" 173

wondering how he would have performed in the greatest series baseball had ever known.

And while the players left the city which had embraced them, the fans stayed, many going a short distance from the park to McGreevey's Third Base Saloon to drink beer and talk about the series they had helped make, and which would take a place in the imaginations of young boys playing in fields and on city streets. Or, as Murnane wrote, "The series was the greatest event in baseball history and paved the way for a grand series of games each fall." The establishment had been festooned in decorations for the champions, and it was full, indeed, with happy patrons who drank and laughed and talked and rejoiced in the win of the hometown team.

After all, the barroom was still only about a home run away from the Huntington Avenue Grounds, now dark and cold and empty, except for the soft, lilting strains of a song called "Tessie" floating somewhere in the air, echoing, the chords growing more distant, until they would be played again.

Someday.

NINE

Echoes of the Game

On opening day in 1904, at the Huntington Avenue Baseball Grounds in Boston, Jimmy Collins helped raise the first World's Championship flag, showing that the club he led as manager had won the first World Series. It was another grand celebration for what would turn out to be another grand year for the Boston Americans.

In 1904, Boston got its third owner in three years. Killilea, criticized for his tightwad methods and for making the baseball writers and Pittsburg owners and officials pay for their own tickets to the games in Boston, was prompted by Ban Johnson to sell the team to Charles Taylor, owner of the *Boston Globe*, who named his son, John I. Taylor, president of the team. Taylor paid $145,000, outbidding John "Honey Fitz" Fitzgerald by $5,000.

The 1904 season was even more thrilling in the American League. The Boston Americans went to New York and beat the Highlanders on the last day of the season to clinch the pennant for a second straight year. They expected to meet the National League champion New York Giants for the World Series. Boston won when New York pitcher Jack Chesbro — the former Pirate — threw a wild pitch in the ninth inning, after a sterling year in which he had won 41 games. The Americans led both leagues by drawing an astounding 623,295 fans in 1904, while their rivals in Boston, the Beaneaters, drew only 140,694 fans.

The Giants were still owned by an old Ban Johnson nemesis, John Brush, and managed by an even angrier foe of the American League president, John McGraw. Brush had been incensed that Johnson had put a team in New York to compete with the Giants. He was afraid the Highlanders would win the pennant and force a World Series between the two New York teams, which he did not want to face. John Taylor issued a challenge to the

Giants for another World Series. McGraw refused outright, citing what he called the inferiority of the American League, a laughable charge given what happened to the Pirates in 1903. But the real reason was his hatred for Johnson, with whom he had had so many run-ins when McGraw was in the American League. Brush feared that a World Series with his Giants would end his team's popularity in the city should they lose to the upstarts, as the Pirates had to the Americans the year before.

"There is nothing in the playing rules or the constitution of the National League which requires its victorious club to submit its championship honors to a contest with a victorious club in a minor league," he said in high-minded fashion. The taunting and the public outcry started immediately and was vicious against the Giants, who were called "cowards" and worse for refusing to play. Chicago White Sox owner Charles Comiskey humiliated the National League team further when he said, "If the Giants do not want to play the champions of the American League, the followers of the game can draw their own conclusion."

There was a lot of feeling, however, that McGraw, bristling at being called a coward, wanted to take on the American Leagues, but by then Brush could not back out of his refusal, especially since he had said in September that winning the National League pennant was "the greatest honor that can be obtained in baseball." Dreyfuss sided with the American League and went so far as to approve a postseason series between the Pirates and the Cleveland entry in the American League, who had finished fourth there. Then Dreyfuss infuriated McGraw and Brush even more when he issued a statement that accused Brush of reneging on an agreement made by a joint scheduling committee in the spring. McGraw fumed and responded that Dreyfuss was licking Johnson's boots, but the Boston media and fans demanded that the World Series be played again.

Dreyfuss was not moved. "It was the National League schedule committee, or a majority of it, which meant the whole, which passed its word to the American League that postseason games would be played. I never agreed to play Cleveland until now. I agree to play the team that finished in the same American League notch that my team did. The American League managers understood this, all along the line, I think, and I will keep my word with them as far as the Pittsburg club is concerned."

The Pittsburg-Cleveland series paired two of the game's greatest players, Wagner and Cleveland star Nap LaJoie, who had jumped from the Phillies in 1901 during the player raids and the baseball war. It was a curious series that ended with Cleveland winning two, Pittsburg one, and two others ending in ties, including a 3–3 affair called because of darkness. But it wasn't the World Series, and there wasn't one in 1904, despite all the pressure put on McGraw and the Giants.

Shortly after the season ended, and after he said he wouldn't play the American Leaguers, it was Brush who proposed that a World Series be made mandatory. And for 90 years it was, until the strike season of 1994 cancelled it.

The Pirates, still reeling from their humbling loss in the World Series in 1903, finished fourth in the league at 87–66, a commendable season but a setback for them.

Boston's business manager Joseph Smart was criticized roundly after the series for how many tickets wound up in the hands of speculators and for the third-game fiasco in which so many people had swarmed the field. Johnson helped ease him out of his job in 1904 and had him replaced by a Chicago baseball writer, Carl Green.

Lou Criger played with Boston until 1908, when he went to the St. Louis Browns for a year, then to the New York Highlanders. He finished his professional career with the Browns again in 1912. He played in 1,012 games and finished with a fielding average of .970. He was on the first Hall of Fame ballot in 1933, but by then many of the sportswriters who had seen him play had passed away and he did not get in. When Criger was traded to St. Louis before the 1909 season, breaking up his battery with Young, the Boston pitcher lamented the loss. "St. Louis will get one of the greatest catchers that ever donned a glove. I've pitched to him so long that he seems a part of me, and I am positive no one will suffer from his departure more than I." They had played together for 12 years. Criger had to endure questions about his first game performance in the first World Series and unfounded suspicions of taking money, talk that dogged many players of the time.

In 1907, Tim Murnane wrote, "I would like to see someone pick out the equal of Criger." He did not fare well after leaving baseball. He moved to a 40-acre farm at Bair Lake near Jones, Michigan, but failing health made him move to the arid climate of Tucson in Arizona in 1924, the same year he provided an affidavit to Ban Johnson detailing his claims of how gamblers had tried to influence him to throw the first World Series. Johnson responded by giving him a lifetime pension from baseball, but critics said they thought Johnson was as much motivated by his hatred toward McGraw as compassion for Criger.

Criger suffered from an old knee injury where he was hit by a baseball, and from tuberculosis, and his left leg was amputated above the knee. Then he became a spokesman for Dr. Miles Anti-Pain pills. He had taken to using morphine while still playing. There was a special day for him in Boston in 1930 with a scroll signed by many players: the first two were Cy Young and Ty Cobb. He died on May 15, 1934 in Arizona.

On December 31, 1916, a two-paragraph item appeared near the bottom of the sports page inside the *Boston Globe*. It told of a sad demise. "Ed Doheny, a Once Great Pitcher, Dead."

Ed Doheny, the old-time pitcher of the New York Giants and Pittsburg baseball teams, died at the Medfield State Hospital Friday evening. He was 42 years old and a native of Vermont. The cause of death was pulmonary tuberculosis. Doheny was a great pitcher in his day. He broke down mentally while a member of the Pittsburg club in 1903, a short time before the World's Championship between the Pirates and the Red Sox [sic].

That was all that was written about him.

On February 6, 1917, as he was attending a performance at the Shubert Theater in Boston, Tim Murnane, the foremost chronicler of the first World Series, collapsed and died. He had been the *Globe*'s sports editor for the previous 30 years. Murnane had worked until 7 P.M. and rushed to the theater to join his wife, and had seemed well, stopping to chat with a number of men in the lobby. While his wife descended the stairs to the ladies' room to check her coat, he stayed in the foyer. When she came back a few minutes later, her husband had fallen to the floor near the ladies' room and a crowd had gathered around him as she fled to his side, distraught at the sight.

Three doctors who were in the theater quickly came to his aid, but Murnane was dead as soon as he hit the floor. And, as his own newspaper reported the next morning, "Thus went away the sunniest man in all the newspaper world and one of the best-known writers of sporting news in the country." Murnane was 65, described as

> a man of the utmost simplicity of character and of wonderful ideals, which survived all the experiences of a life that makes most men cynics. He saw men truly, but he idealized the game with which most of his career was bound up. He believed in baseball sincerely as a former of character and as a great factor in making Americans better men. He preached baseball....
>
> He lived baseball. When he talked with his friends, his very gestures threw a ball or swung a bat. He saw the need of insistence on clean, high standards, and to him in a great measure may be given credit for building the greatest National sport in all history.

He and Walter Barnes, who later became the *Globe*'s baseball editor, were elected to the Hall of Fame.

Buck Freeman played four more years in the major leagues, all with Boston. One of the most feared sluggers of the turn-of-the-century era, Freeman finished with a batting average of .293 and 82 home runs over 11 seasons. He died in 1949, at age 77, in Wilkes-Barre, Pennsylvania.

The curly-haired and feisty Patsy Dougherty was traded from Boston to the New York Highlanders halfway through the 1904 season, and thus played for both teams as they went down to the wire and the final day of that season to determine the pennant winner. In 1906, he was traded to the

Chicago White Sox and finished his career with them in 1911, and with a solid lifetime batting average of .284. He died in 1940 in Bolivar, New York, at age 63.

Chick Stahl had the darkest end of any of the players. In 1906, he finished his playing career with Boston and became a player-manager after Collins got hurt and had a falling-out with the Taylor family. The team finished 49–103 and lost 20 consecutive games at one point, but Stahl was told he would be the manager in 1907. That fall, he married a local girl, Julia Harmon, and they went to Buffalo on their honeymoon and visited his old friend Collins, who told Stahl to accept the manager's job. Stahl's new wife returned to Boston, but he went to his home in Fort Wayne, Indiana, and they were living apart. Stahl had developed a reputation as a womanizer at the same time he was becoming a very good ballplayer who held a number of Boston and American League records, a sign of his consistency and perseverance.

In March of 1907, as the team was preparing for the season and barnstorming its way back home, the 34-year-old Stahl was showing some Doheny-like signs of mental difficulties and stress. On March 25, in Louisville, he complained that the job was too much pressure and that he was having trouble eating and sleeping. He said he wanted to leave but agreed to stay on until a replacement could be found. On March 27, the Americans arrived by train in West Baden, Indiana, a resort community near French Lick, and checked into their hotel.

It was raining and Stahl went into the lobby and sent his wife a telegram that said, "Cheer up little girl and be happy. I am all right now and able to play the game of my life." He was sharing a suite with Collins and the next morning he ate breakfast and went to a local drugstore and bought a small bottle of carbolic acid, used often at the time as an antiseptic or muscle rub, but also as a frequent choice of those who wanted to kill themselves in those days. He went back to the suite and Collins later said he heard his friend choking and trying to vomit. Stahl fell on the bed, holding the empty bottle of acid, choking out his last words: "I couldn't help it. I did it Jim. It was killing me and I couldn't stand it." Collins ran for help, but the drug caused massive internal bleeding and Stahl was dead within a few minutes.

The suicide was big news in Boston, but Murnane quickly reported that baseball was the least of Stahl's problems. Eighty-three years later Boston baseball historian Glenn Stout reported that Stahl had had an affair the previous year in Chicago in which he got a woman pregnant, and that she was blackmailing him. Stahl apparently couldn't take it. He had played 10 years in Boston, for the Beaneaters and the Americans, and finished with an average of .305.

Collins, acclaimed as the greatest third baseman of his time, saw his star fade in Boston too. After being the pennant winners of 1903 and 1904, the team slipped badly in 1905, and he played only 37 games in an injury-riddled 1906, when he was fighting with John Taylor all the time. He was sent to Philadelphia of the American League a fourth of the way into the 1907 season and finished his career there in 1908. He entered the Hall of Fame in 1945.

Hobe Ferris stayed with Boston through the 1907 season and then went to St. Louis in the American League for 1908 and 1909, when he finished his career. He died in Detroit on March 18, 1938, at the age of 60.

Freddy Parent, the feisty little shortstop who outplayed the great Wagner for one series, stayed with Boston through the 1907 season and then played for Chicago in the American League from 1908 to 1911. He was the last survivor of both teams of the First World Series and came back to Northeastern University, now on the spot where the games in Boston were held, more than 70 years later for a ceremony marking the event. He died in Sanford, Maine, on November 2, 1972 at the age of 96.

Big Bill Dinneen, whose two shutouts captured the First World Series, pitched a no-hitter against Chicago in 1905, and was traded to St. Louis of the American League early in 1907, staying until 1909 when he went directly to becoming one of the most respected umpires in baseball history. He worked in that position for 29 years, umpired 45 World Series games and was awarded a cash prize for the umpire whose games were the quickest, just the way he worked on the mound. He died on January 13, 1955, in Syracuse, New York, where he was born. He was 78.

Candy LaChance died on August 18, 1932, at his home in Waterville, Connecticut, at 62. Early in 1905, only 12 games into a season in which he was hitting 6-for-41, he was cut and later went to Montreal of the International League, and the next year went to Providence and then to play with minor league teams in Waterbury and New Haven until he retired in 1908. He umpired in the Connecticut League in 1909 and played for the Waterbury Independents until 1911, when he retired. The next time he wore a uniform was in 1930 when he went back to Boston to play in a benefit game between players of all-Boston teams of his day. "He never lost his interest in the national pastime and attended all games in Waterville and was known to furnish advice to many youngsters on the game he loved," wrote the *Waterbury Republican* on his death. He worked in a plant in his hometown until he became ill.

Cy Young played five more years with Boston, including for the Red Sox in 1907 and 1908, winning 97 more games. He went to Cleveland in the American League from 1909–1911, before coming back to Boston — this time with the National League — to finish the 1911 season before retiring at age 44, losing his last game, 1–0, to a rookie sensation with Philadelphia named

Grover Cleveland Alexander, who won 374 games in 20 years and was elected to the Hall of Fame in 1938. Young had three no-hitters in his career, and had a perfect game in 1904, a year in which he also pitched a 20-inning game against Philadelphia without allowing a walk. He won 30 games five times and finished with 511 career victories, the most in major league history.

In 1908, "Cy Young Day" was hosted in Boston and the major leagues suspended their schedule so an all-star team could play the Red Sox in an exhibition game. More than 20,000 fans jammed the Huntington Avenue Grounds and 10,000 more were turned away. Young pitched the first two innings but was so overcome by the emotion of the day, the *Boston Post* reported, that "he could make no response to the presentation speeches." He was elected to the Hall of Fame in 1937. After he retired, he worked for a while as a greeter at Fred Putnam's hotel on Huntington Avenue, becoming the manager there when he was 71 years old. In 1953, he threw out the first pitch of the World Series between the Brooklyn Dodgers and the New York Yankees, to Yankee catcher Yogi Berra. He later returned to a farm in Peoli, Ohio, where he spent his last years sitting in a favorite armchair looking out over the pasturelands. He died on November 4, 1955, at 88 years old.

Pirates manager Fred Clarke was elected to the Hall of Fame in 1945. He stayed with the Pirates, true to his word, the rest of his baseball career, finishing in 1915 after having led them to the 1909 championship in the World Series, six years after their ignominious defeat by Boston. That team won 110 games, eclipsing even his great 1902 team, but he never got over the injury-plagued 1903 season and the loss of the World Series. He spent 21 years in the major leagues and finished with a career batting average of .312. He died at his farm in Winfield, Kansas, in 1960 at age 87.

Ginger Beaumont stayed with the Pirates until 1907, when he was traded to the Boston Beaneaters through 1909 and finished his career in 1910 with Chicago in the National League. He played 12 years and finished with a career average of .311 and 39 home runs. He died in Burlington, Wisconsin, on April 10, 1956, at the age of 79.

Jimmy Sebring, whose 11 hits in the 1903 series were the best for both teams, didn't last long in the major leagues. He was traded from Pittsburg to Cincinnati in the 1904 season and stayed with them until 1905, when he left to play for a team near his home of Williamsport in Pennsylvania because his wife was ill. Organized baseball did not usually allow players who played for so-called outlaw leagues to come back, but he returned in 1909 to Brooklyn and Washington, and he died in Williamsport on December 22, 1909. He was only 27 years old.

Claude Ritchey, a clever fielder and hitter, led the National League second basemen in fielding percentage five times. He stayed with the Pirates through 1906 and went to the Boston Beaneaters from 1907 to 1909, where he teamed again with Ginger Beaumont. He died in his hometown of Emlenton, Pennsylvania, on November 8, 1951, at the age of 78.

Tommy Leach, the diminutive wonder, said he never got over the sound of "Tessie," and said he could hear it constantly after the games ended. Decent and shy, he was also remarkably resilient and strong, lasting 19 years in the major leagues. He stayed with the Pirates until part way through the 1912 season, when he was traded to Chicago in the National League, where he stayed for 1913–14 before playing for Cincinnati in 1915 and leaving baseball. But the Pirates brought him back for one last year in 1918, although he played only 30 games. He died on September 29, 1969, in Haines City, Florida, at the age of 91.

Kitty Bransfield played with the Pirates only one more year, then went to Philadelphia of the National League from 1905 to 1911, finishing his career with three games that last year in 1911 with Chicago in the National League. He died in his hometown of Worcester, Massachusetts, on May 1, 1947, at the age of 72.

Deacon Phillippe died in 1952 at age 79; he was remembered as one of the first stars of the first World Series, and as much for his shy, unassuming manner as his pitching ability.

Honus Wagner, more than 100 years after he played, is still generally believed to be the best shortstop the game has ever seen. In 1912, New York Giants pitcher Christy Matheson wrote in his book that Wagner carried the stigma of 1903 forever, although he went on to have a brilliant career. What hurt Wagner the most, Matheson wrote, was the "coward" tag some gave him. "This grieved the Dutchman deeply, for I don't know a ball player [who exhibits] less quit to the ton than Wagner.... This was the real tragedy in Wagner's career. Not-withstanding his stolid appearance, he is a sensitive player, and this hurt him more than anything else in his life ever has."

In the spring of 1904, Wagner was supposed to have sent his portrait to National League President Harry Pulliam for a "Hall Of Fame" of batting champions, but the Dutchman was reluctant to do so. "I was too bum last year. I was a joke in that Boston-Pittsburg series. What does it profit a man to hammer along and make a few hits when they are not needed only to fall down when it comes to a pinch? I would be ashamed to have my picture up now."

The Pirates won the World Series in 1909, and Wagner, in a memorable showdown with Detroit's Ty Cobb, smacked him in the face with a tag, bloodying Cobb's face when the ferociously tempestuous Tiger tried to steal second after challenging Wagner. The Pirates won the series in seven games, as Wagner hit .333, redeeming himself from the 1903 series, and earned his World Series title. Wagner's baseball card became the most valuable in history and in 2000 was sold for $1.1 million on an Internet auction. He finished

Pittsburg great Honus Wagner with glove in hand ready to play defense (courtesy Carnegie Library, Pittsburgh).

his career as a player in 1917, having hit .300 or better for 17 of his 20 years in the major leagues, winning eight batting titles and leading the league in stolen bases five times and finishing with 722 stolen bases, being caught only 15 times — all in one year, 1915 — after 17 consecutive years and 684 stolen bases.

He served as sergeant-in-arms for the Pittsburg state legislature and was in the first class of players inducted into Baseball's Hall of Fame in 1936. He married late in life and died in his sleep on December 6, 1955, a month after Cy Young passed away. He and Young were named to baseball's All-Century team in 1999.

McGreevey kept a scrapbook detailing his continued association with the Americans and as they became the Red Sox, traipsing after them with his Rooters. He sold his saloon with the onset of Prohibition in 1929 and it later became an annex of the Boston Public Library. Today, the spot is a parking lot next to the new Boston police headquarters.

Ban Johnson was president of the league he created until 1927, when he retired in anger after a clash with baseball's commissioner, Judge Kenesaw Mountain Landis, who had been brought in as a czar after the 1919 Chicago White Sox were found to have thrown the World Series. Landis' rule even outweighed that of Johnson, who had been an autocrat for years. What hurt Johnson was another budding World Series scandal in 1924, compounded when he released an affidavit from Criger, who talked about the attempted fix of the 1903 first World Series. In 1926, there surfaced yet another fix scandal, with charges that Ty Cobb and Tris Speaker had been involved in fixed games in 1919. Johnson believed the story, but Landis made the story public, infuriating Johnson. The American League owners were weary of scandal talk and they stripped Johnson of his remaining powers. He lived only four more years, dying of diabetes in 1931, but was elected to the Hall of Fame in 1937. The two eight-team leagues of 16 teams continued in the format set by Johnson for 50 years.

The Hotel Langham, where the Americans stayed, was razed in 1964, after going through decades of disrepair and abandonment, ruined when a elevated subway was built along Washington Street. It turned a fine avenue into a road where nobody wanted to live and where second-rate commercialism almost destroyed one of the city's finest neighborhoods of elegant brownstones and brick residences. Toward the end, tacked-on neon signs for liquor stores and run-down businesses ruined its stately appearance. By the time it was razed, it had become so decrepit that it was condemned. Neglected and weather-beaten, the marble slabs of the exterior were so weakened they had to be shored up while the building was being taken down.

The Vendome, where the Pirates argued with Boston fans in its stately lobby, was altered frequently over the years until June 17, 1972, when, after a massive fire was put out, a wall collapsed, killing nine fire-fighters. In 1997, a memorial sculpture was erected in their memory on the tree-lined median, which runs the length of Commonwealth Avenue. The hotel became a condominium complex.

The Boston Americans, after being sold and renamed the Red Sox in 1907, moved to a new field, Fenway Park, in 1912, and became a dynasty during that decade, winning world championships in 1912, 1915, 1916 and 1918. The final year was the last time "Tessie" was sung for them, and the last time they won the World Series. By the end of the 20th century, after decades of frustration, narrowly losing in the seventh game of the series in 1946 and 1967 against the St. Louis Cardinals, in 1975 against the Cincinnati Reds, and in 1986 against the New York Mets, the talk had turned in Boston to razing of the old stadium. When Fenway Park was built in 1912, the infield sod was moved there from the Huntington Avenue Grounds.

The Pirates, who played in Three Rivers Stadium after Exposition Park and Forbes Field were razed, moved to another new facility in 2001. They defeated the New York Yankees in one of the greatest games in baseball history, the seventh game of the 1960 World Series, on Bill Mazeroski's ninth inning home run into the left field seats.

Early in 2002, the Boston Red Sox were sold to a new business group, but talks of a new field to replace Fenway Park became mired in the infamous politics of a city where it is said the three biggest games — apart from baseball and the Old Towne Team — were "politics, sports and revenge."

CONCLUSION

The Bronze Man

Just outside Churchill Hall, the building that houses the president's office at Northeastern University in Boston, stands a silent sentinel to the games that changed the American way of life. It is the bronze sculpture of Denton True "Cy" Young, a representation of the 6' 1", 210-pound winningest pitcher in the history of baseball, whose brilliance and 511 wins would come to be so symbolic that the annual award for the game's best pitcher in each league is named after him. He looks as he appeared in 1903 when pitching for the new Boston Americans of the American League. He is hunched slightly forward, a deep contemplation furrowed in the metal of his forehead, the ball resting just behind his right hip, the too-tiny gloves that were common at the turn of the 19th century resting on his left knee. He is looking now only past a patch of green, the home plate of his day just another building now, surrounded by more gray brick buildings on the urban campus that nearly a century ago echoed with the shouts of scores of thousands of fans lured by the irresistible idea of the champions of the two leagues — Boston and Pittsburg — meeting to decide the championship of the world. Thousands of students pass by every day, most not paying attention anymore to the statue, sponsored by the Yawkey Foundation, named for Tom Yawkey, the late owner of the Boston Red Sox. Few read the proclamation in front of the statue, or see some feet away an engraved photograph of what used to be on the site: the Huntington Avenue Baseball Grounds. The Americans were considered the flagship team when the American League became a major league in 1901, and were carrying the sports and financial hopes of a new generation of fans.

The pathway leading between buildings on the huge, sprawling brickwork campus is called World Series Way, and Churchill Hall also houses the office of the board of trustees of Northeastern. The engraved photo shows thousands of fans strolling across a huge outfield, bedecked in 19th century clothes as quaint as the way they spoke and wrote. It was mostly men, of course, but there were women in dresses that made them look like they were going to a ball instead of a baseball game. The industrial nature of the city could be seen in the brick buildings and smokestacks beyond, and there is a glimpse of the South End Grounds very nearby, the home of the rival National League Beaneaters, whom the Americans had displaced in attendance and attention for the city's fans. The Beaneaters eventually became the Boston Braves, but by the 1950s, their following had fallen off and they moved to Milwaukee and then to Atlanta.

The mystique of the Boston Red Sox and the curse that followed them after the 1918 World Series championship they won before trading Babe Ruth didn't exist in the first few years of the franchise, which were good years indeed. After that came decades of frustration.

In Pittsburg, the 1903 games have been remembered with a marker that was unveiled in September of 1998, on the spot where home plate stood at Exposition Park, outside the center field wall of the former Three Rivers Stadium. The games themselves were called the wildest World Series ever played because of the pomp and circumstance given them by the fans and sportswriters, and by the owners of the two leagues, vying for respectability and bragging rights — and revenues brought in by a rapt audience. Just when baseball was struggling early in the 20th century, along came the idea of the World Series to revitalize the game and the country, and bring the sense of symmetry and history to the sport when it seemed it might lose some of its popularity because of the infighting of National League owners.

In its history, the World Series has had many dramatic moments: Enos Slaughter's charge around the bases to beat the Red Sox in the seventh game of the 1946 series for the St. Louis Cardinals, Mazeroski's homer in 1960, Carlton Fisk's 12th-inning sixth-game home run for the Red Sox to beat the Cincinnati Reds in 1975; Bill Buckner's error that cost the Red Sox the 1986 World Series and continued disappointment for Boston fans; the 1955 Brooklyn Dodgers finally defeating the Yankees, the magical and improbable 1997 seventh-game extra-inning victory of the Florida Marlins, and the New York Yankees losing in the ninth inning of the seventh game in 2001 to an expansion team, the Arizona Diamondbacks.

But it was the first World Series which created a lasting love affair with the game of baseball, which brought in new fans and set up a structure for the sport that would endure into the 21st century, thriving from the dead-ball era of 1903 to the live-ball home run derbies of today. At stake was not only whether the American League would survive, but whether baseball would become the preeminent sport for America. The first World Series came at the start of a new century, in a year when man — the Wright Brothers — would first fly, when the St. Louis World's Fair would fascinate the world, when *The Wizard Of Oz* was published, when America would start its movement to industrial and technological might.

All those events were moments in history, moments that helped define the beginning of the 20th century. The next step, it seems, would be for the event to become truly a world's championship (the Toronto Blue Jays' wins don't count because there were, after all, no Canadians on those teams) and, eventually, for the winner of the major leagues in the Americas perhaps playing the winner of the Japanese major leagues — or even expanding into a third league, an International League, which would become to baseball in this century what the American League was at the start of the last.

Famed pitcher Cy Young. Note the B A on his uniform for Boston Americans (courtesy Boston Public Library).

Imagine the excitement of, say, the Boston Red Sox meeting the Havana Cubans in the first *real* World Series and the day when the all-foreign teams become amalgamated into a worldwide game of baseball. Teams could have, perhaps, a Dominican shortstop, a Puerto Rican second baseman, a Mexican pitcher, a Japanese third baseman, Australian and Dutch outfielders, a Russian, a Venezuelan, an Ecuadorean, a Filipino, a Taiwanese, a Chinese, and even a native-born American. With worldwide cable revenues, with new stadiums being built in places where there are now rocky, bumpy fields, where the game could be brought to the next generations of players and fans, where children would — with monies available from the major leagues — have equipment and places to play, where political differences between countries would be blurred by the commonality of the games that changed America, baseball could — maybe — change the world.

Appendix: 1903 World Series Statistics

Box Scores, Line Scores and Running Scores (Home Team in Bold)

Thursday, October 1: Pittsburg 7, **Boston 3**
WP: Phillippe, LP — Young, Attendance: 16,242, Time: 1:55

Friday, October 2: **Boston 3,** Pittsburg 0
WP: Dinneen, LP — Leever, Attendance: 9,415, Time: 1:47

Saturday, October 3: Pittsburg 4, **Boston 2**
WP: Phillippe, LP — Hughes, Attendance: 18,801, Time: 1:50

Tuesday, October 6: **Pittsburg 5**, Boston 4
WP: Phillippe, LP — Dinneen, Attendance: 7,600, Time: 1:30

Wednesday, October 7: Boston 11, **Pittsburg 2**
WP: Young, LP — Kennedy, Attendance: 12,322, Time: 2:00

Thursday, Oct: 8: Boston 6, **Pittsburg 3**
WP: Dinneen, LP — Leever, Attendance: 11,556, Time: 2:02

Saturday, October 10: Boston 7, **Pittsburg 3**
WP: Young, LP — Phillippe, Attendance: 17,038, Time: 1:45

Tuesday, October 13: **Boston 3,** Pittsburg 0
WP: Dinneen, LP — Phillippe, Attendance: 7,455, Time: 1:35

Game 1

Thursday, October 1, 1903, at Boston
Pittsburg 7, Boston 3

Pittsburg	AB	R	H	RBI	Boston	AB	R	H	RBI
Beaumont, cf	5	1	0	0	Dougherty, lf	4	0	0	0
Clarke, lf	5	0	2	0	Collins, 3b	4	0	0	0
Leach, 3b	5	1	4	1	C.Stahl, cf	4	0	1	0
Wagner, ss	3	1	1	1	Freeman, rf	4	2	2	0
Bransfield, 1b	5	2	1	0	Parent, ss	4	1	2	1
Ritchey, 2b	4	1	0	0	LaChance, 1b	4	0	0	2
Sebring, rf	5	1	3	4	Ferris, 2b	3	0	1	0
Phelps, c	4	0	1	0	Criger, c	3	0	0	0
Phillippe, p	4	0	0	0	a-O'Brien	1	0	0	0
					Young, p	3	0	0	0
					b-Farrell	1	0	0	0
Totals	40	7	12	6	Totals	35	3	6	3

									R	H	E
PIT	4	0	1	1	0	0	1	0	0	7	12	2
BOS	0	0	0	0	0	0	2	0	1	3	6	4

	IP	H	R	ER	BB	SO
PITTSBURG						
Phillippe	9	6	3	2	0	10
BOSTON						
Young	9	12	7	3	3	5

a-struck out for Criger in ninth. b-grounded out for Young in ninth. E — Ferris 2, Criger 3, Leach, Wagner. LOB — Pittsburg, 9, Boston, 6. 3B — Freeman, Parent, Leach 2, Bransfield. HR — Sebring. SB — Wagner, Bransfield, Ritchey. HBP — By Phillippe (Ferris). PB — Criger U — O'Day (N.L.) and Connolly, (A.L.). T —1:55 Attendance: 16,242.

Game 2

Friday, October 2, 1903 at Boston
Boston 3, Pittsburg 0

Pittsburgh	AB	R	H	RBI	Boston	AB	R	H	RBI
Beaumont, lf	3	0	0	0	Dougherty, lf	4	2	3	2
Clarke, lf	3	0	1	0	Collins, 3b	4	0	1	0
Leach, 3b	3	0	0	0	C. Stahl, cf	4	1	1	0
Wagner, ss	3	0	0	0	Freeman, rf	4	0	2	1
Bransfield, 1b	3	0	0	0	Parent, ss	3	0	1	0
Ritchey, 2b	3	0	1	0	LaChance, 1b	2	0	0	0
Sebring, rf	3	0	1	0	Ferris, 2b	4	0	0	0
Smith, c	3	0	0	0	Criger, c	3	0	0	0
Leever, p	0	0	0	0	Dinneen, p	2	0	1	0
Veil, p	2	0	0	0					
a-Phelps	1	0	0	0					
Totals	27	0	3	0	Totals	30	3	9	3

										R	H	E
PIT	0	0	0	0	0	0	0	0	0	0	3	2
BOS	2	0	0	0	0	1	0	0	-	3	9	0

	IP	H	R	ER	BB	SO
PITTSBURG						
Leever (L)	1	3	2	2	1	0
Veil	7	6	1	1	4	1
BOSTON						
Dinneen W)	9	3	0	0	2	11

a-Struck out for Veil in ninth. E — Smith, Veil. DP — Pittsburg, 2, Boston 1. LOB — Pittsburg 2, Boston, 11. 2B — Stahl HR — Dougherty, 2. SB — Collins, 2. SH — LaChance, Dinneen. HBP — By Veil (Dougherty). U — O'Day,(N.L.)and Connolly (A.L.)T — 1:47. A — 9,415.

Game 3

Saturday, October 3, at Boston
Pittsburg 4, Boston 2

Pittsburgh	AB	R	H	RBI	Boston	AB	R	H	RBI
Beaumont, cf	4	1	0	0	Dougherty, lf	4	0	0	0
Clarke, lf	4	0	1	0	Collins, 3b	4	2	2	0
Leach, 3b	4	1	1	1	Stahl, cf	3	0	1	1
Wagner, ss	3	1	1	0	Freeman, rf	3	0	0	0
Bransfield, 1b	3	0	0	0	Parent, ss	4	0	0	1
Ritchey, 2b	4	1	1	1	LaChance, 1b	3	0	1	0
Sebring, rf	3	0	1	1	Ferris, 2b	4	0	0	0
Phelps, c	4	0	2	1	Criger, c	3	0	0	0
Phillippe, p	4	0	0	0	Hughes, p	0	0	0	0
					Young, p	3	0	0	0
Totals	33	4	7	4	Totals	31	2	4	2

										R	H	E
PITT	0	1	2	0	0	0	0	1	0	4	7	0
BOS	0	0	0	1	0	0	0	1	0	2	4	2

	IP	H	R	ER	BB	SO
PITTSBURG						
Phillippe (W)	9	4	2	2	3	5
BOSTON						
Hughes (L)	2*	4	3	2	2	0
Young	7	3	1	1	0	2

E — Collins, Young. P — Boston 1. LOB — Pittsburg 6, Boston, 3. 2B — Collins, LaChance, Clarke, Ritchey, Wagner, Phelps, 2. SB — Leach. SH — Bransfield. HBP — By Young (Wagner). PB — Criger. U — O'Day (N.L.) and Connolly (A.L.). T — 1:50. A — 18,801.

*Pitched to three batters in 3d.

Game 4

Tuesday, October 6, at Pittsburg

Boston	AB	R	H	RBI	Pittsburgh	AB	R	H	RBI
Dougherty, lf	4	0	0	0	Beaumont, cf	4	2	3	0
Collins, 3b	4	1	1	0	Clarke, lf	4	1	1	0
Stahl, cf	4	1	2	0	Leach, 3b	4	1	2	3
Freeman, rf	4	0	1	1	Wagner, ss	4	0	3	1
Parent, ss	4	1	1	1	Bransfield, 1b	4	0	1	1
LaChance, 1b	4	0	1	0	Ritchey, 2b	3	0	0	0
Ferris, 2b	4	0	1	0	Sebring, rf	4	0	0	0
Criger, c	3	0	1	1	Phelps, c	4	0	1	0
a-Farrell	1	0	0	1	Phillippe, p	3	1	1	0
Dinneen, p	3	0	0	0					
Totals	36	4	9	4	Totals	34	5	12	5

										R	H	E
BOS	0	0	0	0	1	0	0	0	3	4	9	1
PITT	1	0	0	0	1	0	3	0	—	5	12	1

	IP	H	R	ER	BB	SO
BOSTON						
Dinneen (L)	8	12	5	5	1	7
PITTSBURG						
Phillippe (W)	9	9	4	4	0	1

a — Flied out for Criger in ninth, Parent scoring after the catch. b — Flied out for Dinneen in ninth. E — Dougherty, Bransfield. DP — Boston 1, Pittsburg 1. LOB — Boston 5, Pittsburg 6. 3B — Beaumont, Leach. SB — Wagner U — O'Day (N.L.) and Connolly (A.L.). T — 1:30. A — 7,600.

Game 5

Wednesday, October 7 at Pittsburg
Boston 11, Pittsburg 2

Boston	AB	R	H	RBI	Pittsburgh	AB	R	H	RBI
Dougherty, lf	6	0	3	3	Beaumont, cf	4	1	1	0
Collins, 3b	6	0	2	0	Clarke, lf	4	1	0	0
Stahl, cf	5	2	1	0	Leach, 3b	4	0	2	2
Freeman, rf	4	2	2	1	Wagner, ss	4	0	0	0
Parent, ss	5	1	2	0	Bransfield, 1b	4	0	0	0
LaChance, 1b	4	2	1	1	Ritchey, 2b	4	0	1	0
Ferris, 2b	5	2	1	2	Sebring, rf	4	0	1	0
Criger, c	3	1	0	0	Phelps, c	3	0	0	0
Young, p	5	1	2	3	Kennedy, p	2	0	1	0
					Thompson, p	1	0	0	0
Totals	43	11	14	10	Totals	34	2	6	2

									R	H	E
BOS	0	0	0	0	0	6	4	1	0	11	14	2
PITT	0	0	0	0	0	0	0	2	0	2	6	4

	IP	H	R	ER	BB	SO
BOSTON						
Young (W)	9	6	2	0	0	4
PITTSBURG						
Kennedy (L)	7	11	10	4	3	3
Thompson	2	3	1	1	0	1

E — Parent, LaChance, Clarke, Leach, Wagner 2. LOB — Boston 9, Pittsburg 6. 2B — Kennedy. 3B — Leach, Dougherty 2, Collins, Stahl, Young. SB — Collins, Stahl. SH — Phelps, Criger. U — Connolly (A.L.) and O'Day (N.L.) T — 2:00 A — 12,322.

Game 6

Thursday, October 8 at Pittsburg
Boston 6, Pittsburg 3

Boston	AB	R	H	RBI	Pittsburg	AB	R	H	RBI
Dougherty, lf	3	1	1	0	Beaumont, cf	5	1	4	2
Collins, 3b	5	1	1	1	Clarke, lf	5	0	2	0
Stahl, cf	5	1	2	1	Leach, 3b	5	0	0	1
Freeman, rf	5	0	0	1	Wagner, ss	3	0	0	0
Parent, ss	4	2	1	0	Bransfield, 1b	3	0	1	0
LaChance, 1b	4	0	1	1	Ritchey, 2b	3	0	0	0
Ferris, 2b	4	0	2	1	Sebring, rf	4	1	2	0
Criger, c	4	0	1	0	Phelps, c	4	1	1	0
Dinneen, p	4	1	1	0	Leever, p	4	0	0	0
Totals	38	6	10	5	Totals	36	3	10	3

										R	H	E
BOS	0	0	3	0	2	0	1	0	0	6	10	1
PITT	0	0	0	0	0	0	3	0	0	3	10	3

	IP	H	R	ER	BB	SO
BOSTON						
Dinneen (W)	9	10	3	3	3	3
PITTSBURG						
Leever (L)	9	10	6	5	2	2

E—Criger, Leach 2, Wagner. DP—Boston 1, Pittsburg 1. LOB—Boston 8, Pittsburg 9. 2B—Clarke, LaChance. 3B—Stahl, Parent. SB—Beaumont 2, Clarke, Leach, Stahl. HBP—By Leever (Parent). U—O'Day (N.L.) and Connolly (A.L.). T—2:02. A—11,556.

Game 7

Saturday, October 10, at Pittsburg
Boston 7, Pittsburg 3

Boston	AB	R	H	RBI	Pittsburg	AB	R	H	RBI
Dougherty, lf	5	0	1	0	Beaumont, cf	5	0	1	0
Collins, 3b	5	1	1	0	Clarke, lf	5	1	1	1
Stahl, cf	4	1	2	1	Leach, 3b	5	0	0	0
Freeman, rf	4	1	1	0	Wagner, ss	3	0	0	1
Parent, ss	4	2	2	1	Bransfield, 1b	4	1	3	0
LaChance, 1b	3	1	0	0	Ritchey, 2b	4	0	0	1
Ferris, 2b	3	1	2	0	Sebring, rf	4	1	2	0
Criger, c	4	0	2	3	Phelps, c	3	0	1	0
Young, p	4	0	0	0	Phillippe, p	4	0	2	1
Totals	36	7	11	5	Totals	37	3	10	3

										R	H	E
BOS	2	0	0	2	0	2	0	1	0	7	11	4
PITT	0	0	0	1	0	1	0	0	1	3	10	3

	IP	H	R	ER	BB	SO
BOSTON						
Young (W)	9	10	3	2	1	6
PITTSBURG						
Phillippe (L)	9	11	7	5	0	2

E — Collins, Parent, LaChance 2, Wagner, Phelps, Phillippe. DP-Boston 1, Pittsburg 1. LOB — Boston 4, Pittsburg 9. 3B — Clarke, Bransfield, Collins, Stahl, Freeman, Parent, Ferris. SH — Wagner, LaChance, Ferris. WP — Phillippe. U — Connolly (A.L.) and O'Day (N.L.). T — 1:45. A — 17,038.

Game 8

Tuesday, October 13, at Boston
Boston 3, Pittsburg 0

Pittsburg	AB	R	H	RBI	Boston	AB	R	H	RBI
Beaumont, cf	4	0	0	0	Dougherty, lf	4	0	0	0
Clarke, lf	4	0	1	0	Collins, 3b	4	0	1	0
Leach, 3b	3	0	0	0	Stahl, cf	4	0	0	0
Wagner, ss	4	0	1	0	Freeman, rf	4	1	1	0
Bransfield, 1b	3	0	0	0	Parent, ss	4	1	0	0
Ritchey, 2b	2	0	0	0	LaChance, 1b	3	1	1	0
Sebring, rf	3	0	1	0	Ferris, 2b	4	0	2	3
Phelps, c	3	0	0	0	Criger, c	3	0	2	0
Phillippe, p	3	0	1	0	Dinneen, p	3	0	1	0
Totals	29	0	4	0	Totals	33	3	8	3

										R	H	E
PITT	0	0	0	0	0	0	0	0	0	0	4	3
BOS	0	0	0	2	0	1	0	0	—	3	8	0

	IP	H	R	ER	BB	SO
PITTSBURG						
Phillippe (L)	8	8	3	3	0	2
BOSTON						
Dinneen (W)	9	4	0	0	2	7

E — Wagner, Bransfield, Phelps. DP — Boston 1. LOB — Pittsburg 4, Boston 7. 3B — Freeman, LaChance, Sebring. SB — Wagner. SH — LaChance. U — O'Day (N.L.) and Connolly (A.L.). T — 1:36. A — 7,455.

Composite Batting Averages

Boston Americans

Player—Pos	G	AB	R	H	2B	3B	HR	RBI	BA
Stahl, cf	8	33	6	10	1	3	0	3	.303
Ferris, 2b	8	31	3	9	0	1	0	6	.290
Freeman, rf	8	32	6	9	0	3	0	4	.281
Parent, ss	8	32	8	9	0	3	0	4	.281
Collins, 3b	8	36	5	9	1	2	0	1	.250
Dinneen, p	4	12	1	3	0	0	0	0	.250
Dougherty, lf	8	34	3	8	0	2	2	5	.235
Criger, c	8	26	1	6	0	0	0	4	.231
LaChance, 1b	8	27	5	6	2	1	0	4	.222
Young, p	4	15	1	2	0	1	0	3	.133
Farrell, ph	2	2	0	0	0	0	0	1	.000
O'Brien, ph	2	2	0	0	0	0	0	0	.000
Hughes, p	1	0	0	0	0	0	0	0	.000
Totals	8	282	39	71	4	16	2	35	.252

Pittsburg Pirates

Player—Pos	G	AB	R	H	2B	3B	HR	RBI	BA
Kennedy, p	1	2	0	1	1	0	0	0	.500
Sebring, rf	8	30	3	11	0	1	1	5	.367
Leach, 3b	8	33	3	9	0	4	0	8	.273
Beaumont, cf	8	34	6	9	0	1	0	2	.265
Clarke, lf	8	34	3	9	2	1	0	0	.265
Phelps, ph-c	8	26	1	6	2	0	0	1	.231
Wagner, ss	8	27	2	6	1	0	0	3	.222
Phillippe, p	5	18	1	4	0	0	0	1	.222
Bransfield, 1b	8	29	3	6	0	2	0	1	.207
Ritchey, 2b	8	27	2	3	1	0	0	2	.111
Leever, p	2	4	0	0	0	0	0	0	.000
Smith, c	1	3	0	0	0	0	0	0	.000
Thompson, p	1	1	0	0	0	0	0	0	.000
Veil, p	1	2	0	0	0	0	0	0	.000
Totals	8	270	24	64	7	9	1	23	.237

Composite Pitching Averages

Boston Americans

Pitcher	G	IP	H	R	ER	BB	SO	W	L	ERA
Young	4	34	31	13	6	4	17	2	1	1.59
Dinneen	4	35	29	8	8	8	28	3	1	2.06
Hughes	1	2	4	3	2	2	0	0	1	9.00
Totals	8	71	64	24	16	14	45	5	3	2.03

Pittsburg Pirates

Pitcher	G	IP	H	R	ER	BB	SO	W	L	ERA
Veil	1	7	6	1	1	4	1	0	0	1.29
Phillippe	5	44	38	19	16	3	20	3	2	3.27
Thompson	1	2	3	1	1	0	1	0	0	4.50
Kennedy	1	7	11	10	4	3	3	0	1	5.14
Leever	2	10	13	8	7	2	3	0	2	6.30
Totals	8	70	71	39	29	13	27	3	5	3.73

Bibliography

Newspapers

All year dates 1903 except as noted.

Boston Daily Advertiser

September 25. "Boston-Pittsburg Series Is Declared 'Off.'"

Boston Evening Record

August 29. "A Pittsburg View of It."
September 24. "Series Looks Doubtful."
October 12. "Doheny Insane."
October 13. "Does Basketball Wreck Health of the Girls of College Age?"

Boston Evening Transcript

May 11, 1938. "Cy Young Back to Stay, Calls Old Baseball Best."
September 2. "War on Football Dancing."
September 25. "Curleys Found Guilty."
October 2. "The Making of Journalists."
October 3. "The Woman Journalist."

Boston Globe

March 4, 1901. "Stahl and Dinneen Reported Officially to Have Jumped."
March 21, 1901. "American League Will Open Baseball Season."
March 22, 1901. "Many a Clash."
March 23, 1901. "Johnson Talks, Says Conflict of Dates Was Unavoidable."
March 23, 1901. "Somers Here, Owner of New Boston Club in Town."

March 29, 1901. "Cy Young Solid, Reiterates His Loyalty to American League."
April 1, 1901. "Cleveland Regards Him Highly."
April 1, 1901. "Baseball Opens, Both Boston Nines Begin Their Practice in South."
April 26, 1901. "American League Opens with Boom in Baltimore."
May 6, 1901. "Baseball and Religion."
May 9, 1901. "American League Season Opens Here Today."

Boston Globe, Evening Globe

March 19. "Cy Young Will Pitch for Collegians, Which Will Make It Interesting."
March 21. "Rain Prevents a Game."
March 29. "All Hit Hard, Americans Get in Some Lively Batting."
April 2. "Joseph Smart Chosen."
April 7. "Stahl's Hit."
April 12. "Americans Defeat Evansville, 9 to 1, By Clever Stickwork."
April 12. "Dreyfuss Satisfied."
April 18. "Americans Have a Close Call."
April 18. "Each Plays a Double Bill."
April 21. "Huntington Avenue Crowd of 27,568 Broke Attendance Records."
April 21. "Same Fortune."
April 24. "Cy on Deck, He Proves a Puzzle to the Champions."
April 26. "An Army at Work."
April 29. "Gibson Wild, Passes to First Help to Beat Him."
May 3. "Fail to Hit, Boston Americans Are Shy of Plank."
May 4. "Baseball Crazy, Nearly 36,000 Persons See the Two Games in Chicago."
May 4. "Ferris Turns the Trick."
May 6. "General Belief That He Is Alive Somewhere."
May 7. "'Twas All Cy, Young Took Notion to Turn Batsman."
May 18. "Boston's Run a Pure Gift."
May 18. "Boston's Run a Pure Gift."
May 29. "Collins and His Boys Help Out Dinneen."
May 29. "Boston Nationals Fail to Hit Mathewson."
June 2. "Jumps Ahead, Boston American Team Is the Pacemaker."
June 2. "Get the Brush, New Yorkers Cannot Hit Billy Dinneen."
June 3. "Boston Americans, with Cy in the Box, Turn the Trick in New York."
June 5. "Dunkle at His Worst."
June 5. "Four Shutouts, Pittsburg Makes a World's Record."
June 6. "In a Slugging Match."
June 7. "Three Straight from White Sox, and Team's 10th Successive Victory."
June 7. "Ends in a Riot, Umpire Shamefully Treated by Haverhill Mob."
June 10. "Timely Stickwork"
June 16. "Here to Make Stickwork."
June 17. "Cleveland Wins Easily."
June 18. "Great Games and Big Crowds."
June 18. "Seen by 50,000 on Common, Liberty Bell Taken to Plymouth."

Bibliography

June 19. "Pittsburg Wins from Boston Nationals."
June 21. "Neck and Neck Race."
June 23. "All Disciplined."
June 25. "Detroit Got the Rubber."
June 26. "Baseball War?"
June 28. "Two Shutouts, Boston Americans Win the Doubleheader in St. Louis."
July 1. "All Over After First."
July 2. "Mighty Cy, He Shuts Out Chicago for 10 Innings."
July 5. "Boston Wins Both."
July 9. "Plague of Mosquitoes."
July 11. "Warm, But the Game Goes On."
July 14. "Prospects of War, National League, It Is Said, Will Take the Initiative."
July 16. "Get an Even Break."
July 17. "There'll Be No War."
July 17. "Clinched It Right Away."
July 18. "Only One Run Made."
July 18. "Rube Makes a Scene."
July 18. "Famous Artist Makes a Scene."
July 20. "President Pulliam Says His Course in Davis Matter Must Be Sustained."
July 21. "Peace in Baseball."
July 21. "Another Shutout, Long Tom Hughes Shows Up in Great Form Against New York."
July 22. "Brush Did Not Attend Meeting."
July 29. "Baseball Championship."
July 30. "Slugging Matinee."
August 1. "Darkness Stops It."
August 2. "Pitches 18 Innings, McGinnity, 'The Iron Man,' Wins Both Games."
August 2. "They Get a Split."
August 7. "Collins Wanted to Play."
August 8. "Win the Last One."
August 9. "Never Have a Chance."
August 9. "Boston Gets Deciding Run in the 12th."
August 9. "Rube Didn't Come."
August 11. "Cy Gets Even."
August 11. "Ban Johnson at the Game."
August 12. "Boston Wins Again."
August 15. "His Blows Have No Sting in Them."
August 16. "Collins' Boys Out in Their Hitting Togs."
August 16. "Pulitzer's Gift, Provides for a School of Journalism."
August 19. "Americans Versus Nationals."
August 19. "Men of Boston Not Especially Perplexed By His Curves."
August 24. "Two for Boston, Collins' Band Tightens Its Grip on First Place."
August 27. "Finish Sizzled, Collins' Men Won Out in Hot Windup."
August 28. "Gets Series, Boston Wins Its 11th from Champions."
September 1. "They Lose and Win."

September 2. "It Was a Close Call."
September 2. "In Fine Form."
September 2. "Series of Games, Killilea Will Soon Confer with Dreyfuss Regarding Boston-Pittsburg Match."
September 3. "Collins' Team at Home."
September 3. "Collins Ready to Play, Pleased with Prospect of a Series of Games with Pittsburg."
September 4. "It Was a Long Battle."
September 5. "Machine Rival of Pitchers."
September 6. "Heavy Hitting."
September 8. "Use the Brush."
September 9. "Forlorn Hope, Buck Freeman Tries to Tie Game with a Homer."
September 10. "Hughes and Winters Do the Stints in the Box, Are Well Backed Up."
September 11. "Buck's Bat Did It."
September 12. "Gibson in Good Form."
September 13. "Cinching Their Lead in Pennant Race."
September 13. "As to the Post Series."
September 15. "Hits and Errors."
September 16. "Heavy Hitting, Collins' Boys Have a Picnic with Tannehill."
September 19. "LaJoie at Fall River."
September 19. "Grand Finish, Boston Plays an Uphill Game and Wins in Ninth."
September 19. "Pittsburg Again Wins the Championship."
September 20. "Post-Season Series."
September 22. "Boston Americans Win in 12th Inning."
September 23. "Altrock, the Discard, Shuts Out Boston."
September 24. "Players Protest."
September 25. "Boston Players Call It Off."
September 25. "Dreyfuss Won't Have It So."
September 25. "Killilea Says It's Off."
September 26. "Boston Team Will Play."
September 26. "Played to a Tie."
September 26. "Giants Will Hold Ames."
September 27. "Give and Take, Boston Has Nothing on the St. Louis Browns."
September 27. "Going with the Team."
September 27. "Ban Johnson Came On."
September 28. "Boston Team Closes with Doubleheader."
September 29. "Both Ready for the Great Test."
September 30. "How They Size Up By Figures."
September 30. "Leach May Not Play."
October 1. "Ready to Battle for the World's Championship."
October 1. "Play Ball, By M.E. Webb."
October 2. "Boston Beaten By Score of 7 to 3."
October 3. "Boston Shuts Out the Pittsburgers."
October 3. "Swarm on the Field, By M.E. Webb."
October 4. "We Lose Again to the Pirates."

October 5. "125 Rooters Go with Team."
October 5. "No Game at Pittsburg."
October 6. "The Pirates Win Another, 5–4."
October 7. "Boston Even Money Has Few Takers."
October 7. "Boston Wins 11 to 2."
October 7. "Charley Lavis Refuses to Be Held Up By Band."
October 9. "Another Glorious Victory for Boston."
October 9. "Globe Offers Medals."
October 9. "Game Goes Over a Day."
October 9. "Collins' Protest Made Without Any Effect."
October 9. "Royal Rooters Had No Lawyer But Did Very Well."
October 10. "Baseball Battle Is On."
October 11. "Boston Wins Again, 7 to 3."
October 12. "To Renew the Struggle."
October 12. "Royal Rooters Back Again."
October 12. "Rain Gives Nines a Rest."
October 13. "Dinneen Will Go In."
October 13. "Big Betting, More Than $50,000 Will Change Hands."
October 14. "Boston Americans Are the Champions of the World."
October 14. "Get About $1280 Apiece."
October 14. "We Were Beaten Fairly and Squarely."
October 15. "Nice Rakeoff."
October 15. "Players Getting Away."

Boston Globe—T.H. Murnane Column "Murnane's Baseball"

March 1, 15, 29   July 5, 12, 19, 26
May 17, 24   August 2, 6, 9, 16, 23
June 21, 28   September 4, 6, 11, 13, 19.

Boston Herald

October 2. "Pittsburg Whitewashed in Second Game."
October 2. "Great Ball Playing By the National Champions."
October 3. "Honourables Take City By Peaceful Invasion."
October 4. "Jimmie Collins, Or Three in One."
October 4. "Rooters Leave Here Sanguine."
October 4. "Boston Players Confident."
October 4. "Pirates Welcomed."
October 4. "Blocked By Crowd, Boston Loses to Pirates."
October 4. "The Throng at the Game."
October 7. "Cy Young Twirls the Sphere in Gilt-Edge Style."
October 8. "Standing of the Clubs."

Boston Post

September 1. "Revere Is Startled By Naked Swimmer."
September 20. "Boston Americans-Pittsburg Games to Begin Here."

September 25. "Pittsburg Series Off, Says Owner Killilea."
September 26. "Pittsburg Games On."
September 27. "Johnson Believes Americans Will Win."
September 28. "Hans Wagner Strikes Terror in Hearts of the Hub's Fans."
September 29. "Big Bets on Pittsburg-Americans Series, with Locals Favorites."
September 30. "15,000 People Expected to Attend Tomorrow's Ball Game."
October 2. "We Lose First Game for World's Champions."
October 2. "Opinions of the Game."
October 2. "$50,000 Wagered on Game."
October 3. "10,000 People See Boston Defeat Pittsburg 3 to 0 in 2d Championship Game."
October 4. "Young Failed to Save the Game."
October 4. "As Viewed By an Expert."
October 4. "Betting Was Light."
October 4. "Wild Scenes at the Game."
October 5. "50,000 Have Seen Boston-Pittsburg Games."
October 7. "Rally in Ninth Inning Set Collins Rooters Wild."
October 8. "They Didn't Do a Thing but Turn City Upside Down."
October 9. "Clubs Tied and Coming Monday."
October 10. "Boston Players and Rooters Disgusted Over Postponements."

New York Times

April 1, 1947. "800 Join in Tribute to Cy Young" (Associated Press).
November 11, 1955. "Cy Young Is Dead" (Associated Press).

Pittsburg Bulletin

January 17.
April 25.
April 23, 1904.

Pittsburg Chronicle Telegraph

October 1. "Champions of Two Leagues Ready for the World Play."
October 2. "Capt. Clarke Compliments Winning Boys"; "Happy Pulliam"; "A Loyal Rooter to the Front"; "Collins Promises Better Arguments."
October 3. "The Champs Beaten By Excellent Pitching."
October 5. "Initial Baseball Game Here Is Postponed."
October 4. "Hughes Forced to Retreat Before Pittsburg Heavy Hitters."
October 6. "Boston People Anxious to Recoup Their Losses."
October 7. "Boston Players Are Given a Scoring."
October 9. "Personality Worth Over $17,000,000."
October 9. "Bostons Win Another Game, Are Now Even with Pittsburg."
October 12. "Baseball Popular in All Sections"; "Hard on Leever."
October 14. "Boston Baseball Club Holds World's Championship."

Pittsburg Daily Dispatch

September 29. "With Betting Against Them, Confident Champs Go East."
October 11. "Boston Team Wins Another, Champions Are Now Behind"; "Rooters Help Boston to Win"; "Cy Young Too Much for Pirates."
October 12. "Players Mingled on the Way to Boston Town"; "Pulliam Reviews the Past Season"; "Denounces Basketball."
October 13. "Doheny Crazed Over Pittsburg's Recent Defeats"; "Bad Weather Spoiled Game."
October 14. "Frenzied Crowd Sees Boston Win"; "Phil Sorry He Lost Two"; "Doheny's Last Sane Thoughts Were of a Small Debt."
October 16. "Each Pittsburg Champion Got Check for $1,316.25."
October 17. "Wives of the Married Got Post-Season Checks"; "Boston Champs Are in Disrepute."

Pittsburg Gazette

October 1. "Pirates in Fine Shape to Face Boston Americans"; "Pirates Ready for Hard Games."
October 2. "Pirates Capture the First Game."
October 3. "Dinneen Proved the Real Thing."
October 4. "Monster Crowd Watches Champion Pirates Defeat Champion Bostons"; "Pirates Made a Great Record."
October 5. "Champions Home to Play Boston."
October 6. "Rain Prevents Opening Game."
October 7. "Poor Playing Brought Defeat."
October 9. "Dinneen Showed His Finest Form"; "The Real Test to Be Played Today."
October 11. "Boston Leads World Series"; "Figures Show Very Poor Work."
October 12. "World Series May Be Stopped."
October 13. "Hard Day's Rain Rest Pirates."
October 14. "Boston Team Wins the Title of Being the World's Champion"; "Dinneen's Curves Fooled Pirates."
October 18. "Clarke Remains Pirate's Leader."

Pittsburg Leader

October 1. "The Pirates Begin Big Baseball World Series with the Bostons."
October 5. "Three Out of Four Is Clarke's Hope."
October 7. "Deacon Again Turns Trick."
October 9. "The Rooters and the Band"; "Cold Weather Knocks Out Game."

Pittsburg Post

March 22. "Hans Wagner Hurts Hand"; "Clarence Beaumont, the Champion Batsman of the League, Joins the Pirates."
March 24. "Tommy Leach Hitting the Ball Well."

April 3. "Ed Doheny Makes a Fine Record in the Pitcher's Box."
April 4. "Outfielder Sebring Bitten by a Centipede."
April 17. "Champions Nearly Shut Out the Reds."
April 18. "Find Little to Be Admired in America"; "Doheny Holds the Cincinnati Batsmen Down to Two Little Runs."
April 20. "Champion Pirates Make Clean Sweep."
April 22. "Pirates Lose Before Home Multitude."
April 24. "Jim Sebring Performs the Unique Feat."
April 29. "Champions Lose a Light Batting Game."
May 1. "Tommy Leach Makes a Home Run at St. Louis with the Bases Full."
May 5. "Champions Capture a Pretty Contest."
May 7. "Fierce Slaughter in Ninth Inning."
May 9. "Game of Baseball Is Too Mild"; "Hans Wagner Suspended for Three Days by President Pulliam of the League."
May 17. "Largest Crowd to See a Ball Game."
May 19. "Doheny Outpitches Iron Man McGinnity."
May 20. "Captain Fred Clarke Emphatically Denies That His Health Is Breaking Down."
May 26. "Fred Clarke a Sick Man."
July 4. "Pirates Take Two from Phillies in Heat and Rain."
July 6. "Clarke's Shoulder Is Dislocated."
September 6. "Man Tarred and Feathered."
September 30. "Champions Go to Battle in Pretty Bad Shape."
October 1. "Pittsburg Money Scares Boston."
October 2. "Pirates Wallop the Beaneaters."
October 11. "Cy Young Too Much for Pirates."
October 12. "Ed Doheny Fells Nurse with Poker"; "More Pirates Are Crippled."
October 13. "Hans Joins List of Cripples."
October 14. "Autos Run with Terrific Speed on Course from Erie to Cleveland"; "Dinneen Shuts Out the Pirates"; "Pirates Fast Fielding"; "Pirate Team Disbands."
October 15. "Pirates Travel Home Like Victors."
October 16. "Dreyfuss Is Given Watch by Players."
October 17. "Champs Scattered."

Pittsburgh Post-Gazette

May 15, 1950. "Mrs. Dreyfuss, Pirate Owner's Widow, Dies."
April 27, 1961. "Barney Dreyfuss' Gifts to Baseball Remain Foremost."

Pittsburg Press

September 30. "Tommie Leach May Not Play."
October 1. "Pittsburg and Boston Ready to Play."
October 2. "Criger Was Up in Air"; "Champs Wallop Boston."

October 4. "Throng Defied the Police."
October 5. "Both Teams Await Fray."

Pittsburgh Press

February 5, 1932. "Word of Death Phoned Here to Relatives."

Pittsburg Times

October 1. "Unbounded Enthusiasm."

The Sporting News

July 19, 1902. "False to Friends."
January 3. "Has Not Been Idle."
January 17. "Saviors of Game."
July 4. "Refuses to Talk."
July 11. "Search for Body of Delahanty."
July 18. "Waddell Repents"; "Delahanty Dazed."
July 25. "Wave of Disorder."
August 1. "Saved Baseball."
August 15. "In Better Shape."
August 22. "Teams Compared."
August 29. "New Agreement."
September 5. "Foul Strike Rule"; "Brush's Attitude."
September 12. "Pirates Win."
September 19. "Cinch for Boston"; "Chesty or Tired."
September 17, 24.
September 26. "Hitch in Series"; "Series Arranged"; "Saved for Boston"; "Liberal Enough"; "Intense Interest."
September 30.
October 3. "Phillippe Faces Young"; "No 25-Cent Seats."
October 24, 31. November 6, 13.

Other Sources

Asinof, Eliot. *Eight Men Out: The Black Sox and the 1919 World Series.* New York: Henry Holt, 2000.
Berry, Harold and Henry Berry. *The Boston Red Sox: The Complete Record of Red Sox Baseball.* New York: Macmillan, 1984.
Boston Public Library. The McGreevey Collection.
Browning, Reed. *Cy Young: A Baseball Life.* Amherst: University of Massachusetts Press, 2000.
CNN/SI.com.

Cohen, Richard M., Davis S. Neft, and Roland T. Johnson. *The World Series*. New York: Dial Press, 1976.
Cunningham, Bill. "Cy Young's 80th Birthday." *The Boston Globe*, April 1, 1974.
Daley, Arthur. "Baseball Immortal." *New York Times*, 1945.
Dickey, Glenn. *The History of American League Baseball Since 1901*. New York: Stein and Day, 1980.
_____, *The History of the World Series Since 1903*. New York: Stein and Day, 1984.
Encarta Concise Encyclopaedia.
Fortnightly Review of Sports. September-October 1903. Rockville Centre, N.Y.: Past Press Productions, 1978.
Gershman, Michael. *Diamonds: The Evolution of the Ballpark*. Boston: Houghton Mifflin, 1993.
Hittner, Arthur D. *Honus Wagner: The Life of Baseball's Flying Dutchman*. Jefferson, N.C.: McFarland, 1996.
Honig, Donald. *The Boston Red Sox: An Illustrated History*. New York: Prentice Hall, 1990.
Johnson, Dick, and Glenn Stout. *Red Sox Century*. Boston: Houghton Mifflin, 2000.
Lieb, Fred. *The Boston Red Sox*. New York: Putnam, 1947.
_____. *The Pittsburgh Pirates*, New York: Putnam, 1948.
Northeastern University, Boston. The World Series Collection.
Okkonen, Marc. *Baseball Memories, 1900–1909*. New York: Sterling, 1993.
_____. *Baseball Uniforms of the 20th Century*. New York: Sterling, 1991.
Ritter, Lawrence S. *The Glory of Their Times*. New York: William Morrow, 1984.
Seymour, Harold. *Baseball: The Early Years*, New York: Oxford University Press, 1960.
Stout, Glenn. "The Royal Rooters," *Boston Sunday Herald Magazine*, October 3, 1983. Available on TotalBaseball.com.
Total Baseball. Viking Press, New York.
Ward, Geoffrey C. *Baseball: An Illustrated History*. New York: Alfred A. Knopf, 1994.

Index

Abbott, Dr. 139
Albany, New York 88, 141, 169
Alexander, Grover Cleveland 180
All-Century Team 183
Allegheny, Pennsylvania 33
Allegheny River 89, 129
Alliance, Ohio 93
Altoona 45
America 17
American League 1, 3, 11, 18, 22, 30, 40, 43, 46, 52, 55, 57, 70, 83, 114, 118, 149, 151, 164, 167, 171, 174–176, 178–179, 185–186; minor 21; premier season 25
American Revolution 170
American Undertaker 143
Ancient and Honourables 10, 75
Anderson 92
Anderson, Will 92
Andover, Mass. 7, 46, 53, 57, 138, 147
Andover Townsman 139
Antharis 88
Arizona 176
Arizona Diamondbacks 186
Arnold, Benedict 40
Athens of America 10
Atlanta 186
"Auld Lang Syne" 129
Avenue Theater 99
"Away Down South in Dixie" 129

Baby Trust 145

Back Bay 66
Back Bay Station 88
Bair Lake, Michigan 176
Baltimore 18, 23, 26, 28–29, 92
Barnes, Walter 19, 90, 177
Baseball as Taught at Harvard 5
Baxter 87
Beaumont, Ginger 2, 4, 6–7, 16, 31, 53, 64, 67, 70, 75–77, 82, 127, 166; with Boston Beaneaters 181; death 180; eighth game 152–153, 156; fifth game 107, 109; fourth game 96–97, 99; goes to Wisconsin 169; saves woman 81; seventh game 131–133; sixth game 114–115
Beaver Falls, Pennsylvania 128
Bellaire, Ohio 103
Bender, Chief 49
Berra, Yogi 180
Birmingham, Dr. R.M. 139
Blairsville, Pennsylvania 128
Bolivar, New York 178
Boston 5, 7, 10, 15, 17–18, 20–23, 26, 29, 47, 63, 65, 73, 87, 89–90, 94–95, 103, 119–120, 122, 125, 129, 136, 141, 151–152, 160, 170, 173–174, 176, 178–180, 184–185
Boston Americans 2, 8–10, 14, 16, 28, 30, 40–42, 45, 49–50, 52–53, 56, 58, 61–62, 66–67, 90, 94, 120–121, 124–128, 137–138, 140, 143, 145–146, 148–150, 166, 170–172, 174, 176,

178–180, 183–185; chase Dinneen 28; eighth game 151–153, 155–160, 162–165; fifth game 103, 105–110; first World Series game 67, 69–75; fourth game 95–100; second World Series game 75–78; series with Pirates 48; seventh game 129–136; sign players 25; sixth game 112–116; talk of Pirate series 48, 50; third game 80–86; thirteenth consecutive win 44

Boston Beaneaters 3, 5, 7, 10, 14, 20–26, 31, 35, 39, 42–45, 56, 62, 74, 87, 125, 172, 174, 178, 180, 186; outdrawn at box office 29

Boston Daily News 65

Boston Globe 3, 5, 17, 19, 22–24, 28, 35, 38–39, 41–44, 64, 80, 84, 87, 99, 117, 121, 125, 127, 131, 146, 149–150, 166, 171, 174, 177; on Doheny 176–177; offers medals 124; on Series dissension 58–59; team comparison 64

Boston Harbor 20, 22

Boston Herald 19, 88, 90, 118, 148, 150, 166

Boston Journal 90

Boston Latin 20

Boston Post 13, 60, 64–66, 81, 170, 180; talk of Series fix 62, 86

Boston Public Library 183

Boston Red Sox 177, 179–180, 183–184, 186–187

Bowerman, Frank 34, 36–37

Brahmins 107

Bransfield, Kitty 14, 31, 69–70, 88, 126–128, 142; death 181; eighth game 153, 155; fourth game 96–97; seventh game 130, 133; sixth game 114; third game 82–84

Breen, H.A. 127–128

Brooklyn 17, 30, 57

Brooklyn Dodgers 180, 186

Brush, John 41–42, 174–176

Buckner, Bill 186

Buffalo, New York 24, 88, 128, 171, 178

Bunker Hill Monument 73

Burlington, Wisconsin 180

Burton, Tom 92

Cambridge, Mass. 22

Carisch 167

Carnegie, Pennsylvania 136, 169

Charleroi, Pennsylvania 128

Charles River Park 22

Chesbro, Jack 2, 30–32, 34, 165, 174

Chicago 21, 23, 29, 43, 52, 60, 62, 178, 180

Chicago Colts 33, 35, 44, 54, 181

Chicago White Sox 73, 175, 178–179, 183

Churchill Hall 185

Cincinnati 32, 45, 128; peace talks 40

Cincinnati Commercial Tribune 19, 90, 144

Cincinnati Red Stockings 32, 34, 53, 73, 93, 180–181

Cincinnati Reds 184, 186

Civil War 30

Clarke, Fred 2, 4, 9, 13–14, 16, 31–32, 34–35, 37, 51, 53–54, 56, 63–65, 88–89, 93, 121–122, 125–127, 137, 143–146, 149, 166–169; attacked by Bowerman 36; confronts Doheny 45–46; death 180; eighth game 151–153, 155–157, 163, 165; elected to Hall of Fame 180; fifth game 103, 105, 107, 109, 111; first World Series game 67, 70, 72, 74; fourth game 96; hurts leg 57; injured 36; predicts Pirate win 94; second World Series game 75–77; seventh game 130–134, 136; sixth game 114–115, 117; third game 81–82, 85; visits Doheny 147; warns against betting 7

Cleveland 23, 29, 31, 44–45, 48, 50, 52, 56, 93, 169, 175, 179

Clifton 88

Cobb, Ty 176, 181, 183

Cohen, "Slap" 87, 95

Collins, Jimmy 5, 8–9, 13–14, 24, 28, 39, 41–42, 48–50, 54, 56–57, 63, 65, 87, 88, 90, 93–95, 100–101, 120–123, 125, 128, 142, 145–146, 148, 170–171, 174; eighth game 151, 153, 156–157, 162, 164–165; elected to Hall of Fame 179; fifth game 103, 105–107, 109, 111; fired 178; first World Series game 69–70, 73; fourth game 96–99; goes home to Buffalo 171; ready for series 52; says games were not fixed 170; says Series off 59–61; second World Series game 75; Series on 62; seventh game 129,

131–132, 136; signs with Boston 25; sixth game 112–114, 117; third game 81–86
Collins, Patrick 11
Colonial Theater 164
Columbia Park 49
Columbus, Ohio 128
Columbus Day 145
Comiskey, Charles 21, 24, 175
Commonwealth Avenue 6, 66, 143, 184
Conant, Arthur 23
Connecticut 39
Connecticut League 179
Connellsville, Pennsylvania 128
Connolly, Tom 14–15, 82, 97, 105, 107, 131, 134, 152
Conroy, Dr. E. C. 138–139
Copley Square 75
Cornelius, Buck 119
Criger, Lou 13, 28, 43, 45, 58, 64, 83, 92, 101, 126; affadavit on fixing World Series 183; death 176; eighth game 153, 156–157, 160, 162, 171; fifth game 107–109; first World Series game 67, 69–71, 73; fourth game 96–98; gets Dinneen's ball 170; second game 76–77; seventh game 133–135; sixth game 115; third game 84

Daly 125
Danvers State Mental Hospital 139
Davis, Ralph 165
Deer Island 160
Detroit 23, 28, 44, 61, 128, 179, 181
Dinneen, Bill 11, 25–26, 28, 44, 49, 52, 64, 74, 88, 90, 122, 128, 142, 145–146, 172; death 179; eighth game 152–153, 155–160, 162, 165–166, 170; fifth game 105–106, 109, 111, 136, 151; fourth game 95–98, 101; jumps to Americans 39; second World Series game 75–78; sixth game 112, 114–116
Dr. Miles Anti-Pain Pills 176
Doheny, Ed 2, 16, 30–33, 35–37, 44, 51, 54, 57, 64, 74–75, 88, 93, 103, 109, 117, 136–137, 142–145, 148, 151, 163, 165, 167, 173, 178; back from Andover 53; death 176; goes berserk 138–140; going mad 4; loses to Homestead 45; quarrel with Dreyfuss 55; suspended 34; visit from Clarke 147

Doheny, Mrs. 55, 138–140, 147, 163
Dominican 187
Donovan 148
Dougherty, Patsy 7, 9, 13, 16, 39, 69, 83, 93, 126; eighth game 153, 156–157; fifth game 107–108; fourth game 96–97, 100–101; goes to Troy, New York 171; second World Series game 75, 77; seventh game 131; sixth game 112, 117; third game 84; traded to New York Highlanders 177
Dreyfuss, Barney 1–3, 8–9, 17, 25, 36, 51, 53, 57, 66, 77–78, 85, 89, 95, 99, 110, 119–120, 122–123, 126–128, 134, 136, 147, 163–164, 169, 171–172, 175; builds juggernaut 30; on Doheny 148; eighth game 157; fifth game 103; first World Series game 70–74; gives Pirates game receipts 166; keeps American League team out of Pittsburg 40; presented watch 167–168; quarrel with Doheny 55; Series dissension 60–61; sixth game 114–117; supports Pulliam 32; visit from Killilea 55; worries about American League 21; writes Killilea 47
Duquesne Theater 94–95

Egan, Pat 117, 149
Elkhart, Indiana 170
Elysian Fields 166
Emerson, Ralph Waldo 5
Emlenton, Pennsylvania 181
Ethics of Baseball 5
Europe 1, 17, 19
Exposition Park 34–35, 56, 89, 94, 103, 112, 129, 184, 186

Faneuil Hall 170
Farrell, Duke 71, 88, 98, 101, 125, 135, 157
Fenway Park 184
Ferris, Hobe 13, 51, 69–71, 75, 77, 128, 142, 166; death 179; eighth game 153, 155–157, 162; fifth game 106, 108–109; fourth game 96–98, 100; goes to Providence, Rhode Island 171; seventh game 132–134; sixth game 112–116; third game 83–85
Filipino 187
First World Series 179, 181

Fisk, Carlton 186
Fitzgerald, Mayor John Honey 21, 174
Florida Marlins 186
Fools of Nature 78
"For He's a Jolly Good Fellow" 168
Forbes Field 184
Fort Pitt Tunnel 32
Ft. Wayne, Indiana 171, 178
Freeman, Buck 13, 16, 67, 69–71, 75, 77, 166, 177; eighth game 153, 155–156, 158; fifth game 106–108; fourth game 98, 101; goes to Wilkes-Barre, Pennsylvania 171; seventh game 131–132; sixth game 112–113; third game 84–85
French Lick, Indiana 178
Fullerton, Hugh S. 169

Geer, George 40
Germanic 17, 20
Gibson, George 63, 126, 135
"Goodbye My Bluebell" 92
Goodfriend, S. 149
Grand Opera House 110
Grandview Avenue 103
Greater Pittsburg Band 92, 110–111, 136
Green, Carl 176
Grillo, J. Ed 19, 90, 144
Groetzinger, John, Alderman 110, 123–124
Gruber, John H. 7, 19, 33, 71–72, 77, 90, 114, 117, 143, 170
Guenther, Prof. W. William 123–124
Gwilliam, Shad 168

"Hail, Hail, the Gang's All Here" 119
Haines City, Florida 181
Hall of Fame 179–181, 183
Handelberg, Moses 105
Handrahan 87
Harmon, Julia 178
Harvard 13, 20
Havana Cubans 187
Hoboken, N.J. 166
Holliday, Bugs 34
Homestead, Pennsylvania 45, 93
Hot Springs, Arkansas 63
Hotel Langham 183
Howarth, Oberlin 138–139
Hughes, Tom 49–52, 64, 75, 82–83, 90, 105, 141, 171–172

Huntington Avenue 8, 13, 20, 22–24, 26, 29, 64, 71, 77, 79–80, 94, 150
Huntington Avenue Grounds 5, 11, 23, 26, 41, 78, 81–82, 89, 126, 150–151, 155, 159, 173–174, 180, 184–185
Huntington Station 143, 180
Hyams, Sam 91

"In the Good Old Summertime" 152
Indiana, Pennsylvania 128
Indianapolis 18
Industrial Revolution 17
International League 179
Irish immigrants 17
Irwin, Arthur 29

Jamaica Plain 87
Johnson, Ban 3, 11, 17, 19, 22–23, 27–28, 30, 32, 40, 42, 45, 48, 50, 54, 57, 78, 103, 151, 164–165, 171, 174, 176; death 183; new American League 18, 24; offers National Leaguers more money 25; ultimatum to Killilea 47; vows to end rowdyism 33; World Series trouble 62
Jones, Michigan 176

Kansas City 18
Keenan, John 91
Kennedy, Bill "Brickyard" 4, 57, 75, 78, 94, 168; fifth game 103, 105–109, 111, 117, 151; goes to Ohio 169
Killilea, Henry 3–4, 13–14, 41, 52, 78, 85, 101, 103, 122, 126, 163, 166, 172, 174; letter from Dreyfuss 47–48; on Series 56–62; visits Dreyfuss 55
Knowles, Fred 36
Krueger, Otto 7, 57, 64, 90, 167–168

L Street Brownies 20
LaChance, Candy 7, 9, 11, 39, 69–71, 73, 75, 77, 88, 128, 141; death 179; eighth game 155–157; fifth game 106–109; fourth game 96–98; goes to Waterbury, Connecticut 171; seventh game 132–134; sixth game 112–113, 115, 117–118; third game 82–84
LaForce, Ed 167
LaJoie, Nap 16, 24–25, 31, 175
Landis, Judge Kenesaw Mountain 183
Lavis, Charlie 61, 87, 92, 95, 98, 128,

142, 146; fifth game 106, 108, 110–111, 119, 129; testifies about band 123–124
Lawrence, Massachusetts 139
Leach, Tommy 8, 33, 67, 70, 75–76, 127–128, 144, 166; death 181; eighth game 152–154, 156, 158, 162; fifth game 105–106, 108–109; fourth game 96–97; goes to Cleveland 169; seventh game 132, 134; sixth game 112, 114, 116; third game 83–84
Leever, Sam 4, 16, 35, 57, 74–75, 78, 89, 93–94, 136–137, 143, 148, 169; fifth game 103, 105, 109, 111; sixth game 112–115, 117
Letter Carriers Band 146, 152, 155
Locke, W.H. 167, 169
Louisville, Kentucky 9, 33, 128, 178

MacBreen 87
Mack, Connie 28, 50
MacKay, Jerry 84
MacQuade 87
Madeira 88
Mahoning Valley, Ohio 128
Marlowe, Julia 78
Massachusetts 46
Massachusetts Avenue 80
Mathewson, Christy 16, 37, 181
Mazeroski, Bill 184, 186
McBreen 150–151
McCool, Peter 105
McGillicuddy 152
McGinnity, Joe "Iron Man" 28, 34, 37, 52
McGraw, John 33–36, 42, 47, 91–92, 120, 165, 171, 174–176
McGreevey, Mike "Nuf Ced" 10–11, 14, 20–21, 24, 29, 62, 74–75, 87, 90, 93, 95, 98, 115, 123–124, 142, 170, 172–173, 183; eighth game 152, 155; fifth game 105–106, 108, 110; sends Lavis to find band 92; seventh game 130, 133–134
McKenna, "Doc" 87
McQuiston, Frank 19, 51, 54–55, 90, 101, 137, 169
Medfield State Hospital 177
Merrill, H.G. 41
Miah Murray's 96
Miller 151
Milwaukee 13, 23, 28, 39, 60, 186

Minneapolis 18
"Mr. Dooley" 152
Monongahela, Pennsylvania 128
Monongahela Hotel 92, 99–100, 119, 123, 135
Montreal 179
Monument Hill 128
Moore, Col. Alec 63, 72
Morse, Jake 90, 118, 148
Mount Washington 32, 89, 105, 128
Murnane, Tim 3, 19–20, 22, 25–26, 29, 38–39, 42, 45–46, 50, 54, 90, 95, 146, 149, 166, 171–173, 178; Boston-Pittsburg series 48, 50–51, 56–58, 65; on Criger 176; death 177; eighth game 152–153, 160, 162–163; first World Series game 67, 69, 72–73; predicts Boston win 91; seventh game 131; World Series prospects 53; on Young 43
"Murnane's Baseball" 39
Murphy, John 167
"My Country 'Tis of Thee" 129
"My Maryland" 129

National Agreement 22, 41
National Board of Arbitration 38
National League 1–4, 6, 9–10, 16–19, 21, 24–26, 30, 38–41, 43–44, 58, 70, 83, 91, 101, 118, 137, 141, 149, 165, 172, 174–175, 179–181, 186
Naugatuck, Conn. 38
New England 60
New England Conservatory of Music 80
New England League 38
New Haven, Connecticut 179
New York 28, 34, 40–41, 52, 107, 126, 146, 172
New York Evening World 78
New York Giants 33–37, 42, 48, 51, 53, 62, 78, 91, 171, 174–176, 181
New York Highlanders 31, 42–43, 52, 54, 174, 176–177
New York Mets 184
New York Yankees 180, 184, 186
North Pole 160
Northeastern University 179, 185–186
Noonan, "Kid" 87

O'Brien, Jack 71, 98–100, 135, 171
O'Day, Hank 14–15, 105, 109, 112–113, 152

Index

Ohio 131, 169
Old Glory 42
O'Neil, J. Palmer 94

Pacific 48
Parent, Fred 13, 56, 69–71, 77, 120, 128, 141, 166; death 179; eighth game 153, 155–156, 162; fifth game 106–109; fourth game 98, 100; goes to Sanford, Maine 171; seventh game 131–135; sixth game 112–115, 117–118; third game 83–84
Patriots' Day 41
Pennsylvania 31
Peoli, Ohio 180
Phelps, Ed 69, 81, 83, 107, 114, 127; eighth game 155–156; goes to Albany, New York 169; seventh game 131–132, 134
Philadelphia 18, 22–23, 48, 126
Philadelphia Athletics 2, 28–29, 40, 42–43, 48–50, 52–54, 73, 171, 179–180
Philadelphia Phillies 3, 28, 31, 36, 41, 51, 73, 175, 181
Phillippe, Deacon 4, 7, 15–16, 30–31, 33, 35–36, 57, 78, 89, 94–95, 116–118, 120–123, 127–128, 137, 142–143, 166–167, 169, 172; death 181; eighth game 151, 153, 155–157, 162–165; fifth game 103, 105, 109; first World Series game 69, 71–73; fourth game 95–99; seventh game 129–130, 132–134, 136; third game 82–85
Pickering's Furniture Store 13
Pilgrims, Boston 26
Pink, William 124
Pittsburg 1, 10, 15, 17, 20, 25, 30, 37, 47, 63, 65, 73, 87–90, 93–96, 105, 107, 117–118, 120, 124, 129–131, 135–136, 147, 151, 159, 162, 167, 170, 186; growing 32
Pittsburg Chronicle Telegraph 100, 136
Pittsburg Dispatch 19, 51, 54, 89, 101, 137
Pittsburg Gazette 10, 72–73
Pittsburg Leader 6
Pittsburg Pirates 1, 6–11, 13–14, 17, 21, 30, 32, 34, 36–37, 40, 44, 48, 52–54, 56, 62–64, 66, 88, 90, 101, 119–121, 123, 125–126, 128–129, 137–138, 140–141, 143, 145–146, 148, 150, 166, 168, 170–172, 174–176, 180, 184–185; eighth game 151–153, 155–160, 162–165, 177, 180–181, 183; fifth game 103, 105–110; first World Series game 67, 69–74; fourth game 95–100; picture in Boston Globe 64; scoreless streak 35; second game 76–78; seventh game 129–136; sixth game 112–116; talk of Boston series 48, 50–51, 57, 59–61; team in 1903 31; third game 80–86
Pittsburg Post 7, 19, 33, 36, 71, 91, 110, 117, 136, 170
Pittsburg Post Gazette 144
Pittsburg Press 86
Pittsburg Times 13, 117
Plank, Eddie 42–43, 50
Plymouth Rocks, Boston 26
Polo Grounds 34
Preston, W.H. 141
Prohibition 183
Providence, Rhode Island 171, 179
Puerto Rican 187
Pulliam, Harry 9, 32, 34, 36, 45, 72, 74, 117, 146, 181; fines Bowerman 37; predicts Pirate win 57, 94; rowdyism edict 41
Punxsutawney, Pennsylvania 129
Putnam, Fred, Hotel 180

Reach's Guide 30
Regan, Mike 96, 98
Richter, Frank 18, 165
Ritchey, Claude 7, 16, 31, 37, 64, 69, 83, 128, 143, 147, 166; with Boston Beaneaters 180; death 181; eighth game 155–157, 163; fifth game 107–110; fourth game 96, 99; second game 77; seventh game 131, 133; sixth game 114; third game 84
"Rocky Road to Dublin" 92
Rose, Frank 84
Roxbury, Mass. 22
Royal Rooters 10–11, 14–15, 24, 29, 52, 69, 75, 87–88, 120–121, 123–124, 126, 137, 141–142, 145–146, 170, 172, 183; eighth game 152, 155–156, 158, 162; fifth game 105–109; fourth game 92–93, 95–99; seventh game 129, 132, 133, 135–136; sixth game 112–115, 118–119

Ruggles Street 20
Russian 187
Ruth, Babe 186

St. Louis 25, 39, 159
St. Louis Browns 44, 51, 62, 73, 176, 179
St. Louis Cardinals 48, 51, 148, 184, 186
St. Louis Globe-Democrat 148
St. Louis World's Fair 187
Sanford, Maine 171, 179
Savannah, Georgia 38
Scandinavian 17
Scranton, Pennsylvania 128
Sebring, Jimmy 7, 16, 32, 56, 64, 69–71; 75, 127, 165, 169; death 180; eighth game 153, 156; fifth game 107; sixth game 114; third game 84
Shea 95
Slaughter, Enos 186
"The Smoke Goes Up the Chimney Just the Same" 119
South Boston 20
South End Grounds 10, 20–21, 23, 35, 41, 44–45, 186
South Station 87, 141
Spalding's Guide to Baseball 40
Spanish-American War 19
Speaker, Tris 183
The Sporting Life 18, 171
Sporting News 18, 40–41, 59, 169–170
Stahl, Charles Sylvester "Chick" 7, 13, 25–26, 67, 69–70, 75; death 178; eighth game 153, 165; fifth game 106–108; fourth game 96, 98, 101; goes to Ft. Wayne, Indiana 171; seventh game 131; sixth game 112–113; third game 83–85
Stahl, Jake 98, 100, 126, 135
"Star Spangled Banner" 129
State House, Boston 5
Steubenville, Ohio 128
Stone, Andrew C. 139
Stout, Glenn 178
Stratford, Conn. 38
Sullivan, Michael 170
Sullivan, Sport 65, 87
Symphony Hall 20
Syracuse, New York 179

Taiwanese 187

Tannehill, Jesse 2, 30–32, 34, 165, 172
Taylor, Charles 174
Taylor, John H. 124–125
Taylor, John I. 174, 179
"Tessie" 92–93, 98–99, 142; eighth game 152, 155–156, 162, 166–167, 173, 181, 184; fifth game 105–110, 123; seventh game 129–131, 133–134, 145–146; sixth game 112; 119, 141
"There'll Be a Hot Time in the Old Town Tonight" 108
Third Base Saloon 10, 21, 142, 173
Thompson 167
Three Rivers Stadium 184, 186
Toronto Blue Jays 187
Troy, New York 171
Tucson, Arizona 176
Twain, Mark 19

Union Depot 88
Uniontown, Pennsylvania 128
United States 1, 17, 19, 120, 159

Veil, Bucky 75, 77, 94, 103, 105, 117, 143; goes to Williamsport, Pennsylvania 169
Vendome, Hotel 5, 66–67, 77–78, 86, 143, 163–164, 183; fire 184
Venezuelan 187
Vermont 177

Waddell, Rube 41–42, 49–50, 52
Wagner, Honus 2, 4–9, 14, 16, 31–34, 46, 48, 51, 54, 62, 65, 74, 88–89, 126, 128, 136, 141, 143, 145, 166, 170, 173, 175, 179, 182; after baseball 18; death 183; eighth game 152–153, 158–159, 160, 162–163, 165; fifth game 105–110; first World Series game 67, 69–70; fourth game 96–97, 99; goes to Carnegie, Pennsylvania 169; hurt leg 55; second game 76–77; seventh game 131–133, 135; sixth game 112–114, 117–118; target of recruitment 25; third game 83–85
Waldron, Charley 123, 135, 142, 145–146
Warner, John 36
Washington 18, 23, 28, 42–43, 49, 52, 180
Washington Express 88

Washington Street 183
Waterbury, Connecticut 171, 179
Waterbury Independents 179
Waterbury Republican 179
Waterville, Connecticut 179
Watson, Jerry 75, 87, 95, 98, 108, 115, 123, 161–162
West Baden, Indiana 178
Western League 18
Westinghouse Company 120
Wheeling, West Virginia 128
Wilkes-Barre, Pennsylvania 171, 177
Williamsport, Pennsylvania 169, 180
Wilson, Tom 145
Winfield, Kansas 169, 180
Winter 126, 135
Wisconsin 169
The Wizard of Oz 187
Worcester, Massachusetts 14, 142, 181
World Series 5, 10, 30, 61–62, 66–67, 96, 120, 131, 174–177, 180–181, 183–184, 186
World Series Way 185

Wright brothers 187

Yale 13
"Yankee Doodle Dandy" 129
Yankees 20
Yawkey, Tom 185
Yawkey Foundation 185
Young, Cy 3, 5–6, 9, 11, 16, 28–29, 39, 41–45, 49–50, 52, 62–64, 88–89, 97, 100–101, 122, 126, 128, 146, 151, 152, 162, 166, 170–172, 176, 179, 183, 185; Cy Young Day 180; death 180; elected to Hall of Fame 180; eighth game 157, 159; fifth game 103, 105, 107–108, 110; in 1902 All-Star game 31; offered bribe 95; recruited 25; relief in third game 83–86; seventh game 130, 132–136; sixth game 112, 115; takes mound for first game 14, 67, 70, 72, 74–75; upset with fix stories 145
Young, Nick 39
Youngstown, Ohio 93, 128

www.ingramcontent.com/pod-product-compliance
Lightning Source LLC
Chambersburg PA
CBHW020814230426
43666CB00007B/1003